Penguin Special
Women's Rights: A Pr

Anna Coote studied Modern History and Politics at
Edinburgh University and graduated in 1968. Since
then she has worked as a feature writer for the
Observer, as a freelance journalist and broadcaster,
and as an activist in the women's liberation movement. She is co-editor of *Civil Liberty: The NCCL
Guide*, a Penguin Special.

Tess Gill was educated at Weston-super-Mare
Grammar School and Manchester University, where
she read Politics and History. Since qualifying as a
solicitor she has worked in a radical law firm dealing
with trade-union and matrimonial matters. She is an
activist in the women's liberation movement.

ANNA COOTE and TESS GILL

Women's Rights: A Practical Guide

Drawings by Posy Simmonds

PENGUIN BOOKS

Penguin Books Ltd, Harmondsworth,
Middlesex, England
Penguin Books Australia Ltd, Ringwood,
Victoria, Australia
Penguin Books Canada Ltd,
41 Steelcase Road West,
Markham, Ontario, Canada
Penguin Books (N.Z.) Ltd,
182–190 Wairau Road,
Auckland 10, New Zealand

First published 1974
Reprinted with revisions 1974

Made and printed in Great Britain by
Cox & Wyman Ltd, London, Reading and Fakenham
Set in Monotype Ehrhardt

Contents

4. Marriage

5. Divorce and Separation

6. Children

7. Housing

The following pages may be of particular interest to you . . .

1. If you are single

2. If you are married

3. If you are divorced

4. If you are separated or getting a divorce

5. If you are living with a man who is not your husband

6. If you have children

7. If you are under 18

We should like to thank the following individuals and organizations for their valuable help:

The Association of British Adoption Agencies
Bill Birtles
British Pregnancy Advisory Service
Barbara Calvert
Catholic Housing Aid Society
Mary Chamberlain
Consumers' Association
Mary Dines
Richard Drabble
Family Planning Association
Lorna Goldstrom
Larry Grant
Patricia Hewitt
Inland Revenue
Christine Jackson
Cecilia Jefferson
Ruth Lister
Betty Lockwood
Beryl McAlhone
Liz Muirhead
Diane Parker
Pat Patten
David Pearlman
Radical Alternatives to Prison
Geoff Robertson
Jane Routh
Geoffrey Sheridan
Alison Truefitt
Julia Vellacott
Women's Abortion and Contraception Campaign
Women's Advisory Committee to the Trades Union Congress
Maureen Wright

This guide has been produced in co-operation with the National Council for Civil Liberties, an independent voluntary organization protecting individual civil liberties and the rights of political, religious, racial and other minorities. The NCCL takes an active interest in the rights of women. It provides legal advice, makes representations to central and local authorities, presses for legal reform through the Parliamentary Civil Liberties Group, and undertakes research through its associated charity, the Cobden Trust. It has groups in many cities and its headquarters are at 186 Kings Cross Road, London WC1.

Introduction

We live in a man-made society. Man devised and built the framework of government that controls our daily lives. Our rulers, representatives and arbitrators have almost all been men. Male judges and justices of the peace compiled our system of common law. Men drafted and interpreted our statute laws. Men constructed a bureaucracy to administer the law. Men cultivated the jungle of red tape which often threatens to engulf us. Men outnumber women in Parliament by twenty-four to one. Over 80 per cent of local councillors are men. Two in three magistrates are men. Juries seldom include more than a couple of token women. Men have an overwhelming majority in the legal profession, in the police force, in the upper ranks of the civil service, and even among trade-union officials.

The authority which men exercise over women is a major source of oppression in our society – as fundamental as class oppression. The fact that most of the nation's wealth is concentrated in the hands of a few means that the vast majority of women *and* men are deprived of their rights. But women are doubly deprived. At no level of society do they have equal rights with men.

At the beginning of the nineteenth century, women had virtually no rights at all. They were the chattels of their fathers and husbands. They were bought and sold in marriage. They could not vote. They could not sign contracts. When married, they could not own property. They had no rights over their children and no control over their own bodies. Their husbands could rape and beat them without fear of legal reprisals. When they were not confined to the home, they were forced by growing industrialization to join the lowest levels of the labour force.

Since then, progress towards equal rights for women has been very slow indeed. There have even been times when the tide seemed to turn against them. The first law against abortion was passed in 1803. It imposed a sentence of life imprisonment for termination within the first fourteen weeks of pregnancy. In 1832 the first law was passed which forbade women to vote in elections. In 1877 the first Trades Union Congress upheld the tradition that woman's place was in the home whilst man's duty was to protect and provide for her.

Nevertheless, the latter half of the nineteenth century saw the gradual acceptance of women into the unions and the informal adoption of resolutions on the need for equal pay. Between 1831 and 1872 the major Factory Acts were passed, which checked the exploitation of women workers by placing restrictions on hours and conditions of labour and by limiting their employment at night. In 1882 married women won the right to own property.

Wartime inevitably advanced the cause of women's rights – women became indispensable as workers outside the home, as they had to keep the factories and government machinery running while the men went out to fight. They were allowed into new areas of employment and were conceded new degrees of responsibility. In 1918 they got the vote. Again, during the Second World War, state nurseries were built on a considerable scale to enable women to go out to work. When peace came, however, women were unable to hold on to their gains. Men reclaimed their jobs, and women were forced back into the home and confined to their traditionally low-paid, menial and supportive forms of work. The government closed down most of the nurseries. Theories about maternal deprivation emerged – women who had been told it was patriotic to go out to work during the war were now told that their children would suffer if they did not stay at home. Little progress was made for the next two decades.

In the wake of the postwar population explosion, men invented the Pill – the first totally effective method of birth control. It was not altogether satisfactory. In its early forms it carried a considerable risk of thrombosis, and its long-term effects are still unknown. For many years it was not available under the National

Health Service. But gradually it began to affect the lives of more and more women. For the first time in history, they were able to decide just when and how often they would give birth – which meant they had greater freedom to decide when to work and when to marry. Meanwhile rising standards of living and the development of household appliances and processed foods made domestic work less taxing. Increasing numbers of married women went out to work. Woman's role was changing. The women's liberation movement was born in Britain in 1968. Its first national conference was held at Oxford in 1970.

It was no coincidence that the late sixties and early seventies saw a series of legislative reforms to improve the position of women. In 1967 the Abortion Act was passed, enabling women to have abortions for 'social' reasons. In 1970, the Equal Pay Act asserted women's right to equal pay for work of equal value. In 1970 the Matrimonial Proceedings and Property Act recognized that a woman's contribution to the family home by her work as wife and mother should earn her a share of the property after divorce. Contraceptive advice was made available free through family planning clinics, and some local councils offered free supplies too. In 1973 the Anti-Discrimination Bill, to end discrimination against women in employment, training and education, *almost* made it through Parliament. In the same year, two new statutes gave mothers and fathers equal guardianship rights over their children, and enabled married women to choose their own domicile; the Law Commission recommended co-ownership of the family home by husband and wife.

However, these have been only token concessions. Women are still treated as men's inferiors and dependants. They are still exploited and oppressed. They do not have equal pay. Their average earnings are little more than half those of men. Employers have avoided the impact of the Equal Pay Act by keeping women in low-paid grades of work or transferring them to 'women's jobs' where they have no chance of comparing their pay and conditions with male workers. They are excluded from certain types of employment and from jobs with a high degree of responsibility. They do not have equal opportunities in education and training. Girls' schools often have inferior facilities, and girls are usually taught domestic and commercial subjects while boys learn technical and mechanical skills. Few young women are able to benefit from apprenticeship or day-release training.

Unless a married woman applies for separate tax assessment, her income is treated as part of her husband's by the Inland Revenue, and he receives any tax rebates due to her. A married woman gets a lower rate of unemployment and sickness benefit than a single person, even though she pays the same National Insurance contributions. Under the government's new pension arrangements, women's earnings-related pensions are set at a rate which is one third lower than men's. A married woman cannot claim supplementary benefit in her own right: her husband must claim it for her. A single woman loses her right to supplementary benefit if she is thought to be living with a man, because she is expected to be supported by him.

The law still does not recognize that a woman has the right to control her own body. The ultimate decision to end an unwanted pregnancy rests with the doctor, not with the pregnant woman. National Health abortions are hard to come by, and many women still pay between £50 and £200 for the operation. Contraceptives are not free: women must pay prescription charges for them. A man can still rape his wife without contravening the letter of the law. A woman cannot legally solicit a man, but a man can legally solicit a woman.

Child-care facilities are so inadequate that women with young children can seldom go out to work without paying considerable fees to nurseries or baby-minders. Despite the good intentions of the Matrimonial Proceedings and Property Act, judges have reverted to the old rule of awarding a divorced woman only one third of the income and capital owned by herself and her husband during the marriage. Mortgage companies are more reluctant to lend money to women than to men. Married women usually find they cannot get credit facilities without their husband's signature, and single women are often asked to provide a male guarantor. If a British woman marries a foreigner, she cannot extend her right of residence to him, so if he doesn't have permission to stay in his own right, she must leave the country in order to live with him.

In addition to these practical inequalities, women suffer discrimination in the form of childhood conditioning. Girls and boys are treated differently by their parents and teachers, and encouraged to behave differently. Toys and books reinforce the traditional male and female roles. Most women are brought up to believe that their main function in life is to marry, have babies and find satisfaction through their children and husbands – rather than to recognize their full potential and to determine their lives according to their real abilities and inclinations.

So, some progress has been made since the beginning of the nineteenth century, but there is still a long way to go. Perhaps the most significant advance made recently is that more and more women have become aware of their oppression and of the need to fight for their rights.

This guide is designed to assist in that fight. Its main purpose is as a practical handbook, to help women gain a useful knowledge of the laws, traditions, rules and regulations which affect their rights – so that they can know best how to defend them when they come under attack.

The material is arranged under broad subject headings. You will find some areas more relevant to you than others, depending on whether you are married or single, with or without children. The special contents table on pp. 8–10 is designed to direct you to the parts of the book most useful for your particular situation. We cannot hope to provide the ideal solution to every problem. In a straightforward situation, we hope we have provided enough information to enable you to take action on your own. If your problem is more complex, we hope the information will give you a basic idea of what your rights are, so that you will be encouraged to seek expert advice – either from a solicitor, or from one of the specialist organizations listed at the end of most chapters or on pp. 317–20. The law is rapidly changing in this field and it is almost impossible to be completely up to date. The last date on which we were able to make any alterations to the text was 1 September 1973.

The guide is also intended to be more than just a practical handbook. It explains aspects of the law which have particular significance for women. It shows where the law can be used to help women to assert and defend their rights. It also points out ways in which the law discriminates against women. For the same purpose it attempts to unravel some of the red tape produced by government machinery. It suggests changes of all kinds that might be made to improve the position of women. In other words it is a self-help guide, a catalogue of evils and something of a manifesto.

Anna Coote
Tess Gill

1. Work

Equal pay

We have an Equal Pay Act but we don't have equal pay. The latest figures from the Department of Employment (October 1973) show that women's average earnings are little more than half men's average earnings:

	Women (18 and over): *average weekly earnings*	Men (21 and over): *average weekly earnings*
Manual workers	£19·7	£38·1
Non-manual workers	£24·7	£48·1

Why? One reason often given is that women work shorter hours than men. But this is certainly not the main reason, as you can see when you compare the average hourly earnings of men and women:

	Women	*Men*
Mechanical engineering	61·73p	89·33p
Food, drink and tobacco manufacture	58·76p	85·44p
Clothing and footwear manufacture	52·28p	80·71p
Electrical engineering	59·79p	88·95p

Another reason given is that women tend to do unskilled work. In fact, employers often give women's work a low grade even when it is quite skilled, and women who are classified as skilled tend to be paid less than most unskilled grades of male workers. Look at the figures for the minimum wage rates in the baking industry (September 1973):

Skilled women	£15·80
Unskilled men	£19·40
Skilled men	£20·60

Some women workers do have equal pay – and have had it for many years. Civil servants and white-collar local authority workers, London Transport workers, municipal and country bus conductors, and Post Office telephonists all had equal pay by 1970. The Equal Pay Act was passed in 1970 (only eighty-two years after the Trades Union Congress first passed a resolution calling for equal pay in 1888!). Since then, women workers in the retail meat trade, the retail multiple grocery trade, the herring industry board, Ford Motor Company and Mobil Oil have all been given equal pay. Unfortunately, the fact that they have 'equal pay' doesn't mean that they have equal opportunities for training and promotion. In some cases it just means that they have the right to be paid at the same rate as the lowest-paid male worker.

What the Equal Pay Act says

The Act, which was passed in 1970, comes into full force on 29 December 1975.

1. It says that women should get equal pay if:
   (a) They are employed on 'like work' with men. 'Like work' is supposed to mean work that is exactly the same or broadly similar to the work done by men, where any differences that do exist between women's and men's work need have no practical effect on their terms and conditions of employment. One has to consider the nature and extent of such differences and the frequency with which they occur when deciding whether they should have any practical effect.
   or
   (b) They are employed on work that is 'rated as equivalent' to men's work. Your work can only be rated equivalent to a man's job by an official 'job evaluation' study. So far only a third of the jobs in industry are covered by job evaluation studies.

2. It says that in addition to equal pay, women should get equal terms and conditions of employment. This means they should get the same basic pay, overtime rates, bonuses, holidays, sick pay and luncheon vouchers.

3. It says that women should continue to be treated differently from men in certain circumstances and still get equal pay – for instance:
   (a) the 'protective legislation' of the Factory Acts prevents most women from doing night work in factories and limits women's working hours;
   (b) maternity leave;
   (c) earlier retirement age (60 instead of 65).

4. In order to negotiate for equal pay, women can compare their pay and conditions with men who are:
   (a) employed in the same place of work; or
   (b) employed by the same employer at another place of work where the same conditions and terms of work apply (this could be at an associated company or at a branch of the same company).

5. If a collective agreement has been made between a trade union and an employer which provides different pay and conditions for men and women, it must be put right so that it provides equal pay and conditions by the end of 1975.

6. Trade unions or employers can refer collective agreements to the Industrial Arbitration Board to make sure that any terms which discriminate against women are removed.
7. If your employer refuses to give you equal pay after the Act comes into force, you will be able to make a claim to an industrial tribunal. You can claim arrears of pay and damages to compensate for unequal conditions. If you leave your job and still want to claim, you must do so within six months of leaving. You cannot claim arrears of pay for more than two years before your claim is heard. It will be up to your employer to prove to the tribunal that he is not discriminating against you.

You can get an appeal form from your local Employment Exchange. If you belong to a trade union, you should consult your local union official, or the union's legal department, before you fill in the form. Otherwise, make sure you get legal advice through the 'green form procedure' described on p. 302.

The wording of the Act is very vague and until some test cases have been brought before industrial tribunals it is impossible to know when or how you are likely to be awarded equal pay.

What the Equal Pay Act does not give you

1. The Act does not give women equal pension rights. (It would be rather embarrassing for the Government if it did, since the pension provisions under the National Insurance Act and the new State Reserve Scheme are most unfair to women.)
2. Women cannot claim for equal pay with men who are working for the same employer at another workplace if the terms and conditions of employment are different there. For example: a company could own two factories and have women in one doing the same work as men in the other. Merely by varying the terms of its agreements with workers in the two factories, it could avoid giving the women equal pay.
3. If a collective agreement (that is, one made between trade unions and an employers' association) applies only to male employees, it need not be extended to women.

4. It does not provide any method of ensuring that women get equal pay if they are doing 'women's work' and there are no men doing 'broadly similar' work with whom they can be compared.
5. It does not prevent job evaluation studies making use of standards that discriminate against women – for example, by giving a high rating to work which requires physical strength and a lower rating to work which requires manual dexterity for intricate or delicate work.
6. It does not stop men being paid more for doing night work and shift work – from which most women are excluded because of protective legislation.
7. It does nothing to counteract the practice of giving extra pay for long service – which can be discriminatory, since women often have to stop work for several years while they are bringing up children.

How employers can dodge the Equal Pay Act

While there is no provision in the Act to give women equal opportunity in training and promotion, it is possible for employers to keep women in low-paid grades of work, or to transfer women employees to 'women's jobs' where they have no chance of comparing their pay and conditions with male workers. It was reported in the *Sunday Times* (25 February 1973) that employers' associations have been sending their members confidential memos on ways of avoiding the impact of the Equal Pay Act: 'In suitably euphemistic language, the memoranda indicate a variety of strategies – such as introducing new job gradings, segregating female employees, and keeping the unskilled rate as low as possible.' A memorandum from the British Paper Box Federation, representing an industry of 26,000 employees, 70 per cent of them women, says:

It has been suggested *seriously* not *cynically* that in the event of proper provision not being made now to provide for an acceptable differential between the take-home pay for men and women, the following discrimination factors are available:

Long Service;
Merit;
Attendance Bonus;
Willingness to work overtime to a given number of hours.

The same memo urges that 'Jobs should be changed now where areas of conflict are likely to arise; i.e. the Lavatory Cleaner'. The *Sunday Times* explains:

The lavatory problem is the central snag for all employers striving to minimise the cost of equal pay legislation. Mr J. B. Winton, industrial relations adviser to the Paper Box Federation, explained that the current practice in most industries is to pay the men who clean the men's lavatories the basic labouring rate, whereas the women who 'do'

I'm the **Gentlemen's Edulcorator** and I earn **£15**

I'm the **Ladies' Lav cleaner** and I earn **£12**

Vive la différence!

the ladies' lavatories are usually on women's unskilled rate – a difference in material terms of £3 a week. It is, of course, difficult to avoid the fact that under the Equal Pay Act these jobs are 'the same or broadly similar'. However, as Mr Winton pointed out, putting up the ladies' lavatory cleaners' money by £3 a week 'could have comparability repercussions at all levels'.

The first report from the Office of Manpower Economics on the implementation of the Equal Pay Act shows employers busily segregating women from men:

In one company, 80% of employees were women engaged on work similar to that of men rated as semi-skilled; they were, however, paid a rate below that for unskilled men. The costs of meeting equal pay within the existing job and pay structure were considered by Management to be prohibitive. With the acceptance of trade union representatives who are concerned about male unemployment in the area, it is therefore now separating men and women into distinct categories of jobs.

For example, the machine shop has had a female day shift and a male night shift; men are now being recruited for daywork and women are being transferred to other departments. The more technical inspection jobs are being allotted to men and the women are being transferred to simple inspection tasks; central packing is becoming a male area, line packing is reserved for women; work in the finishing and paint shops and in the Stores, is to be a male preserve; this also applies to sign-writing, even though many women are considered to be more skilful at this.

White-collar jobs are to be graded into three grades: the lower one predominantly women, the middle one mixed and the upper one predominantly for men. As a result of this re-organization it is expected that by the end of 1972 very little of the work undertaken by women will be even broadly similar to that of men.

Against this sort of opposition, women will remain as far from equal pay as they were before the Act was passed, unless they are prepared to fight to make it effective.

How can women fight for equal pay?

The Equal Pay Act will continue to be a dead letter unless women get together and insist on their rights. An Equal Opportunities

Act would help a bit: if it outlawed discrimination against women in training and promotion, it would, theoretically, give women equal opportunities as well as equal pay. But any Equal Opportunities Act will be just as ineffective as the Equal Pay Act if women do not work together to ensure that it is put into practice.

Here are some suggestions of ways that women can work towards equal pay.

JOIN A TRADE UNION

A lot of women think that trade unions are men's business – often because they have been encouraged to look upon their earnings as 'pin money' to supplement their husbands' wages. In fact, the vast majority of women who go out to work contribute a vital part of the family income and, in any case, they have as much right as men to a fair deal at work.

GET INVOLVED IN THE WORK OF THE UNION

Women are now joining trade unions at twice the rate of men, but few become actively involved in union affairs. This is not because women are apathetic, but because union meetings are often held at times and places which don't suit women with families. If your union meetings are held at awkward times, try to get them shifted to lunch hours; otherwise insist that a créche is provided where women can leave their children during the meetings. Créches have already been set up by several unions, including a telephonists' branch of the Union of Post Office Workers in north-west London, where twice as many women now attend quarterly meetings.

JOIN FORCES WITH OTHER WOMEN TRADE UNIONISTS

Even if women *do* join unions and go to meetings, they still have considerable odds against them. All union leaderships are dominated by men (even those with considerably more women than men as members), and as a result trade unions generally don't take the special problems of women workers seriously. This is partly due to the simple fact that many men still look upon women as inferior beings, and partly due to the way that trade unions tend to operate.

Policies differ from one union to another. Some union officials encourage their members to fight for better pay and conditions. Others dampen their members' demands and press for speedy settlements with management. Unfortunately, the unions which have traditionally organized women are among the least active. This is because women, once unionized, have generally been passive in their attitude and have not put pressure on their officials to take a more militant line. If trade union officials are anxious to settle a deal with management, and if their women members happen to be the least vociferous or threatening, then equal pay and opportunity become the easiest part of a claim to drop.

When women workers at Biba, the Kensington fashion store, wanted to form a branch of the Union of Shop, Distributive and Allied Workers, negotiations dragged on for nine months and it was not until the women took the initiative and threatened a walk-out that the local union official persuaded Biba's manager to sign an agreement recognizing the union.

More active participation by women in trade unions would obviously help to overcome these difficulties. For instance, when 187 women seat-cover sewers at Fords Dagenham went on strike, they gained the support of all Fords' shop stewards, who organized a factory collection to support their fight. The women succeeded in getting 92 per cent of the male rate of pay in all grades, and an immediate increase of 7d. an hour.

Women also need to work together – separately from men – in order to discuss their grievances and plan action without being submerged by their brothers. Some unions, such as the Association of Cinematograph, Television and Allied Technicians and the National Union of Journalists, have appointed special committees to examine and report on the situation of their women members. The Trades Union Congress has an annual women's conference. A lot of resolutions have been passed at a lot of conferences, but this clearly isn't enough. As an example of the sort of action that is needed, the women's committee of the Newcastle Trades Council launched the Tyneside Campaign for Equal Rights in March 1973. A report in the *Guardian* (15 March 1973) described its aims:

> To provide and train speakers for local union branches on all aspects of equal rights; to set up an advice centre to advise and assist working women (especially on how to deal with the gaping loopholes of the Equal Pay Act); to establish a 'flying squad' to rush reinforcements to women in dispute; and to advise unions on how to recruit and involve more women . . . So far two unions have affiliated to the campaign – the General and Municipal Workers', and the Association of Teachers in Technical Institutions. But a number of individuals who have sent in their 50p membership fee have indicated that they will be leaning on their unions to sign up too. The local Labour and Communist Party organisations, as well as Trotskyist and Women's Liberation groups, will also be invited to join.

Women workers and the Factory Acts

In the nineteenth century women, children and men all worked between twelve and fourteen hours a day. The only difference was that women were paid less than men, and children were paid less than women.

The first reform came when the 'ten-hour day' was introduced for women and children. Then children were taken out of the factories and put into schools. Eventually, certain restrictions were placed on working hours and conditions for women – partly out of concern that they might ruin their own health and their children's if they were forced to work long hours in factories as well as run their homes; and partly because male workers were afraid that if women continued to compete for jobs on equal terms, they would bring unemployment and threaten their pay and conditions.

The same restrictions were placed on young people under 18.

They are set out in the Factory Acts and known as 'protective legislation'. They are still in force.

The terms of the Acts apply only to factories: that is, places where people are employed in manual labour, making anything; or breaking up, altering, repairing, finishing, cleaning, or washing anything; or adapting anything for sale. A lot of places that you wouldn't normally think of as factories fit this description – for instance, slaughter-houses and film studios. The terms of the Acts do not apply to women in management jobs who are not doing manual labour.

What do the Factory Acts say?

The Acts are too complicated to be explained in full here, largely because there are so many exceptions to the rules. Here is a broad outline of the ways that women's work is limited:

1. Women cannot work for more than nine hours a day or forty-eight hours a week. (They can work for ten hours a day on a five-day week.)
2. The work period must not be more than eleven hours in any one day and must not begin before 7 a.m. or end after 8 p.m. (or 1 p.m. on a Saturday).
3. They must not work for more than four and a half hours without a break for a meal; but if they have a ten-minute break they can work for five hours without a meal break.
4. *Overtime*. Women are allowed to work overtime under the following conditions:
   (a) they must not work for more than ten hours in a day;
   (b) the work period must not last for more than twelve hours a day and must not start before 7 a.m. or end after 9 p.m. (or 1 p.m. on a Saturday);
   (c) the Secretary of State for Employment is supposed to supervise this overtime, and details must be sent to the Inspector of Factories for the district.
5. *Shift work*. An employer can get permission from the Secretary of State for Employment to employ women on shift work, as

long as their shifts don't start before 6 a.m. or end after 10 p.m. No shift should last longer than eight hours unless it is worked for fewer than five days a week, in which case it can last for ten hours. The Secretary of State will not allow a factory to introduce shift work until a secret ballot of the workers has been taken to see if they agree to it. But this does not apply to new factories which intend to use shift work on a permanent basis.

6. *Night work.* The main restriction of the Factory Acts is that women cannot work nights. However, an employer can apply to the Secretary of State for Employment for an exemption. Before the Secretary of State grants an exemption, he is supposed to be satisfied that 'it is desirable in the public interest to do so for the purpose of maintaining or increasing the efficiency of industry or for the purpose of maintaining or increasing the efficiency of industry or transport.' Under exemption orders in 1969, 21,471 women did night work.

Night cleaners: women who are employed to clean factories are not restricted by the terms of the Factory Acts.

The effects of protective legislation

The existence of protective legislation is often used as a reason for giving women workers less favourable treatment than men: why, it is argued, should women have equal pay and opportunities while their working capacity is restricted? Many people argue that protective legislation should be abolished because it is a discriminatory measure and it stops women from getting better-paid jobs.

However, women have so far resisted any attempts to lift protective legislation. The 1972 TUC women's conference voted to oppose the government's suggestions that limitations on women doing night work in bakeries should be removed. The advantages of the legislation are obvious. Few people enjoy working long hours or at night. Neither women nor men should be forced out of economic necessity to do night work against their will. (Many women are forced to do night work because there is no one to look after their children during the day. This would be avoided if adequate child-care facilities were provided by the state.) There is a strong case for arguing – as most women trade unionists do – that protective legislation should be strengthened and extended to night cleaners and other women who are not protected, and to male workers as well.

Maternity leave

Maternity leave is leave from your job before and after you have a baby. Very few employers in Britain will grant maternity leave, except in the 'public sector' – that is, in local or central government, nationalized industries and other jobs where salaries are paid out of public funds, such as teaching. Even in the public sector, maternity leave is granted mainly to women in 'white-collar' staff jobs.

In other countries where women are accepted and valued as an important part of the labour force, maternity leave is guaranteed by law. In East Germany, for example, women have fourteen weeks off on full pay with their jobs guaranteed when they return to work together with lump sums paid by the state. In Hungary

women have twenty weeks off on full pay, followed by an optional period of up to three years with flat-rate payments of approximately one third of the wage of an unskilled worker, while their jobs are kept open for them. Other countries in the Common Market are far in advance of Britain. By law, women in France get fourteen weeks' maternity leave on full pay and in Italy they get twenty weeks.

In Britain it is still not generally accepted that women should have any special rights because they have babies. If you have a steady, 'white-collar' job and you are covered by a sick-pay scheme which is provided by your employer, you will probably be able to claim sick pay while you are away having your baby and for some weeks afterwards. If you have been employed long enough to qualify for the full rate, you should get up to twenty-six weeks on full pay. But this is not a very satisfactory alternative to proper maternity leave, for the following reasons:

1. You are using up your sick pay, so if you are ill when you go back to work you may find that you are not entitled to any more benefit until you have worked again for a certain length of time.
2. It encourages the argument that women are sick more often than men. Having a baby is a healthy occupation and should not be lumped together with sick leave.
3. Depending on the terms of your sick-pay scheme, you may have to be in your job for a long time before you qualify. Since most women have children when young, this can be a disadvantage.

If you are not covered by a sick-pay scheme the best you can expect is unpaid leave, and this will depend on the 'good will and generosity' of your employer. If you do get unpaid leave and you are contributing to an occupational pension scheme, watch out that it doesn't count as a break in your employment as it could otherwise lead to a decrease in your pension.

The Women's Advisory Committee of the TUC has looked into the question of maternity leave and the various arrangements made for employees in the public sector. It has drawn up the following code of 'Best Practice', showing the most favourable terms for maternity leave, so that unions can negotiate to have them incorporated into collective agreements between trade unions and employers in private industry and commerce.

'BEST PRACTICE' MATERNITY LEAVE ARRANGEMENTS IN THE PUBLIC SECTOR

1. *Eligibility*
The best agreements apply to all women employees, irrespective of marital status, and some include part-time employees provided that they are eligible for sick leave.

2. *Qualifying Period of Service*
Normally 12 months' continuous service at the date of application for maternity leave. The best agreements also make provision for some break in service (example: a period of less than three months between the termination and resumption of employment is not regarded as a break in service).

3. *Application for Maternity Leave*
Normally application must be made not less than three months before the anticipated date of confinement. Some agreements require a declaration at the time of application that the woman intends to resume employment at the expiry of the leave.

4. *Length of Maternity Leave*
The 'best practice' is 18 weeks (but see paragraph 5 below). The period before and after the anticipated date of confinement varies but the best is 11 weeks before and seven weeks after. If the child does not live the period after confinement is sometimes reduced to four weeks. Leave in excess of 18 weeks may be granted in exceptional cases. Further, absence due to, or attributable to, the pregnancy which occurs outside the period of 18 weeks is usually treated as absence on sick leave within the provisions of the sick pay scheme.

5. *Scale of payment*
The outstanding example is undoubtedly one nationalised industry which incorporates maternity leave into the normal sick pay scheme (13 weeks full pay less NI benefit: and 13 weeks half pay without NI deduction). Generally speaking, however, 'best practice' is four weeks full pay less NI benefit (irrespective of whether or not the woman herself contributes to National Insurance) plus 14 weeks half pay without NI deduction – unless the combined total of half pay plus benefit is

more than the normal full pay (in which case payment is that sufficient to bring N I benefit up to full pay).

6. *Relation to Sick Pay Scheme*

Pregnancy is not considered, medically, to be sickness but a number of schemes do incorporate maternity leave payments within the undertaking's sick pay scheme. 'Best practice' is that the period of maternity leave is not taken into account for the purpose of calculating sick pay entitlement.

7. *Resumption of Work*

Most agreements include certain restrictions designed to ensure that the woman will resume employment for a specified minimum period after maternity leave.

'Best practice' is considered to be the withholding of payment for the last four weeks of maternity leave until the woman has been back at work for a minimum period of four weeks. One agreement provides that this payment will not be withheld if the child does not live. Another agreement which withholds payment until the completion of three months' service enables the woman, however, to resume initially on a part-time basis, provided that this is at least half the hours normally worked each week before the pregnancy. No agreement provides for appeal against the withholding of payment of the last weeks of maternity leave if work is not resumed. It is considered that, while it is reasonable to include some restrictions of this nature in the agreement, there should be provision for appeal and that each case should be considered jointly by the appropriate trade union and the management.

8. *Protection of Health*

Only one agreement examined included any protection for the health of the pregnant woman (relating to contact with german measles). Restrictions to protect the woman's health should be kept to the minimum and will vary, according to the industry and the requirements of the particular job. Therefore unions can themselves best judge what protection is desirable for their women members. However, one issue which should be included in all agreements is that pregnant women should be granted leave, without loss of pay, to attend antenatal clinics.

Most areas of the public sector of employment have maternity leave arrangements which come near to 'best practice' – notably, local government, the electricity, gas and water boards, the Post Office, government industry, the U K Atomic Energy Authority, and teaching. But there is nothing comparable in the private sector.

Until the overall situation improves, the best you can do if you want to have your children in comfort without losing your job is to find employment in the public sector. Alternatively, get together with other women at your place of work and demand that your employer introduces a maternity leave scheme.

Further information

A detailed list of maternity leave arrangements in the public sector is available from the TUC Women's Advisory Council, Congress House, 23–28 Great Russell Street, London WC1 (01 636 4030).

Training

Women have few positive rights where job training is concerned. Opportunities for training are scarce, and there is a serious lack of information on the subject. Until anti-discrimination legislation is passed, there is nothing in law to say that women must have equal opportunities with men, and employers are free to discriminate openly. Table 1 shows that only 26·4 per cent of girl school-leavers in 1971 entered jobs providing recognized forms of training, compared with 56·7 per cent of boys. About three quarters of girls' apprenticeships are in hairdressing.

TABLE 1

Type of work	*Boys*		*Girls*	
	Thousands	*Percentage*	*Thousands*	*Percentage*
Apprenticeship or learnership to skilled occupation (including pre-apprenticeship in employment)	95·6	39·5	16·7	7·5
Employment leading to recognized professional qualifications	3·1	1·2	4·1	1·9
Clerical employment	17·6	7·2	78·8	35·8
Employment with planned training, apart from introduction training, not covered in previous columns	38·7	16·0	37·5	17·0
Other employment	87·1	36·0	83·4	37·8

There are still a great many more men than women in all types of government training, except at further education colleges, where most of the training in shorthand and typing takes place. In 1971 there was only one woman for every five men in government training schemes. Table 2 shows how they were distributed.

How does this happen? It boils down to a vicious circle of employers' prejudices and women's conditioning. While girls are at school there are already strong influences at work to restrict opportunities for them. The National Union of Teachers, in

TABLE 2

	Government training centres	Further education colleges	Training 'on the job'	Residential training centres	Total
Men	15,993	3,099	4,528	690	24,310
Women	47	4,107	368	187	4,709
Total	16,040	7,206	4,896	877	29,019

evidence to the House of Commons Expenditure Committee, stated that there were 'mixed schools where, when it comes to anything to do with the vocational course, it is said "The girls go to commerce, the boys to technical", as if that were the rule of life.' The TUC Women's Advisory Committee, in evidence to the same committee, said 'More and more jobs ... require a competence in mathematics and science subjects which girls often do not have. This arises not only from the continuing shortage of women teachers in these subjects, but also, in part, from the different approach to and methods of teaching girls which, in the past, have tended to suggest that subjects other than arts subjects have little practical relevance to the future day-to-day life of women. And so the attitudes of girls themselves have been influenced. They have assumed that there is a "mystique" about mathematics and science subjects.' This sort of conditioning deters girls from applying for serious training outside the conventional female spheres of work. (See p. 222 for discrimination in schools.)

For the few women who get that far, there is little overt discrimination in colleges and universities – though some medical schools and veterinary colleges still exercise 'quotas' limiting places for women to a fixed percentage, regardless of their qualifications. The problem with further education is that girls are channelled through schools in such a way that they don't take the right exams to qualify for entry to traditionally male-dominated fields of study.

Careers advice in schools is often inadequate – there is little incentive for teachers to specialize in this field, and careers teachers are insufficiently trained. We recently heard from an English teacher at a girls' comprehensive in south London that the 'careers room' displayed literature on jobs ranging only from canteen assistant and florist to secretary and nurse – nothing more ambitious.

Bias in the educational system, as well as in society at large, influences the expectations women have of themselves. Most women are brought up to believe that they are destined to be wives and mothers and not primarily workers. Many are discouraged because they know the scope is severely limited for them; some even fail to take up opportunities when they do arise.

There is a tremendous amount of prejudice among employers and employees against accepting women in certain types of work. This is well illustrated by a report from a careers officer: 'A man in insurance was showing some careers officers around. When they asked him about the opportunities at a higher level for girls, he said "Well, we have solicitors, but of course it is very difficult work and women would not want to do it." It is this sort of thing that will remain as an attitude, however many doors one opens.'

Employers still argue that women are a bad investment because they leave their jobs to get married and have children. In fact, that argument has long been discredited, since it has been found that a large and ever-increasing proportion of married women return to work; and that training leads to greater satisfaction at work, which encourages women to stay in their jobs.

It is also clear that by and large men simply don't want women in powerful positions – 'The boardroom is no place for a woman.'

What can you do about this?

CAREERS ADVICE

First of all, make sure you get good careers advice. If you're at school or in full-time education you have a right to a free advice session with a careers officer – careers offices are run by local education authorities in most major towns and cities, and their addresses can be found in local telephone directories. It's worthwhile taking advice as early as possible, as some forms of training require certain O or A levels, for which you will need to plan ahead.

For people over eighteen, the state runs an 'occupational guidance service'. This can be especially helpful for women who want to go back to work in later life and don't know what to do. It's available free at forty-four centres in Britain – you can arrange an interview through your local Employment Exchange.

Whether the careers advice you get is more helpful than telling you to become a sales assistant rather than a factory-hand will depend largely on the individual officer. Careers services are often understaffed, and the advice you are given in one quick interview may be rather superficial. If you feel you need more guidance, ask for further interviews. Remember to keep a critical attitude to what you are told: careers teachers or officers may have a sexist bias, causing them to channel you into a 'female' job, or an occupational bias – tending to give advice in terms of the labour needs of the area: if there is a shortage of office staff, for example, they may suggest you become a typist, and that may not be the best thing for you.

JOBS WITH GOOD TRAINING FACILITIES

If you're thinking about in-job training, it's worth choosing carefully where you start work – some kinds of employment provide better opportunities than others. The civil service and local government are two examples where a wide variety of technical as well as commercial training is available for women.

TRADITIONAL WOMEN'S JOBS

There are of course ample opportunities to train for the jobs that women normally do – social work, teaching, nursing and secretarial work, to name the most common. Some of these have low status because they are 'women's jobs', but they are not necessarily less rewarding. It has been argued that shorthand and typing should be regarded as a proper commercial apprenticeship, with day release and adequate in-job training for men and women. This sort of approach might begin to solve the problem of low status and correspondingly low pay.

GOVERNMENT TRAINING SCHEMES

If you're going back to work or want to retrain in later life, find out about government training schemes. These are designed for people whose skills have become outdated or who missed an earlier opportunity to train for a job – such as women returning to work after raising a family. The scheme offers free full-time training on courses lasting up to one year in a variety of subjects at colleges of further education, government training centres and 'on the job'. During the training, tax-free allowances are paid which are not affected by your husband's income – though the allowances for women are consistently lower than those paid to men. They say they help you find work afterwards – the only problem is that employers tend to think that a craft apprenticeship with experience on the shop-floor is more valuable than a shorter spell of government-sponsored training.

Finally it must be said that very few doors are completely closed to women these days – one keeps hearing of the 'first women' to go into all sorts of unlikely jobs. It is not so much the formal restrictions that hold women back, rather people's attitudes. A woman who has a proper understanding of her own abilities and the persistence to fight against these odds can train for almost any type of work.

A law to end discrimination against women

At the time of writing, it seems possible that some sort of anti-discrimination law may be passed within the next few years. In 1972–3, two almost identical anti-discrimination bills were under discussion in Parliament: one had been introduced into the House of Lords by Baroness Seear, the other into the Commons by Labour MP William Hamilton. Both bills were referred to Select Committees and a huge amount of evidence was collected from the public and from government sources, which provided ample proof that a law of this kind was needed. But since both bills were sponsored by private members, they stood little chance of becoming law without the backing of the government of the day.

At first, it looked as though the Conservative government was prepared to give its support. On 14 February 1973, William Hamilton's bill passed its second reading and went into a Select Committee: never before had an anti-discrimination bill progressed so far through Parliament. But in September that year, the Hamilton bill was shelved when the Conservative government published a 'consultative document' (Green Paper) which set out its own proposals for an 'Equal Opportunities' law. These proposals were a great disappointment. They concentrated on the field of employment and virtually ignored education and other important areas of discrimination; they did *not* propose to include trade unions or professional associations, pensions or retirement, housing, goods, facilities or services; and the enforcement machinery was very weak indeed.

Then in February 1974 the Conservatives were defeated and replaced by a minority Labour government. Amid the political upheavals that followed, the 'Woman's Question' took, as usual, a back seat: the future of anti-discrimination legislation was not at all clear.

An Act of Parliament will not *end* discrimination; but it will be an important statement about the way people are expected to behave. For centuries, discrimination on grounds of sex has been perfectly legal. An Act would state for the first time that it is against the law. It could provide an incentive to women to take positive and collective action to ensure that the spirit of the Act is carried into practice; and if it is adequately enforced it could be of practical use to women who at present suffer discrimination.

What kind of law do we need?

We need a law that prohibits discrimination on grounds of *sex and marital status*. This would mean, for example, that a woman could not be refused promotion because her employer expected her to have children and leave. It would also mean that benefits available to married women and children could not be withheld from single mothers. The Conservatives' document did not include discrimination on grounds of marital status.

The law should cover discrimination in the following areas:

I. EMPLOYMENT

 (i) Women should have equal opportunities with men to obtain job qualifications. This would cover, for example, apprenticeships and day-release training.
 (ii) Women should not be refused jobs because they are women.
(iii) They should be offered, and given, equal terms and conditions of employment, including fringe benefits.
(iv) They should be given equal opportunities for in-job training and promotion.
 (v) They should not be sacked just because they are women. This would prevent the current practice of laying-off married women first when there are redundancies to be made.

Exemptions

The Conservatives' document included a long list of types of work that were to be exempted from the new law. Let-out clauses of this kind are dangerous because they provide loop-holes for employers who wish to practise discrimination.

Only one exemption is really necessary: that is where there is a need for *authenticity*, for instance, in acting or modelling. In addition, there could be a list of specific jobs (such as the clergy, miners working underground, midwives and prison workers) which are exempted. This list should be regarded as a temporary measure, until opinions can be changed to accept women (or men) in these jobs. It should be kept as short as possible and reviewed annually in Parliament.

Private households and establishments employing not more than four people should not be covered by the law.

Protective laws

Sections of the Factory Acts which limit the hours that women can work and exclude them from night work should *not* be repealed by the new Act. The Conservatives proposed to do this as a price for 'Equal Opportunities' legislation. The Labour Party and the TUC appear to be committed to retaining the protective laws, but it is unlikely that we have heard the last of the debate. If protective laws are abolished, working-class women will find themselves forced to work in shifts and at night and the result will be more exploitation, not less. (More about the Factory Acts on pp. 30–33.)

2. TRADE UNIONS AND PROFESSIONAL ASSOCIATIONS

It should be illegal for these bodies to discriminate, not only in admission to membership, but also in admission to office or to any job controlled by them. This would mean, for instance, that the Post Office Workers' Union could no longer prevent the full-time employment of postwomen.

3. PENSIONS AND RETIREMENT

 (i) Women should be allowed to join occupational pension schemes on the same terms as men.
 (ii) It should be unlawful to give women lower pensions because of their longer life expectancy. This would apply to state and occupational pensions (see pp. 97–9).
(iii) It should be unlawful to make a woman retire earlier than a man, if she wants to go on working. This would mean that women could go on working after the age of sixty – but only if *they* chose to do so.

4. ADVERTISING

It should be illegal to advertise jobs as 'men's jobs' and 'women's jobs' unless they are specifically exempted from the new law.

5. HOUSING, GOODS, FACILITIES AND SERVICES

All these areas should be covered by the law, to include:
  (i) Access to places where members of the public are generally allowed (such as bars and billiard halls which are not private clubs).
 (ii) Renting and sale of accommodation.
(iii) Hotels and boarding houses.
 (iv) The services of banks, insurance and finance companies.
  (v) Hire Purchase and other credit facilities.

6. EDUCATION AND TRAINING

Women and girls should be treated equally with men and boys by all schools, colleges and other places which provide education and training. It would become illegal, for instance, to segregate girls into domestic and commercial classes while boys followed mechanical and technical courses; and it would become illegal to provide inferior laboratory facilities in girls' schools.

The government will probably be under a lot of pressure to exempt single-sex schools. We see no reason why single-sex education should continue, but if necessary the Act could exempt *existing* single-sex schools while preventing the opening of any new ones.

It should be the duty of the Equal Opportunities Board (which we describe below) to investigate the content of courses and educational material used by schools and colleges, and to remove any discriminatory bias by having text books rewritten and courses reorganized.

How should the law be enforced?

An anti-discrimination law should include strong machinery for enforcement if it is to be at all effective. We suggest:

1. AN EQUAL OPPORTUNITIES BOARD

This should have the following powers:
  (i) To initiate its own investigations in all areas of discrimination on grounds of sex.
 (ii) To require employers to provide documents and information, either for investigations or for statistical use; to summon witnesses and to carry out surveys.
(iii) To bring complaints to a tribunal or court on behalf of an individual (see below).
 (iv) To carry out educational and promotional activities.
  (v) To refer contracts which discriminate against women to the courts, to be revised.
 (vi) To review new and existing laws, and recommend any amendments that are necessary to end discrimination.
At least half of the members of the Board should be women.

2. CONCILIATION OFFICERS

These would be appointed by the Equal Opportunities Board and any complaints of discrimination would first be referred to them to investigate and attempt a conciliation. There should be a time limit of four weeks on this procedure. If this fails, the case would be referred to the Equal Opportunities Tribunal (see below).

3. EQUAL OPPORTUNITIES TRIBUNALS

These should deal with all cases of discrimination on grounds of sex, including unfair dismissal and equal-pay cases.

To ensure that an adequate number of women sit on the tribunals, the three members could be picked from a single panel at least half of whom are women, chosen for their specialist knowledge of the areas covered.

Complaints should be brought to the tribunal by the individual concerned, by the Equal Opportunities Board, or by another organization acting on behalf of the individual. Any conciliation agreement that is reached should be filed with the Equal Opportunities Board, which could apply to the tribunal to have it enforced.

When a case is brought before a tribunal, the employer should bear the burden of having to prove that he has not discriminated unlawfully. The woman who complains to the tribunal should only have to prove that something has happened (e.g. dismissal or refusal to promote); the employer would then have to prove that his action did not involve unlawful discrimination.

The tribunals should have the power to award compensation and back-pay. Compensation should be heavy enough to make it uneconomical for employers to discriminate. Costs should not be awarded against the complainant, under any circumstances. Tribunals should also have the power of declaring the rights of parties to dispute, and to recommend a course of action, e.g. that a woman who has been refused promotion should be promoted.

Any act of retaliation against a woman who complains to the tribunal (such as harassment or threats of demotion) should be made illegal.

Employers should be required to display a notice giving details of the law and how to go about making a complaint.

A woman whose case goes before the tribunal should have the right to be represented. The problem with tribunals at present is that legal aid is not available (although advice is available under the 'green form procedure', see p. 302). This means that a woman who doesn't have a trade union or other organization to act for her has to put her own case to the tribunal. Legal aid should be available for cases brought before the Equal Opportunities tribunals, and for all others.

When a law is eventually passed

The battle will have just begun. There will be no miraculous end to discrimination just because a law has passed on to the statute book. One of the greatest dangers is that it will encourage women to sit back and think that everything will be all right. On the contrary, it will be up to women, particularly through trade unions and women's organizations, to see that the law is enforced. Otherwise we shall be little better off than we were when it was first thought of.

2. Money

Tax

Tax is a complete mystery to most people. If you work for an
employer your tax is probably deducted before you get your take-
home pay, so you may never think about how much you are paying
or why. It's worth knowing how your tax is calculated – you may
even find that you are paying too much.

Basically what happens is this

1. You earn a certain amount of money each year.
2. You get what are called 'allowances', which means that some of the money you earn is tax-free and you get all of it.
3. You can get extra tax-free personal allowances for a number of different reasons – for instance, if you are supporting children or paying off a mortgage.
4. The rest of your income is taxable. This normally means that you pay 30 per cent (almost one third) of it in tax, unless you are very rich, in which case you pay more.
5. What's left after that is yours to spend.

The government department which deals with tax is the Inland Revenue. Normally your tax will be dealt with by the local Inspector of Taxes. The system of having your tax deducted before you get your take-home pay is known as PAYE (Pay As You Earn). Most people who work for an employer pay tax through PAYE.

As you might expect, the Inland Revenue does not go out of its way to see that everyone pays as little tax as possible. You won't get any extra tax-free allowances unless you claim them. You do this by filling in your 'income tax return' form from the Inland Revenue. If you pay tax through PAYE, the Inland Revenue will send you a tax form every one to three years, depending on how stable they think your financial circumstances are. If you don't pay through PAYE (for instance, if you are self-employed) you will probably be sent a tax form regularly each year. Each year, you should also receive a 'coding notice' – this explains what your tax allowances are and gives you what is called a 'code number', indicating the rate of tax you should pay.

Are you paying too much tax?

There are several reasons why you may be paying too much tax. You may not have filled in a tax return form since you became eligible for certain allowances. You may have changed jobs and failed to tell the local tax office what your code number is. You may have been given the wrong code number (a recent survey showed that 25 per cent of all code numbers were incorrect). Don't rely on your employer to sort out your tax for you.

If you think you are paying too much tax, the first thing to do is to find out the address of the local tax office which deals with your tax. It will be the one which covers the area where you *work* (not the area where you live, if the two are different). You can ask the accounts department at your place of work for the address of the tax office, or look it up in the phone book, where it is listed under 'Inland Revenue'. Once you have the address, write to the local Inspector of Taxes and ask for a P46 form. This is a very simple form, on which you write your name and address. When you have sent it back to the tax office, you will be sent a tax return form. You must then fill in the tax return form, claiming all the tax allowances you think you should have, and supplying the relevant information. Don't be intimidated by the formality of it – the form is really quite simple to complete, if you take it slowly. If you don't understand anything, or can't remember details that you are asked to supply, you can always write 'I don't understand' or 'I don't remember' on the form, and send a letter to the Inspector of Taxes, explaining your situation in your own words.

If you move around from job to job and you think you may be paying too much tax, keep a list of all your employers and their addresses, and how much you were paid by each one. If you can't remember what you were paid, you can always write to your previous employers and ask for the dates of your employment and the amount you were paid: they will probably have records of this.

You get any excess tax back in the form of a 'tax rebate'. If you don't claim it back soon after you have paid it, it isn't lost. You can reclaim tax up to six years after you have paid it, and it will be paid back to you eventually.

If you start a new job where you pay tax through PAYE, the wages department will ask you for your Form P45. This is a form which you should have been given when you left your last job: it says how much you earned, how much tax you paid and what your code number is. It is very important to keep your Form P45 in between jobs. If you give it to the wages department at your new place of work, they should continue to deduct tax at the rate you were paying before (unless the wages clerk makes a mistake, which sometimes happens, so check when you get your pay packet).

If you have lost your P45, or you don't have one because this is your first job, then you will have tax deducted at the 'emergency' rate until you have filled in a tax return form and the Inland Revenue has worked out how much tax you should be paying. Emergency tax is the same as the rate of tax paid by a single person who has no extra tax-free allowances – it is fairly high, so that if you go down to a lower rate when you get coded you will get a tax rebate. You will probably be sent a tax return form shortly after you start your new job. If not, tell the wages department that you want a P46 form and they will arrange it. If they don't, write to the local tax office as explained above.

How much tax will you have to pay?

As is the habit of most government departments, the Inland Revenue treats single women and married women as two completely different species. They treat single women like single men and married women like inanimate objects attached to their husbands. If you are separated from your husband, you may have particular difficulties with your tax, as explained below (p. 59).

Single women

As a single woman, your tax position is the same as a single man's. You don't pay tax on the first £595 you earn each year. This is known as a 'personal allowance' and you usually get it automatically without having to put in a claim.

There are extra tax-free allowances you may be able to claim, depending on your circumstances. Here are the main ones:

1. *Additional personal allowance.* If you are bringing up children single-handed, whether or not you are getting maintenance payments from their father, you can claim an 'additional person allowance' of £130 a year. This does not alter according to how many children you have. If you are financially responsible for your children you will also be able to claim *child tax allowances*, as explained below.

2. *Housekeeper allowance.* If you are widowed and you have a woman living with you who acts as a housekeeper, you may be able to claim an allowance of £100 a year. But you cannot claim this as well as the additional personal allowance. You can only claim one of the two.

3. *Daughter's services allowance.* If you have a daughter living with you and you are financially responsible for her, you may be dependent on her 'services' (for instance, her help with housework or with looking after younger children). If so, you may claim an allowance of £55 a year. You can't claim this for a son, though.

4. *Dependent relative allowance.* If you have any relatives whose income is not more than £457 a year and to whom you are giving some sort of financial help, you may be able to claim a 'dependent relative allowance' of up to £145 a year, depending on how much you are helping them. (The help may be in the form of goods, not just money.) There is no limit to the number of dependent relatives you can have.

5. *Life assurance relief.* If you have a life assurance policy you will probably be able to claim an allowance for part of the premiums you are paying. This is rather complicated to explain here, but you should be able to get advice from the life assurance company.

6. *Tax relief on occupational pension contributions.* If you are paying into an approved occupational pension scheme (that is, one run by a private company and not by the state), your contributions are deducted before your earnings are assessed for tax and this is taken into account in your code number.

7. *Other tax allowances.* You can claim tax relief on any interest you are paying on a mortgage or on a loan from a bank or

finance company. Write to the company to whom you are paying the interest and ask for a 'certificate of interest', which you then forward to the Inland Revenue. You can also claim tax relief on any expenses you have incurred 'wholly, necessarily and exclusively' in the course of your employment, which have not been reimbursed by your employer.

IF YOU ARE RECEIVING MAINTENANCE FROM A FORMER HUSBAND OR THE FATHER OF YOUR CHILDREN

Where the maintenance is for you:
If the man is making payments to you under a legal separation agreement or under a court order, the rule is that he should deduct the standard rate of income tax (30 per cent) from all payments. He must account to the Inland Revenue for the tax he deducts. You may claim any tax allowances you are eligible for (for example, an additional personal allowance), and (depending on your total income) you may receive a tax rebate. The tax deducted by the man will be looked upon by the Inland Revenue as though it had been paid by you.

If the man is paying maintenance under a court order which amounts to less than £12 a week or £52 a month, the rule is that he doesn't have to pay tax on it at all but pays it gross. *You* may have to pay tax on it if your total income is high enough to be taxable.

Where the maintenance is for your children:
If the maintenance order says that the maintenance is to be paid to the child, the money will not be added to your income for tax purposes, so you will not have to pay tax on it. In effect, what this means is that the child has an independent income, although the money is paid to you to administer for the child.

CHILD TAX ALLOWANCES

If you are looking after children on your own and you are financially responsible for them, you should be able to claim tax allowance for them. If the children's father is supporting them, the allowance will be paid to him. In fact, he can claim the allowance even if he is not supporting them. Here are the rates:

Child under 11 – £200
Child over 11 and under 16 – £235
Child over 16 – £265.

The allowance for a child over 16 will only be paid if she or he is in full-time education or on a full-time training course that lasts at least two years. If the child's own income is more than £115 a year, the allowance will be reduced.

If you and the children's father both apply for child tax allowance, the situation can get more complicated. See below (p. 59).

Tax on family allowance (single and married women)

If you have more than one child, you will get family allowance. But then the tax allowances received by you (if you are single) or by your husband (if you are married) are reduced by £60 for each child for whom family allowance is paid. So you will only get the full benefit of family allowance if your income (or your combined income, if you are married) is not high enough to be taxed. But one advantage of the system is that, with a married couple, it redistributes money from the husband to the wife.

Your tax allowances will not be reduced in this way if you are getting a widow's allowance, a widowed mother's allowance, a retirement pension or a child's special allowance.

Married women

For tax purposes, your income is treated as part of your husband's. This means that your husband has to fill in the tax form with details of your income and his. He is responsible for paying any tax that either of you owes to the Inland Revenue. But if a tax rebate is due, whether on his income or yours, it will be sent to him, unless he signs a letter to the Inland Revenue telling them to send the rebate to you. If you are paying tax through PAYE, your husband will only be responsible for paying tax on your unearned income – if you have any.

If you are earning, you are entitled to a 'personal allowance' of £595 and your husband gets a married man's allowance of £775. If you help your husband with his business, you cannot claim this relief unless you are paid proper wages for the work you do.

Married couples have a slight tax advantage over two single people if the wife is earning because her husband will still get his married man's allowance of £775. That means they will get £180 more in tax allowance than two single people. They would not have this advantage if their joint income were large enough to be liable for a higher rate of tax (higher tax rates begin at over £5,000 for a married couple's joint net income). But in that case they would benefit from the new form of separate assessment which is explained below.

IF YOU WANT YOUR TAX TO BE
SEPARATELY ASSESSED

You may prefer to deal with your own tax affairs. If so, you must make a special application for separate assessment. There are two ways you can do this:

1. *The old scheme* has been going for several years. You have to apply for separate assessment by writing to your local Inspector of Taxes before 6 July in the year you want to be separately assessed. (The tax year starts on 1 April.) This will enable you to fill in your own tax form, while the tax will be divided between you and your husband according to your income and allowances. Your husband is usually able to claim tax allowances for the children and for mortgage payments. This scheme does *not* affect the total amount of tax you have to pay between you.

2. *A new scheme* was introduced in 1972 which enables you and your husband to be taxed on your earned income as two single people. But the only couples to benefit financially are those

whose joint incomes are large enough to be in the higher tax bracket (that is, over £5,000 for most married couples). If you want to be assessed under this scheme, you and your husband must both make written applications to the local Inspector of Taxes. You would then be assessed on your earned income as a single person, with a personal allowance of £595. Your husband would also receive a single person's allowance. He would claim tax allowances for children and mortgage payments. If you had any unearned income it would continue to be assessed as part of your husband's income.

Neither scheme gives you any real privacy, as your husband can still find out what your income is.

TAX EXAMPLE ONE

Sarah is an unsupported mother with two children aged 6 and 9. She works as a computer punch-card operator and earns £24 a week (£1,250 a year). She receives family allowance of 90p a week (£47 a year).

Her total income with wages and family allowance is: £1,297·00
She has the following tax allowances:

1. personal allowance	£ 595·00
2. child allowances	400·00
3. additional personal allowance	130·00
These add up to:	£1,125·00

She loses some tax allowance
because she is getting family
allowance. This amounts to: £ 60·00
Her total tax allowance is: £1,065·00

So her total taxable income is: £1,297 − £1,065,
which comes to: £ 232·00
Tax at 30 per cent of £232 amounts to: £ 69·60
So her net income after tax is: £1,297·00
− 69·60

£1,227·40

TAX EXAMPLE TWO

Carol is married to Fred Marshall. They have no children. They have not applied for separate tax assessment as their incomes are not high enough to benefit from it. Carol works as a quality supervisor in a sweet factory and earns £1,100 a year. Fred works as an engineer and earns £2,000. They are paying interest on a mortgage at £300 a year, which is tax-free.

Their total earnings are:	£3,100·00
They have the following tax allowances:	
1. married man's allowance	£ 775·00
2. wife's earned-income allowance at seven ninths of her earnings with a maximum limit of £595	£ 595·00
3. mortgage interest	£ 300·00
Their total tax allowance is:	£1,670·00
So their total taxable income is £3,100 – £1,670, which comes to:	£1,430·00
Tax at 30 per cent of £1,430 is:	£ 429·00
So their net income after tax is:	£3,100·00
	– 429·00
	£2,671·00

IF YOU ARE SEPARATED

If you separate from your husband and he stops supporting you, notify the Inland Revenue: you should become eligible for the same tax allowances as a single person. If your husband continues to claim a married man's tax allowance while not supporting you, he could find himself in serious trouble – the penalty is up to nine months in prison.

If you have children, there is nothing to stop your husband from continuing to claim, and receive, child tax allowances, long after the separation, even if he is not supporting them – unless you make a positive counter-claim. If you are supporting the children, whether partly or wholly, you should write to the local Inland Revenue office and tell them (a) that you and your husband have separated; (b) that you want to claim tax allowances; and (c) that you want to complete an income tax return form.

If you can reach an agreement with your husband as to how the allowance is to be divided between you, you should both write to the Inland Revenue and tell them what you have agreed. If you can't reach an agreement, you should write to the Inland Revenue and ask for the matter to be brought before the Commissioner of Taxation (this is an appeal body, like a tribunal, which will consider both your claims and decide how the allowance should be divided). It will almost certainly be up to you, the wife, to take the initiative at this stage, since your husband will be the one who is getting the full tax allowance.

Before the matter is considered by the Commissioner, you must prepare a detailed statement of everything you spend on the children. You can make your claim retrospectively, from the date of the separation. You will be sent notification of the date and place of the hearing. It's important to attend if you possibly can – don't be intimidated, it's a fairly informal occasion. Husbands often give up at this stage and fail to present their side of the case to the Commissioner. If you feel you can't handle this alone, get an accountant to help you.

If you are self-employed

You can claim the same tax allowances as an employed person. You do not normally pay tax through PAYE, but through the 'Schedule D' system. You can claim tax relief on all sorts of expenses incurred in your work – heating, phone, rent, equipment, etc. It's often worth getting help from an accountant – if she or he is efficient and you don't earn a great deal, you may end up paying very little tax, or none at all. Get a written estimate first; some of them charge extortionate rates.

Tax relief for the elderly

If you are over 65 and your total income is not more than £700 (if you are single) or £1,000 (joint income if you are married), you will not have to pay any tax.

The proposed tax credit system

While this book was being written, the government's proposals
for a new system of taxation called tax credits were under discussion. It is not yet certain whether the new system will ever
see the light of day. If it does, it is not certain when it will be
introduced, or in what form. But the tax credit proposals have
provoked such a storm of controversy that we thought it would be
helpful to include a brief description.

Under the new system, some tax allowances, family allowance
and the family income supplement (FIS) will be replaced by
tax credits.

WHAT ARE TAX CREDITS?

The difference between tax credits and tax allowances is as
follows: tax credits are like tax-free sums of money added to
your wages after tax has been deducted; a tax allowance is
money that you earn but don't pay tax on.

Here is an example (the rates mentioned are hypothetical, so
don't assume they are the rates you would actually pay). Say
you earn £30 a week and, under the present system, you have a
tax allowance of £624 a year, i.e. £12 a week. This means you
pay tax on £18 a week at a rate of 30 per cent – i.e. £6 tax,
leaving you with £24 to spend. Under the tax credit system you
would get a credit of £4 a week – that's money in the hand. On
the entire £30 that you earn per week you pay tax at a rate of
30 per cent, i.e. £10 tax. This leaves you with £20 plus the £4 tax
credit which comes to £24.

HOW MUCH TAX CREDIT WILL BE PAID AND WHO WILL
GET IT?

The rates the government has been talking about are £4 a week
for a single person and £6 for a married couple, but there is no
guarantee they will be as high as this. Credits will be paid to all
men and single women who fulfil *one* of these conditions:

1. They are working for an employer and earning £8 a week or more.
2. They are receiving National Insurance benefits such as unemployment or sickness benefit.
3. They are receiving a retirement pension.

The personal tax allowance of £595 for a single person and £775 for a married man will be abolished for people getting tax credits. But other tax allowances, such as the additional personal allowance, dependent relative allowance, and tax relief on mortgage payments can still be claimed.

How will they be paid? Tax credits will be paid through the PAYE system. Employees will receive them in their pay packets. People getting National Insurance benefits or pensions will receive them together with those payments.

People getting tax credits will pay a flat-rate tax of 30 per cent on *all income and* on National Insurance benefits and pensions. Only people with an income over £5,000 a year will pay a higher rate.

Married women will not get tax credits. Instead they will get earned-income relief as they do now: that is, a yearly tax allowance of seven ninths of their earnings, up to a maximum of £595. In exceptional circumstances, where the woman is the family breadwinner and her husband is not entitled to tax credits, she will probably be entitled to receive them.

CHILD TAX CREDITS

Initially, the government proposed paying child tax credits at a suggested rate of £2 a week per child to single women and married couples with children who were eligible to receive tax credits because they fulfilled one of the three conditions listed above. It was uncertain whether the child credits would be paid to the father or to the mother, or be divided between the two. The government favoured paying them into the breadwinner's pay packet along with the other tax credits, because it was administratively simpler. For most families this would have meant that the husband received the child tax credits: the wife would lose her right to draw family allowance and would get nothing to replace it unless she could rely on her husband to pass the money on to her. It would also have meant that families who were not eligible for tax credits would receive nothing in place of family allowance or the family income supplement.

However, a select committee was set up to hear evidence from the public on this issue, and in the face of a determined campaign by the women's movement and organizations such as the Child Poverty Action Group, the government conceded that child credits should be paid to the mother. It now looks as though child credits may be paid as a universal benefit, to all mothers, not unlike the present system of family allowances.

WHAT ABOUT PEOPLE WHO ARE NOT ELIGIBLE FOR TAX CREDITS?

The following groups of people will not be eligible for tax credits because they do not fulfil one of the three conditions:

    people living on supplementary benefit;
    the unemployed or sick who are not eligible for unemployment or sickness benefit;
    strikers;
    people with an income of less than £8 a week;
    the self-employed (who will continue to be taxed under the old system);
    married women.

If child credits are paid as a universal benefit, mothers who fall into any of these categories will receive them.

This new system will widen the poverty gap between the low-wage-earner and people living on supplementary benefit – making the latter even worse off than they are now in relation to the wage-earner. It will also penalize strikers and people who do not work regularly: tax will be deducted at the same rate every week, and a person who is out of work for several weeks and then goes back to work won't pay any less tax, even though his income averaged out over the year has been reduced. Under the present system income tax is assessed according to total earnings over the whole year.

TAX CREDIT EXAMPLE ONE

Sarah's income under the present tax system is described in Example One on p. 58. This is how her tax would be worked out under the tax credit system, using the rates initially proposed:

She gets no family allowance, so her total income is	£1,250
She can still claim an additional personal allowance of	130
So her taxable income is	1,120
Tax at 30 per cent of £1,120 is	336
Her income before she gets her tax credits is £1,250 — £336, which comes to	914
She gets tax credits at £8 a week which amount to	416
So her net income is	£1,330·00
Her net income with family allowance under the present system is	£1,227·40

TAX CREDIT EXAMPLE TWO

Carol and Fred Marshall's income under the present tax system is described in Example Two on p. 59. This is how their tax would be worked out under the new tax credit system:

Their total income is	£3,100
Carol gets the maximum wife's earned-income relief, which is	595
They claim tax relief on mortgage interest payments	300
So their taxable income is	2,205
Tax at 30 per cent of £2,205 is	661·50
Their income before they get tax credits is £3,100 — £661·50, which comes to	2,438·50
They get tax credits at £6 a week which amount to	312
So their net income is	£2,750·50
Their net income under the present system is	£2,671·00

National Insurance

The National Insurance scheme is a bureaucrat's dream. It's so complicated that no one really knows why they are paying money into it each week, what they are getting in return, or what they might be missing if they don't pay. (Do you?) The scheme is particularly complicated for women, as it is based on the concept of woman's dependence on man and many of its provisions vary according to whether you are single, married, separated, divorced or widowed.

How the scheme works

The basic idea is that you pay for National Insurance stamps while you are working and in return you get money to live on while you are not working – for instance, while you are unemployed, sick, having a baby or retired.*

Everyone who works is supposed to have a National Insurance card, and to have one stamp stuck in it every week. Most people see their cards very seldom, because they are kept by their employers, who put the stamps on them. But if you've ever been

*Most National Insurance benefits quoted in this chapter were increased in April 1974.

'given your cards' at the end of a job, you'll know what a National Insurance card looks like. In case you don't, here's a picture.

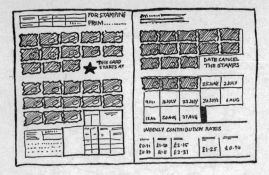

Is it compulsory to pay stamps?

This depends on whether you are single or married.

1. *If you are single or divorced*, you must pay National Insurance stamps for fifty-two weeks each year, whether you are working for an employer, self-employed or not working at all. In certain circumstances you can get stamps 'credited' to you without having to pay for them. Or if your income is very low you can ask to be excused from paying. Otherwise you are legally obliged to pay and you may be prosecuted if you don't.

2. *If you are married (or separated but not divorced)* you have a choice. You can choose whether to pay National Insurance stamps like a single woman, or to 'opt out' so that you don't have to pay. If you opt out you will be insured, in a limited way, by your husband's stamps. If you are working for an employer and you have opted out you must still pay 4p a week insurance against industrial injury.

WHAT ARE THE ADVANTAGES OF HAVING YOUR OWN INSURANCE STAMPS?

You do not have to depend on your husband's insurance. If he has failed to pay his stamps regularly – or if your marriage breaks down – you are less likely to suffer financially. You can draw a pension as soon as you retire at sixty instead of having to wait until your husband retires. If you have Class 1 stamps, you can claim unemployment benefit, sickness and invalidity benefit, maternity allowance, a pension and certain other benefits. If you have Class 2 stamps you can claim all these except unemployment benefit. If you have Class 3 stamps you can claim a pension and certain other benefits. If you have opted out you cannot claim any of these. You may get some National Insurance benefits (at a reduced rate) on your husband's insurance, if he has paid his stamps regularly. But if he hasn't you may find you have to rely on supplementary benefit as your only source of income.

WHAT ARE THE DISADVANTAGES OF HAVING YOUR OWN INSURANCE STAMPS?

(1) You have to pay for the stamps each week. If you are bringing up children and not going out to work you probably won't be able to afford it.
(2) You pay the same money for your stamps as a single woman but you get a *lower* rate of sickness and unemployment benefit. Unlike a single woman you cannot claim additional allowances for your children if you are living with your husband, unless he is disabled and incapable of working.
(3) You may pay the full number of stamps for as many as thirty-five years and still find you that you cannot draw a pension on your own insurance (more about this on p. 86).

HOW TO OPT OUT

If you are working when you get married and you want to opt out of paying insurance, you have to make a special declaration. Ask for form CF9 at your local Social Security office, fill it in and return it to them. If you are self-employed or non-employed when you get married, it's the other way round: you have to make a special declaration if you want to continue to pay insurance, and you do this by filling in the same form. If you change your mind at any time, you can fill in another CF9 form, saying what you want to do, and return it to the Social Security office

3. *If you are widowed*, you also have a choice. Your rights under the National Insurance scheme are in the section on widows' benefits, p. 101.

When can you avoid paying stamps altogether?

If your income after tax is £520 or less a year you can apply for a 'certificate of exception', which means you don't have to pay for National Insurance stamps. If you want to do this, contact your local National Insurance office and explain your situation to them. You don't normally have to pay if you are in full-time training or education. If you have a baby you don't have to pay stamps during your week of confinement and for three weeks after that. If you are excused from paying (and stamps are not 'credited' to you), you may lose your right to claim benefits under the National Insurance scheme. If you want to know more about this, inquire at your Social Security office.

What kind of stamps must you have?

There are three different classes of National Insurance with three different classes of stamps. Which class of stamps you pay depends on your work situation.

Class 1. You must have Class 1 stamps if you work for an employer. You and your employer both contribute to the cost of the weekly stamp. Your contribution is deducted from your wages. The basic rate is 71p. Your employer adds a larger contribution and is responsible for providing the stamp and sticking it on the card.

Class 2. You must have Class 2 stamps if your are self-employed. You pay £1·67 a week, you keep your own card and buy a stamp for each week from the Post Office.

Class 3. You must have Class 3 stamps if you are neither working for an employer, nor self-employed, nor having stamps 'credited' to you; and if you are not excused from paying. You pay £1·23 a week, you keep your own card and buy the stamps from the Post Office.

Sometimes you get stamps 'credited' to you without having to pay for them

If you are getting sickness benefit or maternity allowance, you will be 'credited' with Class 1 or 2 stamps (depending on which you normally pay), which means that you get them without having to pay. If you are getting unemployment benefit you will be credited with Class 1 stamps. If you are out of work for over a year, you will stop being eligible for unemployment benefit, but you may still be credited with Class 1 stamps. If you are under 18 and in full-time education or training, you are credited with Class 3 stamps.

What do you get for your stamps?

The benefits you can claim under the National Insurance scheme depend on which class of stamps you have been paying.

If you have Class 1 stamps you can claim:	*If you have Class 2 stamps you can claim:*	*If you have Class 3 stamps you can claim:*
unemployment benefit		
sickness benefit	sickness benefit	
industrial injuries benefit		
invalidity benefit	invalidity benefit	
maternity grant	maternity grant	maternity grant
maternity allowance	maternity allowance	
retirement pension	retirement pension	retirement pension
guardian's allowance	guardian's allowance	guardian's allowance
child's special allowance	child's special allowance	child's special allowance
death grant	death grant	death grant

But it's not as straightforward as it looks. Before you can get any of these benefits, you must have a certain number of the right class of stamps paid or credited to you over a certain period of time. If you don't have enough stamps, the amount paid to you will be smaller. If you have less than a minimum number of stamps you won't get anything. Sometimes the number of stamps you have to pay and the amount of money you get varies according to whether you are single, married or divorced. The exact requirements vary from one benefit to another.

We will now deal with the different benefits in turn.

Unemployment benefit

This is 'the dole'. You claim it when you're out of work.

HOW MANY STAMPS DO YOU NEED AND WHAT DO YOU GET IN RETURN?

IF YOU ARE SINGLE

You should get the standard rate of unemployment benefit if you satisfy both of these two conditions:

1. You have *paid* at least twenty-six Class 1 stamps during your working life.

2. You have at least fifty Class 1 stamps paid or credited to you during a particular twelve-month period known as your 'contribution year' (see 'What is a contribution year?', p. 73).

If you have fewer than fifty stamps during your 'contribution year' you will get a lower rate of benefit, provided you have *paid* at least twenty-six Class 1 stamps during your working life and you have at least twenty-six Class 1 stamps paid or credited to you during your 'contribution year'. The more stamps you have above that level, the more money you will get. If you don't satisfy both these minimum conditions you will get no unemployment benefit.

Apart from having to pay twenty-six Class 1 stamps at some time during your working life, it makes no difference how few (or many) stamps you have paid at any time outside the necessary 'contribution year'.

Sometimes Class 2 and Class 3 stamps can be counted as Class 1 stamps. If you have paid at least thirty-nine Class 1 stamps during your 'contribution year' any Class 2 or 3 stamps you have during the rest of that year are counted as if they were Class 1 stamps. If you have recently started working for an employer and you have paid at least thirty-nine Class 1 stamps in the year immediately before the date you claim unemployment benefit (*not* your 'contribution year') then any Class 2 or 3 stamps you have *during* your 'contribution year' are counted as if they were Class 1 stamps.

How much do you get? The full rate is £7·35 per week for a single person over 18. You can get extra money if you have dependants. The rates are:

for an adult dependant	£4·55
for the first dependent child	£2·30
for the second dependent child	£1·40
for each other dependent child	£1·30

You may get extra money in the form of an *earnings-related supplement*. This will depend on how much you have been earning and it is explained on p. 79.

IF YOU ARE MARRIED

If you have opted out of paying stamps you are not eligible for unemployment benefit. If your husband is unemployed and has paid the right number of Class 1 stamps, he can claim extra money for you as his dependent wife. The rate is £4·55 a week.

If you have not opted out, you must pay the same number of stamps as a single woman in order to qualify for unemployment benefit. *But* you get less money.

How much do you get?

The standard rate for a married woman is £5·15 a week, which is £2·20 lower than the amount you would get as a single woman, paying exactly the same for your stamps.

If your husband is an invalid and you are supporting him, you can claim the same rate of benefit as a single woman, plus extra for him and your children as your dependants. You cannot claim extra for your children unless your husband is an invalid and incapable of supporting himself.

If you once opted out and later decided to start paying the full stamps, you have to satisfy a special requalifying condition before you can get unemployment benefit. Since you began paying stamps again, you must have paid at least twenty-six Class 1 stamps and you must have had at least fifty-two stamps paid or credited to you.

IF YOU ARE SEPARATED, BUT NOT DIVORCED

You can still opt out if you are separated, in which case you are in the same position as a married woman who has opted out. If your husband is getting unemployment benefit, he can only claim extra for you if he is supporting you.

If you haven't opted out, you must pay the same number of stamps as a single woman before you can claim unemployment benefit.

How much do you get ?

You can claim the full rate of benefit (£7·35) *only if* :

1. You have paid the right number of Class 1 stamps
   and
2. You are not living with your husband
   and
3. You are getting no more than £2·25 a week maintenance from your husband.

If you don't satisfy these three conditions, you get the same rate of unemployment benefit as a married woman (£5·15 a week).

IF YOU ARE DIVORCED

You cannot opt out of paying National Insurance stamps once you are divorced.

If you do not have the right number of Class 1 stamps during your 'contribution year' (see below), you may still be able to claim unemployment benefit if you have *paid* at least twenty-six Class 1 stamps from a date not more than twenty-six weeks before the date of your divorce.

How much do you get ?

The same rate as a single woman.

WHAT IS A CONTRIBUTION YEAR?

Find out which month of the year your National Insurance card begins with. It will be March, June, September or December, according to whether your National Insurance number (marked on your card) ends with A, B, C, or D. Once you know this, you can find out, which is your contribution year, as **Table 3** shows:

TABLE 3

If your National Insurance number ends with . . .	your contribution year runs for 12 months from the first Monday in . . .
A	March
B	June
C	September
D	December

The stamps you pay during one contribution year determine your right to benefit during the year which begins five months after the end of that contribution year – as Table 4 illustrates.

TABLE 4

Your National Insurance number ends with this letter	The stamps you pay during this 'contribution year' . . .	. . . determine your right to benefit five months later, during this period . . .
A	March 1973 to March 1974	August 1974 to August 1975
B	June 1973 to June 1974	November 1974 to November 1975
C	September 1972 to September 1973	February 1974 to February 1975
D	December 1972 to December 1973	May 1974 to May 1975

Here are two examples:

1. You want to claim unemployment benefit in July 1974 and your National Insurance number ends with C. Your contribution year runs from September to September. In order to get the full rate of benefit you must have at least fifty Class 1 stamps paid or credited to you between September 1972 and September 1973.

2. You want to claim unemployment benefit in April 1975 and your National Insurance number ends with D. Your contribution year runs from December to December. In order to get the full rate of benefit, you must have at least fifty Class 1 stamps paid or credited to you between December 1972 and December 1973.

YOU CAN BE DISQUALIFIED FROM CLAIMING UNEMPLOYMENT BENEFIT

In certain circumstances, you are not allowed unemployment benefit, no matter how many stamps you have paid:

1. You get no unemployment benefit for the first three days you are out of work.
2. You get no unemployment benefit for any day you are on holiday or abroad (unless you are looking for work in the Common Market); or when you have done a normal week's work, paid or unpaid. However, a recent test case showed that you might be able to do voluntary work for a charitable organization without losing your right to unemployment benefit.
3. You will probably lose your right to benefit in the following circumstances:
   (a) You were paid for a period of 'notice' at the end of a job but you didn't have to work during that time, in which case you will not get benefit until the period of notice comes to an end.
   (b) They find out that you have a part-time job.
   (c) You are so choosy about the sort of work you are prepared to do that you have no reasonable chance of getting a suitable job.
4. You may be disqualified for up to six weeks in the following circumstances:
   (a) if you turn down a job 'without good cause'; or
   (b) if you left your last job voluntarily; or
   (c) if you lost your last job through 'misconduct'.
5. If you are out of work because of a strike, you will not get benefit for as long as the strike lasts, unless you can prove that

neither you nor others working at the same level as you had any part in the strike.

6. You stop getting unemployment benefit after you have been claiming it for a full year. If you continue to register for work by 'signing on' at your Employment Exchange, they will go on crediting you with Class 1 stamps. If you get work for at least thirteen weeks and then become unemployed again, you should be able to claim benefit for as long as another year.

If you are disqualified from claiming unemployment benefit, you can claim supplementary benefit, as explained below, p. 113.

HOW TO CLAIM UNEMPLOYMENT BENEFIT

It's important to go to your Employment Exchange as soon as you find yourself out of work. If you delay, you may not get any money for the period before your first visit. Take your National Insurance card with you. Your employer should have given it to you when you left your last job. If you haven't got one, call on or write to your local Social Security office and ask for one. You give it to the Employment Exchange and they stamp it while you are registered for work there.

The first thing you have to do is register for work by filling in a form – this is called 'signing on'. If they don't provide you with a job on the spot, they'll give you another form to fill in so that you can claim benefit. You will then be told to come back to the office each week to sign on. They make you do this every week that you want to claim benefit. It's their way of getting proof that you are available for work and therefore eligible for unemployment benefit. Try not to miss a week. If you do, you will have to go through the whole form-filling process again before you sign on the following week.

In all this you will need a lot of patience and perseverance. You may have to put up with hours of waiting and being shuttled from one department to another. The system seems designed to discourage anyone who is not absolutely desperate for money. Don't expect to get paid as soon as you register for work. They have to check up on your record first and you may not get any money for several weeks.

When your money finally arrives, it will either be sent to you through the post in the form of a Giro order which you can cash at any Post Office, or you will be told that you can collect it when you go to sign on.

If you are under 18 and unemployed, go to your local Youth Employment office. You should be able to claim unemployment benefit if you have recently left school and you have paid twenty-six Class I stamps. But you get less money. The standard rate for a single person under 18 is £4·05 a week.

If you are unemployed and not getting unemployment benefit, or if the benefit you are getting is not enough to live on, you can claim supplementary benefit. If you are getting less than £6·55 unemployment benefit a week (as a single person) you should get supplementary benefit to make it up to that level. You should also get extra to cover rent and rates. Ask for Form B1 at your Employment Exchange and take it to your Social Security office. If you are married it's more complicated, because your right to supplementary benefit depends on whether your husband is working and how much he is earning. If you are eligible for supplementary benefit, and your joint income is less than £11·65 a week, the claim must be made by your husband. Supplementary benefit is explained in detail on pp. 113–21.

Sickness benefit

This is what you claim when you are off work because of illness – rather than the dole. Sickness benefit is almost identical to unemployment benefit. You must have the same number of stamps during the same 'contribution year' in order to claim. The rates paid are exactly the same. The only difference is that you can claim sickness benefit if you have Class 1 or Class 2 stamps. Sometimes Class 3 stamps can be counted, in the same way as they can be counted for unemployment benefit.

HOW TO CLAIM SICKNESS BENEFIT

Get your doctor to sign a National Insurance medical certificate
and send it to your local Social Security office within six days of
becoming too ill to work. Your doctor will have the necessary
form and he should be familiar with the procedure. Just tell him
you want to claim sickness benefit. The money will be sent to you
by post in the form of a Giro order that you can cash at any
Post Office.

   You can go on claiming sickness benefit for twenty-eight weeks.
After that, if you are still too ill to work, you become eligible for
invalidity benefit.

Invalidity benefit

You can claim invalidity benefit if you are still too ill to work
after you have been claiming sickness benefit for twenty-eight
weeks, provided you have *paid* at least 156 Class 1 or 2 stamps since
you first started working. It is paid at a higher rate than sickness
and unemployment benefit (£7·75 for a single person), and you
get more for dependent children. If you are under 55 when you
first claim it you get an extra allowance which varies according to
your age. If you haven't paid the necessary stamps to qualify
for invalidity benefit, you can draw sickness benefit for up to
312 days.

Industrial injuries benefit

You can claim industrial injuries benefit if you have Class 1
stamps or if you have opted out as a married woman and you
have been paying the 4p weekly stamp as insurance against industrial injuries. Everyone who works for an employer must be
insured against industrial injuries. The time to claim it is when
you are injured at work or if you contract what is known as a
'prescribed industrial disease'. Complete Section B on the first
medical certificate you send to your Social Security office to claim
sickness benefit.

How much do you get? The rate is higher than sickness benefit: £10·10 a week for a single person. You can claim additional allowances for dependants, in the same way as you can for unemployment benefit. You may also get an earnings-related supplement, as explained below.

If you are assessed as disabled, you will get more money in the form of disablement benefit, and this varies according to how disabled you are. If you want to know more about either of these benefits, ask your doctor, your trade union branch official, or your local Social Security office.

Earnings-related supplement

The earnings-related supplement is extra money you may get if you are claiming unemployment benefit, sickness benefit or industrial injuries benefit. It is based on what you were earning before you stopped working.

The amount of money you get depends on how much you earned and paid tax on through PAYE during the tax year before you claim benefit. Tax years run from April to April. Your earnings in any one tax year determine your right to an earnings-related supplement in the year beginning the following January. So, for example, if you claim unemployment, sickness or industrial injuries benefit in November 1974, the amount you get as an earnings-related supplement will depend on how much you earned between April 1972 and April 1973.

If your taxable earnings during the relevant tax year were more than £520 you will get an earnings-related supplement of approximately one third of the amount by which your average weekly earnings exceed £10, up to a limit of £30, and if you earn more than that, you get an extra 15 per cent of your average earnings between £30 and £42. So if you are earning £30 a week, you should get a supplement of £7 a week, and if you are earning £42 a week, you will get £8·47, which is the maximum. It is paid from your thirteenth day of receiving benefit and continues for up to 156 days after that.

You don't have to make a separate claim for the earnings-related supplement, but if your tax records are incomplete, you may be asked to produce your certificate of pay and tax deducted during the relevant tax year. This is Inland Revenue Form P60, and it should have been given to you by your employer at the end of the tax year. In any case, it is most important that you don't lose this form when it is given to you.

YOU WILL NOT GET AN EARNINGS-RELATED SUPPLEMENT:

1. If you are married and you are only paying the 4p stamp as insurance against industrial injuries.
2. If you are self-employed and paying 'Schedule D' tax.

Maternity benefits

MATERNITY GRANT

This is a sum of £25 to help with the immediate costs of having a baby. You can claim it whether you are single or married if you satisfy the following conditions. If you're married you can claim it if your husband satisfies the same conditions.

1. You must have paid at least twenty-six Class 1, 2 or 3 stamps since you started work.
2. You must have paid or been credited with at least twenty-six Class 1, 2 or 3 stamps during the last full 'contribution year' before the baby is due. (See pp. 73–5 for 'What is a contribution year?')

If you are not married, you cannot claim the maternity grant on the insurance of the baby's father.

You can claim the grant if your baby is stillborn, provided your pregnancy lasted at least twenty-eight weeks. If you have more than one baby at a time, you get an extra £25 for each baby that survives.

Get the claim form BM4 from your local Social Security office or from your maternity or child welfare clinic. You can apply at any time from nine weeks before the baby is due, to three months after it is born.

MATERNITY ALLOWANCE

This is a weekly allowance that you can get for several weeks before and after your baby is born. You can claim it whether you are single or married, but you can only claim it on your *own* insurance, and if you satisfy the following conditions:

1. You must have *paid* at least twenty-six Class 1 or 2 stamps during the year preceding the thirteenth week before your baby is due.
2. You must have at least fifty Class 1 or 2 stamps paid or credited during that year.

If you have at least thirty-nine Class 1 or 2 stamps paid or credited during that year (of which at least twenty-six are *paid*), any Class 3 stamps you have during the rest of that year are counted as Class 1 or 2 stamps.

You will notice that the period during which you need stamps in order to claim maternity allowance is not the same as the 'con-bution year' described on p. 73. The best way of working out whether you have the right number of stamps at the right time is to get a calendar or diary and count backwards. Or ask your local Social Security office. Here is one example to give you an idea of how it works:

> Your baby is due in the week beginning 4 March 1974. The thirteenth week before that date begins on 12 November 1973. So if you are to get the full rate of maternity allowance, you must have at least fifty Class 1 or 2 stamps paid or credited to you between 13 November 1972 and 12 November 1973.

Maternity allowance is *not* paid while you are doing paid work. If you are not working it is normally for eleven weeks before your baby is due, and for seven weeks after it is actually born, with a minimum total of eighteen weeks. If your baby is born later than expected you will get maternity allowance for longer.

How much do you get? The standard rate is £7·35 a week. If you don't have the full number of stamps, you will get less. You can claim additional allowances for your dependent children, but if you are married you cannot claim for your children unless your husband is disabled and incapable of work. You might also get an earnings-related supplement as you do with unemployment benefit. This is explained on p. 79.

Get the claim form BM4 from your local Social Security office or from a maternity or child welfare clinic. You can claim at the beginning of the fourteenth week – and not later than the eleventh week – before the baby is due.

MOTHERS UNDER 16 CANNOT CLAIM MATERNITY BENEFITS

Withholding money does not stop babies being born. Mothers under 16 and their babies need money every bit as much as mothers over 16. Yet the government persists in its inhuman and short-sighted policy of refusing maternity benefits to them.

A mother under 16 cannot even claim supplementary benefit in her own right. The only way to get money is for her parent or guardian to claim supplementary benefit for her as a dependent child.

Local councils have power to give financial help to mothers under 16 under Section 1 of the Children and Young Persons Act (1963). But it is a purely discretionary power and few councils use it.

If you have a baby when you are under 16 – or if you know someone who has – it might be worth approaching the social services department of your local council and asking for help. You may have to remind them of the relevant Act. If you get no help there, contact One-Parent Families (address on p. 320).

Child's special allowance

This is an allowance you can claim in the following circumstances:

1. You are divorced, but not remarried
   and
2. Your former husband has died
   and
3. You are looking after a child
   and
4. Your husband was supposed to be paying at least 25p a week towards the support of the child and, if he wasn't, you had taken reasonable steps to get him to pay.

The rate is £3·80 for the first child, £2·90 for the second child and £2·80 for each other child. If you want to know more about this inquire at your local Social Security office.

Guardian's allowance

You may be able to claim a guardian's allowance if you are looking after an orphan child. The rate is £3·80 a week. Normally both parents of the child must be dead before you can claim, but you can sometimes claim if only one parent is dead, for instance, if the parents were divorced, if the surviving parent is missing or serving a long term in prison. If you want to know more about this, inquire at your local Social Security office.

Your right to appeal

If you disagree with a decision which has been made about your right to any National Insurance benefit, you can appeal to the National Insurance tribunal. The procedure for appealing is described on pp. 311–12.

Further information

The Department of Health and Social Security publishes leaflets on most of the major aspects of the National Insurance scheme. They tend to be bedevilled by jargon and a rather pompous turn of phrase, but they do give all the details. The following are relevant to this section:

NI 12:   *Unemployment Benefit*
NI 16:   *Sickness Benefit*
NI 17A: *Maternity Benefits*
NI 1:   *A Guide for Married Women*
NI 95:   *Guidance for Women Whose Marriage is Ended by Divorce or Annulment*
NI 43:   *Excusals and Credits*
NI 42:   *Guidance for the Non-Employed Person*
NI 30:   *Students*
NI 125:   *Training for Further Employment*
NI 31:   *Apprentices*

The National Council for One-Parent Families is at 255 Kentish Town Road, London NW5 (01 267 1361).
Claimants' unions and the Child Poverty Action Group may help you to claim National Insurance benefits. See p. 119.

Pensions

Most women retire at 60. Do you know what you will live on when you reach that age? Will you have a pension of your own? Will you be able to draw a pension on your husband's insurance? Or will you have to live on supplementary benefit?

The size of your pension is determined by how much money is paid towards it during your working life. So it's important to think about it now and to understand how the pension system works. You may find that you can take a decision now which will make your old age more secure financially. Or you may find that you stand to get so little that it's not worth paying out anything at all.

You will see as you read on that women generally get a worse deal than men where pensions are concerned. In fact, 74 per cent of all pensioners who receive supplementary benefit are women. This means that these women have no pensions, or pensions that leave them below the breadline.

.. and to think .. she would have got her pension in another twenty-eight years

In 1975 the whole pension system will be rearranged, leaving women in an even worse position. We shall describe the current system first and then the new system, and show how you will be affected by the change from one to the other.

How the current pension system works

Under the current system, most people get a flat-rate pension and a graduated pension.* The first is a basic weekly allowance. The second is an additional amount which is related to how much you have earned during your working life.

Flat-rate pensions

The flat-rate pension is paid at the same rate to you as to everyone else, no matter how much you have been earning. It varies only according to how many National Insurance stamps you have.

IF YOU ARE SINGLE

You get the same deal as a single man, except that he retires

*Rates quoted in this chapter were increased in April 1974.

five years later than you, at 65. When you retire you can draw the full flat-rate pension of £7·75 a week, as long as you have accumulated the right number of National Insurance stamps. Throughout your working life you must have *paid* at least 156 stamps. In addition, you must have a yearly average of fifty stamps, either paid by you or 'credited' to you (that is, paid by the state) while you are registered for unemployment or getting sickness or maternity benefit.

As explained in the section on National Insurance (p. 68), there are three different classes of National Insurance stamp: Class 1, 2 and 3. For the purpose of getting a pension, it makes no difference which class of stamp you have collected. Your 'working life' officially begins when you are 16 and ends at 60. If you stay on at school or college after you are 16, stamps are credited to you until your 18th birthday. After that, if you don't have stamps paid or credited to you every week, your pension will be reduced.

As a single woman, you are obliged by law to pay stamps every week unless they are 'credited' to you for the reasons mentioned above, or unless your yearly income is less than £520 and you apply to be excused from paying (more about that on p. 68).

Table 5 shows how your pension is affected by the number of stamps you have accumulated.

For example, if you collected fifty stamps a year for thirty-three years, you will have a yearly average of 37–39 stamps and thus get £5·67 pension per week.

As you can see, you can pay stamps for as many as forty years and still get a pension that is considerably less than you would get if you were living on supplementary benefit (for which you need no stamps). Supplementary benefit for a single person over 60 is £8·15 a week, plus rent and rates; and there may be additional allowances for special needs.

IF YOU ARE MARRIED

As a married woman there are two ways in which you can get a pension when you reach retirement age.

1. You can decide *not* to pay your own stamps and to rely instead

TABLE 5

If you have collected at least 50 stamps a year for approximately this number of years ...	... you will have a yearly average, over your working life (16–60), of *this* number of stamps ...	... and you will get *this* for a weekly pension ...
44 years	50–52 stamps	£7·75 a week
42	48–49	£7·44
40½	46–47	£7·13
38	43–45	£6·82
35½	40–42	£6·26
33	37–39	£5·67
30	34–36	£5·09
26½	30–33	£4·49
23	26–29	£3·88
19½	22–25	£3·31
16	18–21	£2·71
11	13–17	£2·17

on the stamps that your husband has paid during his working life. If he has accumulated the *full* number of stamps necessary to get a full pension you will automatically be entitled to a married woman's pension of £4·75 per week. If he has less than the full number, your pension will be proportionately lower.

2. You can decide to pay your *own* stamps like a single woman. If you accumulate the *full* number of stamps necessary, you will get a single woman's pension of £7·75 a week. If you have less than the full number of stamps, your pension will be proportionately lower.

Even if you are paying your own stamps you are still entitled to a married woman's pension on the stamps your husband has paid. However, it's important to realize that you will only get *one* pension in the end. The pension you get will be the higher of the two. This means that if the pension you can get from your husband's stamps works out in the end to be higher than the one you could have got from your own stamps, all the stamps of your own that you have paid throughout your life will be discounted – rather a waste!

So you should make some calculation as soon as possible to help you decide which is the best type of pension for you. It's worth asking yourself the following questions in each case: firstly, *how much* money is each likely to bring me? and secondly, *when* will I get it?

1. *Relying on your husband's stamps* ('opting out')

How much will you get? As we have seen, the size of your pension will depend on how many stamps your husband has accumulated during his working life. If he has accumulated a yearly average of fifty stamps over forty-nine years between the ages of 16 and 65 he will get £7·75 for his pension and you will get £4·75 a week – a total of £12·50 per week. If he has fewer stamps than that, your pension will be lower. Do you know how many stamps your husband has paid? It's worth finding out. If he doesn't know, tell him to find out from his local Social Security office.

When will you get it? You will not be able to get a pension until your husband reaches *his* retirement age, which is 65. This means that unless he is five years or more older than you, you will not get a pension when you reach *your* retirement age of 60. If, for example, your husband is 60 and you are 65, he will still have another five years to go until he gets a pension, which means that you won't get your pension until you're 70! So timing is something you should take into account if your husband is less than five years older than you. On the other hand, if your husband is older than you by five years or more, so that you are *under* 60 when he retires at 65, he will be able to draw your pension in addition to his own: this means he will get a total pension of £12·50 a week. However, if you are working and earning more than £9·50 a week when he retires (after tax and certain other expenses have been deducted) he will only be able to claim a reduced amount for you – your portion will be reduced according to how much you are earning at the time above £9·50.

2. *Paying your own stamps*

How much do you pay?

If you want to have your own pension like a single woman you must fulfil the following two conditions:

1. You must pay at least 156 stamps at some time during your working life.
2. You must pay or be credited with stamps for at least *half* the weeks between the date of your marriage and your 60th birthday – unless you get married on or after your 57th birthday. If you marry more than once this applies to your last marriage only. This rule can have disastrous results, as the following example shows:

Alice worked from the age of 15 to 48 and paid her full contributions as a single woman. She then married and after two years retired from her job through ill health. She had paid stamps for thirty-five years. When she was 60, she went to collect her pension, but was told she was not entitled to a penny as she had not paid contributions for half her married life.

How much will you get?

If you have fulfilled these two conditions how much money can you get? In order to get the *full* pension of £7·75 a week, you must have a yearly average of fifty stamps paid or credited to you throughout your working life. If you have less than this your pension will be proportionately lower - the table on p. 87 shows how to work out how much less you get.

Don't forget that if your own pension turns out to be *lower* than the married woman's pension you can get from your husband's stamps, then you will only get the latter – which means that you might as well never have paid your own stamps. Think about that – you may be able to save yourself a lot of money.

When can you get it?

If you have your own pension you will get it as soon as you reach 60. If you retire before your husband, you will get whatever pension you have earned from your own stamps until he retires. After that you will get the married woman's pension *or* your own pension, whichever is higher.

When you start paying stamps you may have no idea how your life is going to develop, and this will make it difficult to decide which kind of pension would be best for you. Here are some general points to consider.

If you are worried that your husband won't pay enough stamps to get a full pension for the two of you, you might decide it's worth paying your own stamps so that you will at least get a pension for yourself. If you see yourself going out to work most of your life, earning good money and therefore paying stamps regularly, you might decide to have your own pension for the simple reason that it is higher than that given to married women through their husbands (though it's not all that much higher).

If, like a lot of women, you're having to work because the family income is low you'd do best not to subtract valuable money from your pay packet – if you're going to be seriously short of money when you retire you will probably be eligible for supplementary benefit anyhow.

If you stay at home for a number of years to look after children, or if you go abroad or live on supplementary benefit for several years, you will not be paying stamps during that time. So the pension you will be able to get from your husband's stamps will almost certainly be higher than your own and you would do better to 'opt out' of paying stamps yourself.

IF YOU SEPARATE FROM YOUR HUSBAND

You are in the same position as a married woman as far as your pension is concerned. If you are under 60 when your husband retires, he can still draw extra pension for you, provided he can show the National Insurance officials that he is supporting you financially. But there is one difference: a married woman who is not separated can earn up to £9·59 a week without causing a reduction in her husband's pension. As a separated woman, if you earn over £4·15 a week, your husband will not be able to draw any extra pension for you.

If you are over 60 when your husband retires and you don't qualify for a pension of your own, you can draw a pension on your husband's insurance, but at the married woman's rate only. If this is not enough to live on (which it generally isn't) you can claim supplementary benefit, as explained on p. 113. You would obviously be in a better position if you had your own pension through your own stamps, or if you were divorced.

IF YOU GET DIVORCED

If your husband has paid more stamps than you (both before and after the date of your marriage), you can 'adopt' his National Insurance record to help you qualify for a single person's pension. This means that all the stamps he has paid, from the date of your 16th birthday up to the date of your divorce, are counted as though they were your own. From the date of your divorce, you have to pay stamps like a single woman and when you reach 60 your pension is worked out in the same way as a single woman's. Your pension does not alter if you remarry when you are over 60.

Here is an example of how the rule works:

You left school at 16, but you did not go out to work until you were 20. You married at 24 and opted out of paying stamps when you were 25 because you started a family. You did not start paying stamps again when you went back to work at 35. You divorced at 40. Up to the date of your divorce, you had therefore paid stamps for only ten years. Your husband started work at 16 and paid his stamps regularly right up to the divorce. His insurance record is obviously a great deal better than yours so you are able to adopt it as your own. You will get a pension as though you had paid stamps all the way from 16 to 40. If you pay stamps as a single person regularly for another twenty years until you are 60, you will get a full single person's pension.

However, if you divorce and then remarry *before* you are 60, you cannot count your former husband's stamps towards your pension. Instead, you will draw a married woman's pension on your second husband's insurance in the same way as any other married woman – unless you happen to qualify for a higher pension on your own stamps.

If you divorce when you are over 60, you will get a single

person's pension, based on the number of stamps your husband has paid – unless you qualify for a higher pension on your own stamps – and you will get this even if you and your former husband are both still working.

IF YOU ARE WIDOWED

Your pension rights are explained in the section on widows' benefits, p. 101.

SPECIAL NOTES FOR WOMEN WHO MARRIED OR STARTED WORK BEFORE 5 JULY 1948, WHEN THE PRESENT NATIONAL INSURANCE SCHEME STARTED:

(a) If you started paying insurance before 30 September 1946, you need only have *paid* a total of 104 stamps. The rest can be either paid or credited to you.

(b) If you were married before 5 July 1948, you must have paid stamps for half the weeks between your 60th birthday and *either* the date of your marriage *or* 5th July 1948 *or* the date on which you started work whichever of these things happened last.

(c) In order to get a full pension on your own stamps, you must have a yearly average of fifty stamps between your 60th birthday and *either* 1936 *or* the date you first entered into insurance, whichever happened later.

We reckon anyone who can make head or tail of all that deserves to get a pension! If in doubt, inquire at your local Social Security office.

Graduated pensions

A graduated pension is one that is related to how much you have earned during your working life – the more you earn, the more pension you get. If you are working for an employer, you must pay an extra amount of money each week towards the graduated pension scheme. This is compulsory even if you are married and you have opted out of paying National Insurance stamps. The amount you pay varies according to how much you earn: it is worked out at a rate of 5 per cent of what you earn between £9 and £54 a week. For instance, if you are earning £15 a week, your contribution to the graduated scheme will be 31p; if you are earning £25 a week, it will be 82p. The money is deducted from your wages along with tax and ordinary National Insurance contributions.

However, you can be 'contracted out' of the graduated scheme. This means you pay less money towards it each week. You can only contract out if you belong to an occupational pension scheme (explained below) which is approved by the Government. If you are contracted out, your weekly contribution towards the graduated scheme is only 0·75 per cent of your earnings between £9 and £18 a week. If you earn more than £18 a week, you must pay 5 per cent of your earnings between £18 and £54 a week.

How much do you get? Whether or not you are contracted out of the scheme, your contributions will earn you a graduated pension in addition to your flat-rate pension. It is paid at a rate of $2\frac{1}{2}$p a week for each £9 sum you have paid in graduated contributions. It will be paid to you weekly with your flat-rate pension, or as a lump sum when you retire if you don't qualify for a flat-rate pension. If you divorce your husband when you are over 60, you will get half the graduated pension that he has earned from his contributions – either when you stop working or when you reach 65, whichever happens sooner.

Occupational pensions

An occupational pension is one paid by a private scheme provided by your employer. It is paid in addition to your flat-rate pension. The amount of pension paid varies from one occupational scheme to another. If you belong to one, it is worth finding out what kind of scheme it is and what it provides for you. Most people don't know.

HOW A TYPICAL OCCUPATIONAL PENSION SCHEME WORKS

Here is an excerpt from the pamphlet explaining an occupational pension scheme provided for salaried workers at Ford. While this book was being written, it was replaced by a more equitable scheme as a result of pressure from trade unions (a hopeful sign!), but it is still a typical example of the way pension schemes discriminate against women.

'At the normal retirement age of 65 (60) you will receive a pension equivalent to 1/60th (1/80th) of your average basic salary (excluding overtime, etc.) over the best continuous 5 years' service out of the last 10 years before retirement, for each year of pensionable service. The best continuous 5 years will in most cases be the last 5 years before retirement.

You can calculate what your annual pension will be by following this formula:

$$\frac{\text{Years of service}}{60 \ (80)} \times \text{Average annual basic salary (excluding overtime, etc.) over the best continuous 5 years of last 10 years.}$$

The figures in brackets are the figures for women.

Here are examples of yearly pensions awarded to a man and a woman whose average salaries over the best five years are both £1,200 per annum, and who had both been contributing to the Ford pension fund for thirty years:

Man

$$\frac{30}{60} \times £1,200 = £600$$

Woman

$$\frac{30}{80} \times £1,200 = £450$$

Many private schemes of this kind give women a similarly bad deal. Find out what your employer's pensions are for women – if they are this bad your union may be able to help you negotiate better terms. (See p. 96 for more information.)

If you go on working after you are 60

You can claim your pension and then earn a further £9·50 a week without your pension being reduced.

Alternatively, you can *increase* your pension if you do the following things:

1. You work between the ages of 60 and 65;
   and
2. During that time you give up your right to any pension or widow's benefit you might be getting;
   and
3. You continue to pay National Insurance stamps.

Your pension will be increased at a rate of 6p for every nine stamps you pay. For instance, if you go on working for two and a half years, you can earn an increase in your pension of approximately 84p a week. If you go on working for five years you can earn an increase of almost £1·68 a week (is it worth it?).

You may also get a higher graduated pension if you go on working after you are 60.

If you go on working after you are 65

You cannot earn any further increase in your pension, but you can earn as much as you like without your pension being reduced.

If your pension doesn't leave you enough to live on

You have a right to supplementary benefit.

If you are single and your weekly income is less than £8·15 a week, you can claim supplementary benefit to bring it up to this level, plus extra for rent, rates and certain special needs.

If you are married your right to claim supplementary benefit depends on the joint income of you and your husband. If it is less than £12·85 a week your husband can make a claim for supplementary benefit. But you yourself cannot claim unless you are living apart from him. Each of you can earn £2 a week without any reduction in your benefit.

If you are 80, you can claim an extra 25p a week in supplementary benefit.

You can claim an additional allowance if you need extra heating. But if you claim more money to cover other special needs, such as special foods or heavy laundry expenses, you will only get the difference between what you claim and 50p (if you are aged between 60 and 80), or 75p (if you are over 80).

Further information

The NCCL, 186 King's Cross Road, London WC1 (01 278 4575) has a special fact sheet on occupational pensions. See also Age Concern, p. 101.

The new pension system

A new pension system will be introduced in 1975. It will take effect gradually, and it will not come into full force until the next century. But it will apply – at least partially – to everyone who is below retirement age in 1975. The younger you are the more it will affect you.

Under the new scheme, most people will get two pensions: a basic pension which is like the current flat-rate pension; and a second pension which is related to how much you have been earning. The earnings-related pension will come either from an occupational pension scheme or from the new state-run 'reserve pension scheme'.

THE BASIC PENSION

This is the same as the present flat-rate pension, but with the following exceptions:

1. In order to get a full basic pension, you will have to have National Insurance stamps paid or credited to you weekly for nine-tenths of your working life (16 to 60) – that is, $39\frac{1}{2}$ years. This is fractionally more generous than the current system.

2. The amount you pay for your stamp will vary according to how much you earn, although the pension you get for it at the end will not. If you earn less than £9 a week, you will not pay anything, but this will not entitle you to a pension – you will have to claim supplementary pension instead. If you earn between £9 and £54 a week, you will have to pay 5·25 per cent of everything you earn up to £54 (or one and a half times the national average wage) – for example, £1·05 if you earn £20 a week. If you are self-employed you will pay flat-rate stamps like you do now, plus 5 per cent of any earnings between £1,150 and £2,500 a year, through the Schedule D tax system.

3. Basic pension rates will be more or less the same as the present flat-rate pension. They will be reviewed annually, supposedly so that they can be kept in line with the cost of living. So will the amount you pay for your stamp.

THE EARNINGS-RELATED PENSION

If you work for an employer you will *have* to belong to an occupational pension scheme, or pay into the 'reserve pension scheme', even if you are married and have opted out of paying National Insurance stamps. You do not have to pay towards an earnings-related pension if you are self-employed or if you are not working.

1. *Occupational schemes*

An occupational pension scheme is a private scheme provided by your employer. Every private scheme must meet the following minimum requirements in order to be recognized by the Government.

If you belong to a scheme that is not recognized, you will have to pay into the reserve pension scheme.

(a) *Pension rates*. The scheme must provide you with a yearly pension of at least 0·7 per cent of whatever you have earned each year since you started paying into it. Say, for example, the total of 0·7 per cent of each year's earnings comes to £720, you will get a pension of £720 a year. That is the minimum requirement for *women's* pensions. For men, the pension must be at least one per cent of each year's earnings. Why the difference? It is based on a mathematical calculation which appears to ignore the concept of need. Women retire earlier than men and tend to live longer than men. Their pensions are therefore spread over a longer period. So they get less money each week.

(b) *Protection against inflation.* The scheme must either link the pension to the cost of living index; or provide a set rate of increase; or satisfy the Occupational Pensions Board (set up to supervise occupational schemes) that adequate provision is being made for increases, without laying down a set rate. However, it need *not* do so if it provides a pension which is 25 per cent above the minimum level.

(c) *Transferring pension contributions from one scheme to another.* If you leave a job after belonging to an occupational scheme for at least five years and you are aged 26 or over, the scheme must pay you, when you reach retirement, whatever pension you have earned from the scheme (this is called a 'deferred pension'); *or* transfer your contributions to another scheme. It cannot give you a refund except of contributions paid before 1975; or if you leave a job before 1980. If you leave a job after belonging to an occupational scheme for less than five years, your employer must pay into the reserve scheme whatever you would have paid if you had been contributing to the reserve scheme during that period.

(d) *Provision for widows.* If your husband dies after his retirement, the scheme he belonged to must provide you with a widow's pension of 50 per cent of the minimum he would have received for himself. If he dies before retiring, the scheme can give a lump-sum payment instead.

2. *The reserve pension scheme*

This will be set up by the government and run like an occupational scheme by an independent board of management. If you work for an employer and you do not belong to a recognized occupational scheme you will have to pay into the reserve pension scheme. You cannot pay into it if you are self-employed or if you are not working. Here are the main provisions of the reserve pension scheme:

(a) *Contributions.* You will contribute to the reserve scheme through PAYE, like you pay tax. The amount you pay will be 1·5 per cent of your earnings up to a limit of £54 (or one and a half times the national average wage) – for example, 30p a week if you earn £20.

(b) *Pension rates.* The rates haven't been settled yet, but they will certainly be very low. The amount you get will depend on how much you have contributed and when you started paying into the reserve scheme. Women will get a lower rate of pension than men. If you enter the scheme at 22, and your earnings increase at a rate of 3 per cent a year your pension will be 13 per cent of your earnings in the year before you retire. If a man entered the scheme at the same age and his earnings increased at the same rate, his pension would be 19 per cent of his final earnings. This is based on the same sort of calculation as the requirements for occupational schemes.

(c) *There is no guarantee of protection against inflation,* although bonuses are supposed to be paid periodically.

(d) *A widow's pension* is provided at half the rate of the husband's pension if he dies after reaching pension age, or half the pension he has earned up to his death if he dies before reaching pension age.

What will happen to the present graduated pension scheme?

This will cease to exist in 1975. Any graduated pension you have earned up to 1975 will be 'frozen' and paid to you at a fixed rate when you retire, or in a lump sum. So if you're 35 in 1975 and you retire at 60, you will get a dozen or so years' worth of graduated contributions paid back to you at a rate which is twenty-five years out of date. Rather like cashing Premium Bonds which you bought twenty-five years ago when they haven't won you anything.

COMMENT ON THE SOCIAL SECURITY BILL (1972),
WHICH INTRODUCED THE NEW PENSION SYSTEM,
FROM THE GUARDIAN (5 MARCH 1973)

There is a cold mathematical logic behind this appalling piece of discrimination. Firstly: when we are reduced to statistics, women have a longer life expectancy than men. When a girl is born, she can look forward to 74·7 years of life. A boy can only hope for 68·5 years. So if we are lucky enough to be average, we can grab an extra six years to gasp the polluted atmosphere. Naturally, we have to pay for the privilege. The logic collapses, in fact, when we consider other statistics. Manual workers have a shorter life expectancy than non-manual workers. No one has suggested awarding them a higher pension accordingly.

Secondly: women retire earlier. Well yes, we can't deny it. We unburden the labour market at 60 instead of 65. This was decreed by a predominantly male Parliament in 1940. Before that, women and men both retired at 65, but it was thought to be inconvenient for married couples where the husband was older than the wife, if the wife went on working and left her retired husband at home to fend for himself. The average age difference between husband and wife was then five years. It is now three years – and heaven knows how many variables there are – but no one has seriously considered adjusting the retirement age. Women would not be keen to accept an extra five years' work and the unemployment figures couldn't stand it. The Treasury couldn't stand it if all men suddenly retired at 60. Why shouldn't everyone retire at 62½? It's a bit messy, but it's not unreasonable. Or why not a floating pension age between 60 and 70 so that people could retire when it suited them?

But there we are. Women live longer and retire earlier. The money we have put by for our pensions must be spread over a longer period of time. So, say the mathematical geniuses at the Department of Health and Social Security, we must get less money each week. Let us not forget that it is an earnings-related pension. Women's average earnings are still just over half men's average earnings and the Equal Pay Act is having the impact of a wet flannel on Vesuvius. So we shall get a lower percentage of a lower wage.

It might seem less painful if we had some choice in the matter. But we are retired at 60 by law. We cannot help living longer. It would hardly be fair if we had to compensate by contributing *more* than men to the pensions scheme, considering how much less we earn. If we all promised to hurl ourselves under buses on our 72nd birthdays (thereby ensuring a life expectancy equal to men's on retirement) would we be granted an equal pension? The sight of rows of little old ladies teetering on the edges of the nation's pavements might put the Government to shame. It might even be preferable to eking out an old age on the poverty line . . .

One concept is glaringly absent from the Bill: that pensions should be provided according to *need*, not according to how much people can afford. Far more women than men live alone in their old age; and they live to be older. The older you are, the greater your needs. You need to keep warm and to pay for transport when it is harder to get about; you may need special foods; you will be less able to work to supplement your pension. Once you consider the human factors, it emerges that women need at least as much as, if not more than men.

Further information

Age Concern, 55 Gower Street, London WC1 (01 637 2886): information and campaigning centre for old people's welfare rights. (See also p. 96.)

Widows' benefits

If your husband dies, you will probably be entitled to widows' benefits.* The amount you get and the type of benefit you receive will depend on:

1. How old you are when he dies;
   and
2. The number of National Insurance stamps he has paid.

In order to get any widow's benefit at all, your husband must have paid for at least 156 stamps since he started work. If he has kept up an average of fifty stamps paid or credited to him each year since he started contributing to the National Insurance scheme, then you will get the standard rate of widows' benefits. If he has an average of between thirteen and fifty stamps a year, then you will get a reduced rate. If he has an average of fewer than thirteen, you will get nothing.

* Rates quoted in this chapter were increased in April 1974.

If you remarry or live with a man 'as man and wife', you lose your right to widows' benefits.

**If you are under 60 when your husband dies,
or if you are over 60, but your husband was not
entitled to a retirement pension when he died**

– you get the following benefits:

WIDOWS' ALLOWANCE

This is paid for the first twenty-six weeks after your husband's death. The standard rate is £10·85 a week. You get additional money for any child who is below school-leaving age *or* under 19 and still in full-time education or training. The rates for children are:

£3·80 for the first child
£2·90 for the second child
£2·80 for each other child

These rates are fixed: they do not vary according to how many stamps your husband paid.

(Don't forget you will also get family allowance if you have two or more children. The rate is 90p a week for the second child and £1 for each child after that.)

WIDOW'S SUPPLEMENTARY ALLOWANCE

You will get this in addition to your widow's allowance, for twenty-six weeks, if:

1. Your husband was not entitled to a retirement pension when he died;
   and
2. In the tax year before his death his earnings on which he paid tax through PAYE amounted to more than £450 – that is, £9 a week.

The amount you get depends on your husband's average weekly earnings in that tax year. The rate is worked out in the same way as the earnings-related supplement, which is explained on p. 79.

WIDOWED MOTHER'S ALLOWANCE

You should get this when your widow's allowance runs out after twenty-six weeks, if you have dependent children. The standard rate is £7·75 a week, and you will get increases for your children at the same rate as you got with your widow's allowance. It ceases when you no longer have any children under 16, or under 19 and still in full-time training or education.

WIDOW'S PENSION

You will get this if:

1. You are over 40 when your widowed mother's allowance ends.
   or
2. You are over 40 when your husband dies and you have no dependent children: in this case you get a widow's pension when your widow's allowance ends.

The standard rate depends on your age, as shown in Table 6.

TABLE 6

Your age when your husband died or when your widowed mother's allowance ends	Standard weekly widow's pension
40	£2·33
41	2·87
42	3·41
43	3·95
44	4·50
45	5·04
46	5·58
47	6·12
48	6·67
49	7·21
50 or over	7·75

WILL YOUR BENEFITS BE REDUCED IF YOU ARE WORKING?

There is no limit to the amount of money you can earn while you are getting widow's benefit: your benefit will not be reduced. Widow's benefits are assessed for tax and you must declare them to the Inland Revenue. (Don't worry – if you are only getting widow's benefit, you probably won't have to pay any tax on it.) However, if you are receiving a state grant for education or training, your benefit will be either reduced or withdrawn until the grant ceases.

SPECIAL RULES TO HELP YOU GET UNEMPLOYMENT OR SICKNESS BENEFIT

If, as a married woman, you opt out of paying full National Insurance stamps, you are not normally allowed to claim unemployment or sickness benefit. But if you are widowed, the following rules may make it possible for you to claim, even if you haven't been paying stamps.

1. If you have had a widow's allowance or a widowed mother's

allowance and it comes to an end, you will be able to claim unemployment and sickness benefit *even though* you have not been paying National Insurance stamps. But you will not be able to claim additional benefit for your dependants unless you have paid at least twenty-six stamps of any kind since your widow's allowance or widowed mother's allowance came to an end. So if you have dependants and you're worried you may fall ill or be out of work, make sure you start paying stamps when either of these two allowances comes to an end.

2. If Rule 1 does not help you, you may be able to claim sickness benefit for a limited period, both for you and your dependants, if you have paid at least twenty-six stamps from a date not more than twenty-six weeks before your husband's death.

DOES A WIDOW HAVE TO GO ON PAYING NATIONAL INSURANCE STAMPS?

You do not have to pay National Insurance stamps during the week of your husband's death and during the following twenty-six weeks. After that, you can opt out of paying stamps as long as you are receiving a widowed mother's allowance or a widow's pension. While you are receiving a widow's allowance, widowed mother's allowance, or a widow's pension (in this last case you must be 50 or over), National Insurance stamps are credited to you anyway. If, when stamps are no longer credited to you, you want to know whether it's worth opting out or not, it's best to discuss the matter with the staff at your local Social Security office: they will tell you whether, in your particular case, it is worth paying the full rate of stamps or not.

If, twenty-six weeks after your husband's death, you are not entitled to a widow's pension or a widowed mother's allowance or a widow's pension, you are supposed to pay National Insurance stamps like any other single person.

WHAT HAPPENS WHEN YOU REACH 60

At 60, or at 65 (if you don't retire at 60 but go on working), your widow's pension will be changed to a retirement pension – even if you continue to work after 65.

If you are still entitled to a widowed mother's allowance or widow's allowance and the rate is higher than your pension would be, you can go on receiving that allowance until you cease to be eligible for it.

If you are 60 or over when your husband dies

1. If your husband is *not* entitled to a retirement pension when he dies (for instance, if he is too young), you will get the widow's allowance and widow's supplementary allowance for twenty-six weeks. After that you will get a retirement pension.
2. If you are receiving a married woman's retirement pension when your husband dies, it will be increased to the single person's rate. If you are getting the standard pension, this will mean an increase from £4·75 to £7·75.
3. If you are receiving a retirement pension on your own insurance and your husband is entitled to a retirement pension when he dies, you will either continue to get your own pension, or get a pension on your husband's insurance, whichever is higher.

GRADUATED PENSIONS

If you are over 60 and retired, you may get a graduated pension in addition to your retirement pension. You will get half the graduated pension which your husband had earned, plus any graduated pension which you had earned on your own contributions. When you reach the age of 65, you will receive any graduated pension you are entitled to, whether you have retired or not. Graduated pensions are explained in more detail on p. 92.

UNDER THE NEW PENSION ARRANGEMENTS

Provisions for widows under the new pension arrangements, which are to be introduced in 1975, are explained on pp. 98 and 99.

IF YOU GO ON WORKING AFTER YOU ARE 60

If you are getting a retirement pension, you can earn up to £9·50 a week without it being reduced. If you are over 65, or if you are still getting widow's benefit, you can earn as much as you like without the pension or benefit being reduced.

You can increase your pension by working after 60, as explained on p. 95.

Death grant

This is a lump sum which you claim if either you or your husband has been paying National Insurance stamps. It will probably be £30, but if the insurance record is incomplete, you may get less. Full details are given in leaflet NI 49, which you can get from your local Social Security office.

How to claim all widows' benefits

Fill in the form on the back of the death certificate and send it to your local Social Security office, or visit the office and make your claim in person. Be sure to make your claim within three months of your husband's death.

IF YOU THINK YOU ARE GETTING THE WRONG AMOUNT

You can appeal to the National Insurance tribunal, as explained on pp. 311–12.

If you haven't got enough to live on

Claim supplementary benefit (see p. 113).

Further information

See p. 109.

Widows' inheritance

If your husband has made a will

his money and belongings will go to whomever he has named in the will. Most married couples – if they make wills at all – make 'mutual' wills, so that the husband has one will leaving everything to the wife and the wife has another leaving everything to the husband. There is normally an arrangement to leave everything to the children if husband and wife die together. A will can also appoint a guardian to look after the children.

It's best if you and your husband do make wills, because it can save a lot of anxiety when either of you dies. A will is not valid unless it is properly drawn up, so it's advisable not to rely on a home-made one, but to get a solicitor to do it for you. They normally charge between £5 and £10 for this.

If your husband has made a will but leaves little or nothing to you or your children

you can – unless you have divorced him and remarried – apply to the court to have the terms of the will altered. You will need the help of a solicitor for this, so read pp. 298–301. When the court is deciding how much you should get, it must consider how you and your husband and children have led your lives. For example, if you left your husband in order to live with a well-off man twenty years ago and have not depended on him since, you will probably get nothing. On the other hand, if you and your husband spent most of your lives together and separated only recently, and you were not well off, you and your children will probably be awarded part of your husband's property. If you were divorced and your husband had remarried, this would be taken into consideration and you might get less.

If your husband dies without leaving a will

and you have no children between you, you will get everything.
If you have children by him, you will be entitled to his personal
belongings and to the rest of his property up to the value of
£15,000, free of death duty and legal costs. If his property is
worth more than that, you are entitled to half of everything over
£15,000, after death duties and legal costs have been deducted.
The children will get the rest when they reach the age of 18.

Before you can take over your inheritance

you will probably have to get a 'Grant of Probate' (if he left a
will) or 'Letters of Administration' (if he didn't leave a will).
Both are obtainable from the Probate Registry in the High
Court. If you've inherited a large amount, it's best to instruct a
solicitor to deal with this side of affairs. Your bank may also
advise you. Otherwise, you can make your own application to the
Probate Registry. If you want to know more about this, ask your
Citizens' Advice Bureau.

Further information

National Insurance leaflets NI 51, *Guide for Widows*, and NI 13,
Widows' Benefits, from your local Social Security office.

The Cruse Organization for Widows, 6 Lion Gate Gardens,
Richmond, Surrey (01 940 2660), offers information and advice
for widows, and produces some useful fact sheets and a booklet
entitled *Caring for the Widow and her Family*.

Family allowance

You can claim family allowance if you have two or more children,
whether you are single or married. It is the only money that a
mother has an automatic right to receive. You don't need National
Insurance stamps to claim it. You don't have to fill in any com-

plicated forms or answer questions about your financial resources.

You get no money for your first child, 90p for your second child and £1·00 for every child after that. You go on getting family allowance as long as you have two or more children who are:

1. Under 16 or under 19 and in full-time education or training *and*
2. Living at home with you or being financially supported by you. You may be able to claim family allowance for a child who is not your own but who is living with you and being supported by you.

To get family allowance you have to fill in a simple claim form, which you can get from your local Social Security office. You will be sent a book of money orders which you can cash every Tuesday at your local Post Office. The order book is always sent to the mother, except where she is not living with the children and the father is looking after them and supporting them on a permanent basis.

Family allowance may be abolished if the Government introduces the new tax credit system which it has recently proposed (see p. 62).

Family income supplement

The family income supplement (FIS) is a weekly allowance of up to £6.* It is intended for poor families. In order to get it you have to have the right family circumstances and a low enough income to qualify; and fill in a lengthy claim form with details of your income and circumstances.

Despite massive advertising campaigns, many people do not know of the existence of FIS or, if they do, have difficulty in claiming it. So it is hardly surprising that only about 60 per cent of people eligible for FIS actually claim it. Moreover, FIS encourages people to stay in low-paid employment. It is payable to families (including one-parent families) that have at least one dependent child and a total income which falls below a prescribed

*Rates quoted in this chapter were increased in April 1974.

level; it can only be claimed by families where the 'head of the household' is in full-time work.

In October 1973, the prescribed level was £21·50 for a family with one child, plus £2·50 for each child after that.

When can you claim FIS?

You can claim FIS if you have at least one dependent child living with you *and*:

1. You are single, working at least thirty hours a week, and have an income below the prescribed level.
   or
2. You are married or living with a man 'as man and wife', he is working at least thirty hours a week, and the total family income is below the prescribed level.

If you are married or living with a man you cannot claim FIS in your own right, since the man is considered to be 'head of the household'. He must make the claim, and he can only do so if *he* is in full-time work, unless he is disabled or otherwise incapable of work. You cannot claim FIS when you are employed and the man is not. In this situation, if you haven't enough to live on, the man will have to claim supplementary benefit, as explained on p. 113.

Any children who are under 16, or over 16 and still at school, can be counted as part of your family as long as they are living with you. But you cannot include your own children if they are living away from home.

How much FIS will you get?

This will depend on how little you are earning. It is worked out at *half* the amount by which your total family income falls short of the prescribed level. And when they say 'total family income' they mean *everything* – including gross income of both parents, family allowance and any other benefits you may be receiving. Here are two examples.

1. You are married with two children. Your husband is earning £16·40 a week; you are getting 90p family allowance. You are not working, and the family has no other source of income. Your total income is £17·30, which falls short of the prescribed level (£24·00) by £6·70. You will therefore get £3·40 FIS a week.
2. You are single with one child. You are earning £10 a week and you have no other source of income. Your income falls short of the prescribed level (£21·50) by £11·50. Half that is £5·75, but in fact you will get £5, which is the maximum for families with up to two children.

How to claim

Get the claim form (FIS 1) from your local Post Office. If they don't have it, get it from your local Social Security office. You should also make sure that they give you the prepaid envelope for sending it off. Fill in the form with details of your income. You should enclose your pay-slips for the last five weeks, if you have them. If you are paid by the month, you should enclose the last two monthly pay-slips. But don't delay in sending off the form if you haven't kept them. If you are single, only you need sign the form, but if you are married, or making a joint claim with the man you are living with, you must *both* sign the form. Send it off to the Department of Health and Social Security, Family Income Supplement, Norcross, Blackpool FY5 3TD.

If they decide you are eligible, you will be sent a book of orders which can be cashed at your local Post Office every Tuesday. You will be able to draw FIS for fifty-two weeks, and it will not be affected if your circumstances change during that time. After fifty-two weeks you must renew your claim.

Note

While you are receiving FIS, you are automatically entitled to free prescriptions, free dental treatment and glasses under the National Health Service; free welfare milk and food for children under school age and expectant mothers; free school meals for schoolchildren; and fares refunded for any members of your family going to hospital for treatment. Your F I S book acts as a passport to these benefits.

Supplementary benefit

Supplementary benefit is money you can claim from the state if you haven't enough to live on. It says a lot about the position of women in Britain that over 68 per cent of all people who receive supplementary benefits are women. They include single women who aren't eligible for full National Insurance benefits, unsupported mothers, wives of men claiming supplementary benefit, prisoners' wives, divorced and separated women, widows and women pensioners.

The Supplementary Benefits Commission, which runs the scheme, is hardly a hotbed of generosity. Benefits are very low indeed – scarcely enough to keep you above the breadline. If you are going to make a claim, you need even more patience and perseverance than you would if you were claiming unemployment benefit. It helps if you also have a thick skin, a stubborn disposition and an equally determined friend to back you up when you go to the Social Security office – preferably a member of a claimants' union or the Child Poverty Action Group (more about these at the end of the section, p. 119).

There are detailed regulations which say how much money should be given out, to whom and in what circumstances. The Social Security officials often make all kinds of personal judgements about people without any justification before deciding whether they need benefits. Their judgement is guided by an official manual called the 'A' Code. The 'A' Code is secret, so you never know exactly what their terms of reference are. They seldom if ever tell you how to get the maximum amount that you are entitled to.

However, you have a *right* to supplementary benefit if you haven't enough to live on. So don't be put off. First you must know *how much* you have a right to – including the basic allowance and all the possible extras. Then claim for as much as you can get.

(Supplementary benefit is called 'supplementary allowance' when paid to people under 60 and 'supplementary pension' when paid to people over 60. For the sake of simplicity, we have called it 'supplementary benefit' throughout.)

When can you claim supplementary benefit?

You can claim if you are single, separated, divorced or widowed, and if your financial resources fall below a certain level.

You cannot claim if you are married and living with your husband or if you are living with a man 'as man and wife'. If you are, it is the man who must make the claim. He will receive the rate for a married couple, which is less than the rate for two single people. This particular rule gives rise to a great deal of hardship and confusion when it is applied to single women who are living with men but want to remain financially independent. It is known as the 'cohabitation rule' and is explained in more detail on p. 121.

Under 18. You cannot claim supplementary benefit if you are under 16. If you are 16 or 17, you cannot claim if you are still at school unless you are 'head of a household'. If your parents are claiming supplementary benefit, they can claim extra for you as their dependant. If you are over 16 and not at school, you have the same right to claim supplementary benefit as anyone else, although you get a lower rate if you are not a 'householder' (as explained below).

You may have to register for employment before you can claim. If you have a child under 16 who is living with you; if you are looking after a sick or aged relative; or if you are sick, recently widowed or over 60, you can go straight to the Social Security office and make your claim. Otherwise you are supposed to go to your local Employment Exchange and register for work before you claim supplementary benefit. But they probably won't make you do this if you are over 45.

How much do you get?

The amount of supplementary benefit you get depends on how much you can claim and how much other income you have (if any). It is paid in the form of a weekly allowance to cover regular living expenses, with additional payments (if and when you claim them) to cover extra expenses that crop up.*

HERE IS THE MAXIMUM AMOUNT OF MONEY THAT CAN BE CLAIMED AS A WEEKLY ALLOWANCE:

1. *If you're under 60 :*

(a) A basic allowance to cover day-to-day living expenses for yourself. This is £7·15 for a single person who is a householder (which means someone who is directly responsible for household necessities and rent); £5·70 for a single person who is not a householder, or £4·40 for a non-householder aged between 16 and 18; and £11·65 for a married couple.

(b) Additional weekly allowances for any dependants you have. The rates are –

for a dependant aged 18 or over	£5·70
16 to 18	4·40
13 to 16	3·70
11 to 13	3·00
5 to 11	2·45
under 5	2·05

(c) An amount to cover your rent and rates. These will usually be paid in full, unless the Social Security officials decide that they are unreasonably high, in which case they will pay a contribution towards them.

(d) You can claim further allowances if you have 'exceptional needs', for instance if you need special food or if you have

*Rates quoted in this chapter were increased in April 1974.

heavy laundry expenses, or if you have to make hire-purchase payments for essential items.

(e) If extra heating is a special need, you can get an allowance for this as well.

2. *If you are over 60* OR *if you have been claiming supplementary benefit for over two years and you don't have to register for work :*

(a) The basic allowance is higher – £8·15 for a single person and £12·85 for a married couple. You get the same allowances as a person under 60 for dependants, rent and rates.

(b) If you are over 80 you get an extra 25p a week.

(c) You can claim an additional allowance if you need extra heating.

(d) If you claim any other allowance to cover special needs, you will get only the difference between what you claim and 50p (if you are under 80), or 75p (if you are over 80).

YOU MAY GET LESS SUPPLEMENTARY BENEFIT IF YOU HAVE OTHER MONEY COMING IN

If you have any other income, most or all of it will be deducted from your weekly allowance:

1. If you are receiving family allowance, family income supplement, National Insurance benefits or maintenance payments, these will be deducted in full.

2. You (and your husband or the man you are living with) can each earn up to £2 a week, or £1 if you are required to register for employment before claiming benefit: this income is *not* deducted. All other earnings are deducted in full.

3. In addition, income up to a total of £2 a week from any of the following sources will *not* be deducted:
   disability pension;
   war widow's pension;
   the first £1 of any other income, including 'assumed income' from capital and savings (explained below).

What is counted as 'assumed income' from capital and savings? If you own a home which you live in, this is ignored completely, so there is no 'assumed income' from it. If you have capital of less than £325, this is ignored too, even if it produces an income. Above that, it is assumed that you have a weekly income for 5p a week for each £25 between £300 and £800 and of 12½p for each £25 over £800.

HOW TO WORK OUT HOW MUCH SUPPLEMENTARY
BENEFIT YOU SHOULD GET EACH WEEK

1. Add up the total amount of money you can claim as a weekly allowance.
2. Add up the total amount of other income you have which must be deducted.
3. Subtract (2) from (1). The amount that is left is approximately what you should get as supplementary benefit.

What else can you claim?

You can claim extra payments for clothes, footwear, prams, pushchairs, floorcoverings, bedding, furniture, cooker, heaters and similar essentials (although the weekly allowance is supposed to cover 'normal repair and replacement of clothing, footwear and normal heating costs'). You can also claim financial help with fares to visit relatives in hospital or your husband if he is in prison. Inquire about this at your local Social Security office.

If you are receiving supplementary benefit, you are also automatically entitled to free prescriptions, help with National Health dental and optical charges, welfare milk and vitamins, and free school meals for your children. You may also be able to claim further grants to help support your children while they are at school, if you apply to your local education authority.

If your husband is off work because he is involved in a strike

He is disqualified from claiming supplementary benefit for himself. However, he can still claim benefit for you, at the rate for an adult dependant, which is slightly higher than the rate for a wife. He can claim the normal amount for rent and for any children you have. If he gets strike pay or tax rebates while he is off work, all but the first £1 of the total will be deducted from the supplementary benefit.

How to claim

First of all, look at p. 114 to see if you have to register for employment before you can claim supplementary benefit.

1. If you do not have to register for employment, you should get form SB1 from your local Post Office and ask for the prepaid envelope to go with it. You then fill it in and send it to your local Social Security office.
2. Alternatively you can go straight to your Social Security office and make your claim in person.
3. If you have to register for employment, ask for Form B1 at your Employment Exchange, fill it in, and take it or send it to your Social Security office.

When they get your form the Social Security office will want to interview you and ask you questions about your income and needs. A Social Security official will probably visit your home. If they decide to give you supplementary benefit it will be paid by means of an order book, or by Giro order, which you can cash each week at a Post Office. But if you are in urgent need, you can ask for a Giro order 'over the counter' at the Social Security office.

You will find yourself in a much stronger position in getting your claim if you have someone to help you. Contact your local claimants' union, or the local branch of the Child Poverty Action Group if there is one in your area. If there isn't and you are having difficulty with your claim, go to your Citizens' Advice Bureau, or get help from a social worker: if you are not already in touch with one, contact the social services department of your local council. (The addresses of your local CAB and social services department are both in the telephone directory.)

Your right to appeal

You can appeal to the supplementary benefits appeals tribunal if you don't agree with a decision taken by the Social Security office about how much supplementary benefit you should get. The appeals procedure is explained on pp. 312–13.

Further information

A *claimants' union* is a group of people claiming supplementary benefits or National Insurance benefits who get together to help each other with their claims and to spread information about available benefits. They accumulate experience of how to get the most out of the system and take collective action if Social Security officials prove to be particularly obstructive. There is a growing claimants' union movement, but there are no formal links between the local unions, no structure and no headquarters. If you want to know if there is one in your area, ask the other people waiting in the Social Security office. If there isn't one, you can always start one. One of the most long-standing claimants' unions in London, which may be a possible source of information, is the South-East London Claimants' Union, The Albany, Creek Road, Deptford, London SE8 (01 692 1047).

The Child Poverty Action Group (CPAG) is an organization which fights poverty for adults and children alike. It is a good source of information on all aspects of welfare rights and publishes some useful pamphlets and an invaluable booklet called *National Welfare Benefits Handbook*, price 25p from CPAG, 1 Macklin Street, London WC2 (01 242 3225). If there's a branch of the CPAG near you, the address should be in your local telephone directory.

The Citizens' Rights Office concentrates on helping people with specific claims and with appeals to tribunals. Also at 1 Macklin Street, London WC2 (01 405 5942).

The Penguin Guide to Supplementary Benefits by Tony Lynes, price 40p. A detailed description of how the supplementary benefits system works, which is as lucid as it can be, considering the complexity of the subject.

Supplementary Benefits Handbook. The official word, price 32½p, from HMSO bookshops.

EXAMPLE ONE

Mavis and Bill Jones have three children aged 14, 11 and 6. Bill works as a self-employed house painter, but he is often out of work during the winter. As he is not entitled to unemployment benefit, he has to claim supplementary benefit. This is a summary of what they get, showing how their various sources of income are deducted from the money they receive as benefit.

Benefit before deductions

Basic weekly allowance for a married couple	£11·65
for a child aged 14	3·70
for a child aged 11	3·00
for a child aged 6	2·45
Rent per week	6·00
Weekly HP payments on a cooker	0·90
Total before deductions	£27·70

Deductions

Family allowance for two children	1·90
Mavis works part-time and earns £5 a week, of which she is allowed the first £2	3·00
They have savings of £400, and thus an 'assumed income' on £75 at 5p per £25	0·15
Total deductions	£5·05

Total weekly benefit is £27·70 minus £5·05 =   £22·65

EXAMPLE TWO

Judy is a single mother with two children aged 3 and 5. She has been living on supplementary benefit since the birth of her first child. As she is looking after children, she does not have to register for work before claiming benefit. Her rent is £4 a week. She receives a small amount of maintenance from the children's father. This is what she gets:

Benefit before deductions

Basic weekly allowance for a single person who has been living on supplementary benefit for more than two years, who is not required to register for work	£8·15
Allowance for a child aged 5	2·45
Allowance for a child aged 3	2·05
Rent per week	4·00
Total before deductions	£16·65

Deductions

Family allowance for one child	0·90
Maintenance from the children's father	7·50
Total deductions	£8·40
Total weekly benefit is £16·65 minus £8·40 =	£8·25

The 'cohabitation rule'

'Cohabitation' means living together. The 'cohabitation rule' is applied to women who claim certain welfare benefits. It says that if a woman is living with a man 'as man and wife' she should be treated as the man's wife, even though she is not married to him.

This means that a single woman who is living with a man cannot claim supplementary benefit, widows' benefits or benefits for any of her children. She is expected to rely on the man to support her and her children from his earnings, or claim supplementary benefit for her as his dependent 'wife'. Supplementary benefit paid for a woman as a man's wife (£4·50) is considerably less than that paid to a single woman (£7·15, or £5·70 if she is not a householder).*

What often happens is that a woman loses her right to claim benefit because she is thought to be 'cohabiting', even when she is receiving no money from the man, and when she has no wish to be financially dependent on him.

There appear to be two main assumptions behind the cohabitation rule:

*Rates quoted in this chapter were increased in April 1974.

1. A woman who is married to or living with a man and sleeping with him should be supported by the man.
2. A woman who is married to or living with a man and sleeping with him needs less money to live on than a woman who is living alone, with another woman, or with a man who does not share her bed.

The official justification is that an unmarried couple who live together should not get more money than a married couple.

You may be affected by the cohabitation rule if:

1. You are single, separated, divorced, or widowed;
   and
2. You are claiming supplementary benefit, widow's benefits or child's special allowance;
   and
3. You are living with a man.

How do the Social Security officials decide whether you are cohabiting?

Special investigators are employed to check up on women who are suspected of cohabiting. According to the *Supplementary Benefits Handbook*, they are supposed to consider a number of different facts:

Does the woman use the man's name and do they represent themselves, or are they publicly acknowledged, as man and wife?

Is the partnership a stable one? How long has it lasted?

Is there a common home, in the sense of shared accommodation and household duties?

Have the couple had children? Do they share the same bedroom?

Does the man support the woman financially (as distinct from paying for board and accommodation)?

The special investigators may call at your home and ask to look around. They will be searching for evidence that a man is living with you. If they call at an inconvenient hour – like early in the morning or late at night – you have every right to turn them away or ask them to come back another time. If you refuse them entry altogether, there is a danger that they will take that as evidence that you are cohabiting. On the other hand, if they look around and find nothing, that will weaken their case. They may spy on your home to see if they can catch a man leaving it several mornings a week. They may also question your children and your neighbours. But evidence they collect this way may not amount to proof that you are cohabiting.

The *Supplementary Benefits Handbook* also states:

There is no simple way of deciding the issue. The existence of a sexual relationship is not in itself decisive and certainly occasional sleeping together does not constitute cohabitation. The fact that a man is contributing to a woman's financial support does not necessarily mean that she is cohabiting with him. On the other hand, if he does not support her financially that is not in itself conclusive evidence against cohabitation.

So you are *not* 'cohabiting' if you have a boyfriend who stays with you occasionally. You are *not* 'cohabiting' if you are simply sharing accommodation with a male flat-mate, landlord or lodger and you are not sharing the same bed. Nevertheless, a lot of women *are* accused of cohabiting when they are not.

If they decide that you are cohabiting, your book of money orders will be taken away. But if you have children whose father is not the man you are living with, they may go on paying an allowance for the children for four weeks.

What do you do if your benefit is stopped?

Whatever the circumstances, it is almost certainly worth appealing against the decision.

1. Make a fresh claim for benefit at once to your local Social Security office. If you tell them you are in urgent need, you may be able to get some money while you are waiting for your appeal to be heard. Tell them that this is allowed under 'section 13 of the 1966 Ministry of Social Security Act'.

2. Contact the claimants' union, if there is one in your area, or the local branch of the Child Poverty Action Group. They will help you make an appeal. You should be able to find their addresses through other people waiting at the Social Security office, in the telephone directory or at your local Citizens' Advice Bureau. If you can't find people in the neighbourhood who can help you, it is well worth writing off to the Child Poverty Action Group London office for two very useful leaflets: *The Cohabitation Rule*, and the *Guide to Supplementary Benefit Appeals Tribunals*. They cost 5p each and you can get them from CPAG, 1 Macklin Street, London WC2.

3. Make an appeal. If you were getting supplementary benefit, appeal to the supplementary benefits appeals tribunal. If you were getting widows' benefits or child's special allowance, appeal to the National Insurance tribunal. You can appeal to both if necessary. Do this within twenty-one days of having your benefit stopped. If you don't you will have to explain why you haven't appealed sooner, and the tribunal may refuse to hear your appeal. But if twenty-one days have already gone by, it is still worth trying to appeal.

4. The Clerk of the tribunal will let you know when and where the hearing will be held. He will send you copies of the papers which are to be presented to the tribunal, including details of the 'case against you'. This should give you a chance to prepare your defence. Try to attend the tribunal yourself. You are allowed to take two people with you, and this is always a good idea: take a friend who supports your story or a representative from your claimants' union or the CPAG. Collect together all the evidence you can find that might convince the tribunal that you are not cohabiting – such as rent book, wage-slips and letters. Get witnesses to support your case – such as neighbours, your boyfriend or a social worker. It is particularly useful if you can produce evidence that your boyfriend is living somewhere else; or supporting another family; or that the man in question is in fact your lodger or your landlord. Don't be intimidated by the tribunal. Remember it is up to them to prove that you are cohabiting and the evidence col-

lected by the 'special investigators' can be very flimsy. You should be allowed to cross-question them.

5. If you can't prove that you are not cohabiting, you may be able to plead 'exceptional circumstances'. The tribunal is more likely to accept a plea of 'exceptional circumstances' if you are supporting the children of another man and the man you are living with refuses to support them. But if this doesn't apply to you, you should try it if you feel you are facing any exceptional difficulties. If the tribunal accepts the plea, you will continue to get benefit for the children – but not for yourself.

Here is a true example of how the cohabitation rule can work in practice.

Janice, an unsupported mother of three, relied on supplementary benefit as her only possible source of income. She couldn't work because she was looking after her young son, who was recovering from a serious fall. She had a friend who stayed with her one or two nights a week. He wasn't living with her and he could not support her financially.

Her local Social Security office decided that she was cohabiting and took her supplementary benefit order book away. They based their decision on an anonymous letter and on subsequent inquiries made by one of their special investigators.

The special investigator had visited the office where her friend worked and asked to see the company's books. He had been to the café where she worked for a week and talked to the proprietor about her relationship with the man. He questioned her son about him, referring to him as 'your dad'. Janice lodged an appeal against the decision. The manager of the Social Security office refused to give her an emergency allowance to last her until the appeal was heard, although he was empowered to do so under section 13 of the Social Security Act. When she rang the office later they refused to talk to her on the telephone or to see her in person. She had no money and no idea when her appeal would be heard – they often take weeks. Eventually, she enlisted the support of her local claimants' union. They sent a delegation of ten to occupy the office until the manager agreed to discuss the case with them. His one concession was to set an early date for the appeal.

When the appeal was heard by the supplementary benefits

appeals tribunal, only one independent witness was produced to give evidence against Janice: the caretaker of the half-way hostel where she was living. He claimed that he saw a man leaving her flat every morning after 8 o'clock when he came on duty; that the man drove away in a red car and sometimes in a lorry marked 'Eliot'.

Janice was accompanied to the tribunal by a member of the claimants' union. They pointed out that her friend was a long-distance driver, away for an average of four nights a week. When he stayed with her he usually left as early as 6.00 a.m. He drove a grey car and had no connection with any firm called 'Eliot'. She did not share a common home with the man. Nor did she pool household expenses with him. None of her children were his and she was not publicly acknowledged as his wife.

She won her appeal and her right to draw supplementary benefit was restored.

Further information

See p. 119.

Student grants

You get the standard rate of grant if you are single, married to a *student*, widowed, divorced or separated. The maximum standard grant is £520 if you're a student in London, Oxford or Cambridge; £485 if you're a student anywhere else in the UK; and £390 if you're living at home with your parents. The grant is assessed on your parents' income (even if you are married), unless:

(a) you are over 25;
(b) you have worked for three years between leaving school and going to college;
(c) there are special circumstances – e.g. your parents can't be found.

You may get a higher-value 'mature student's' grant if you start your course when you are over 26: this will depend on how much you have earned in the years before you became a student.

*Rates quoted in this chapter were increased in 1974.

You get the low married woman's rate of grant if you are married to a non-student. This is all of £295, and it may even be assessed on your parents' income if you married during your course and your grant was assessed on their income before you got married; or if you were married and under 21 before you started the course. A male student married to a non-student does not suffer in the same way.

Extra grants for dependent children and adults : A male student can claim allowances for his dependent wife and children. The rates are: £250 for the wife; £105 for the first child; £60 for the second child; and £55 for each other child. But a married woman student cannot claim an allowance for a dependent husband unless he is physically or mentally disabled and incapable of supporting

himself. So if you are married with kids, you will not be able to support your husband if he is looking after them at home. As a woman you cannot claim allowances for your children if you are married or unmarried. You can, however, if you are widowed, divorced or separated. The rates are: £250 for the first child; £60 for the second child; and £55 for each other child. However, if you have a child but you have never been married, the most you can claim is £144·30. This is a shocking anomaly which discriminates against unmarried mothers.

If you are working and your husband is a student you may be able to claim a tax allowance for a dependent relative: if his income is no more than £422 a year, you can claim a tax allowance of up to £145 a year.

If you're in any doubt about what your grant should be, you can get more information by writing to: Grants Adviser, National Union of Students, 3 Endsleigh Street, London WC1 (or phone 01 387 1277).

3. Sex

Sex under 18

Most of the legal restrictions on your sex life are lifted on your 16th birthday. But until your 18th birthday, there are still some things you cannot do without getting into trouble with the law. Once you are 18 you have reached the 'age of majority' and you can officially do what you like.

Sixteen is the 'age of consent'. This means that you can't legally have sexual intercourse until you are 16. The law does not seem very realistic in these days of earlier puberty and greater sexual freedom, but in fact it was not so long ago that the age of consent was 12.

The age of consent was raised to 16 in 1885. The reason was not to stop 15-year-old girls sleeping with their boyfriends, but to make it illegal to procure young girls for prostitution and the White Slave Trade – both flourishing businesses in the mid-nineteenth century.

The scandal of procuring young girls was brought to the public notice by Mrs Josephine Butler. She persuaded a Mr Stead, then editor of the *Pall Mall Gazette*, to dramatically illustrate the situation. With the help of the Salvation Army, he bought a 13-year-old girl for £5, kept her (suitably protected) in a brothel overnight and sent her to Paris the next day. He then published details of the transaction, pointing out that it was all entirely legal, under the title 'The Maiden Tribute of Modern Babylon'. The article caused a tremendous sensation and five days later a Criminal Law Amendment Bill was rushed through Parliament, raising the age of consent to 16. Mr Stead got three months in prison.

The age of consent has stuck at 16 ever since. But some of the effects it has today are not at all what Josephine Butler would have envisaged in 1885. For example:

1. *You may find it difficult to get birth control under 16* (although withholding birth control never stopped anyone having sex). Girls under 16 are less likely to want children than older girls, but – while it is possible for them to get contraceptives from some clinics in a rather 'under-the-counter' way – it is not their right.

Birth control advice, eh? Well, **abortions** now and **contraceptives** later... when you're **16**

2. *If you are pregnant and under 16*, you can get no financial help from the state. You are not eligible for a maternity grant or maternity allowance, nor can you claim supplementary benefit in your own right. (We explain what you can do in these circumstances on p. 82.)

3. *You may find yourself in court if you are under 17 and having sexual intercourse or 'in danger' of having it.* This will only happen if your parents are not looking after you or if they feel they can't cope with you. You can be taken to court if your parents, the police, or the social services department of your local council think that you are in 'moral danger'. 'Moral danger' in the eyes of the law can mean: that you are under 16 and likely to be having sexual intercourse; *or* that you are under 17 and away from home and likely to be having sexual intercourse.

(Incidentally, boys are not taken to court for the same reasons.)

If you are taken to court and it is decided that you are in need of 'care and control', the court will place you under a supervision order or under a care order. There is a full explanation of this, and what to do if it happens to you, on p. 238.

You are *less* likely to get into this kind of trouble if you are living in conventional surroundings and leading a fairly 'normal' life, even if you are having sex. You are *more* likely to if you mix with an unconventional crowd of people; if you have dropped out of school; if you leave home without your parents' consent; or if you are living with a man or in a mixed flat or commune, even if you are not having sex.

4. *A boy or man with whom you have sexual intercourse may be prosecuted.* The laws were designed to protect young girls from seduction. Unfortunately, they may also be used against a boyfriend you cared for and wanted to sleep with. Here is a list of the things a man cannot (legally) do with you if you are under 18.

(a) It is a very serious offence for a man to have sexual intercourse with a girl under 13. He cannot normally defend himself by claiming that she consented or that he thought she was older.

(b) It is an offence for a man to have sexual intercourse with a girl aged between 13 and 16. But if he is under 24, he may avoid being convicted if he can show that he thought she was over

16, unless he has been charged with the same offence before. It is assumed in law that a boy under 14 cannot be found guilty of illegal sexual intercourse.

(c) It is an offence to make an assault, indecent or otherwise, on anyone, but an indecent assault on a girl under 16 is more serious and carries a higher penalty.

(d) It is an offence for a person to let a girl under 16 use premises for sexual intercourse; or to encourage prostitution or illegal sexual intercourse.

(e) It is an offence to take a girl under 16 away from her parents without their consent. This could mean that a boy of 17 (or a man of any age, for that matter) might be prosecuted if he encouraged a girl of 15 to run away with him, even if he didn't have sexual intercourse with her.

(f) It is an offence for a man to take an unmarried girl under 18 away from her parents without their consent if he is taking her 'with intent to have unlawful sexual intercourse'. ('Unlawful' in this case means sex outside marriage.) The only way he can avoid conviction is by claiming that he thought the girl was over 18. So if you leave home and go to live with a boyfriend when you are 17, he may be prosecuted if he encouraged you to leave, even though it is perfectly legal for you to have sex.

WHERE TO GET HELP WITH SEXUAL PROBLEMS IF YOU ARE UNDER 18

The Brook Advisory Centres specialize in helping young people with all sexual problems. There are five Brook centres in London, three in Bristol, and one in Coventry, Birmingham, Cambridge, Liverpool and Edinburgh. If you live in one of these areas, you can find the address in the telephone directory. The head office is at 233 Tottenham Court Road, London W1 (01 580 2991).

Many of the bigger towns and cities now have youth advisory centres. If there is one in your area, the Citizens' Advice Bureau will give you the address. Otherwise if you have a serious problem, try talking to your teacher (if you are at school) or go to the social services department of your local council (address in the telephone directory) and ask to see a social worker.

Contraception

If you are under 16

Although the law says that you should not have sexual intercourse until your 16th birthday, it is not illegal to use birth control. However, some family planning clinics may refuse to prescribe the Pill, or to fit you with a cap or coil.

The legal position is this: it is not illegal for a doctor to give you *advice* about contraception. But in most cases it is illegal for a doctor to give you medical examination or treatment without your parents' consent: this would include prescribing the Pill or fitting the cap or coil. But a doctor can legally examine or treat you if he is 'acting in good faith' and has the opinion of a second doctor. He would have to make a personal judgement, and not all doctors would agree to it.

The result is that your chances of getting contraception depend on the prejudices of your doctor. Some will help you without any hesitation; some will insist that you get your parents' consent first; others will refuse to help you at all. (Some family doctors have been known to tell a girl's parents against her wishes.) A lot of girls get round the problem by saying they are 16 and they usually find that clinics don't check up on them.

The Brook Advisory Centres specialize in helping young girls and boys on all sexual matters. They charge an initial fee of £5. The addresses are given at the end of the section (p. 142). You can rely on them to be sympathetic. They will encourage you to tell your parents, but they will not insist if you don't want to, and they may be able to help you anyway, by getting the opinion of a second doctor.

Likewise, it is the official policy of most family planning clinics not to turn anyone away. They are likely to be more insistent about getting your parents' consent, but they will not tell them if you don't want them to. Whether or not they let you have birth control supplies will depend on the attitude of the doctor at your local clinic. Don't be afraid to approach them.

If you are over 16

Whether you are single or married, you can get birth control advice and supplies from your local family planning clinic. From April 1974, new Area Health Authorities are being set up and they will be advised to take over family planning clinics run by local authorities and, eventually, those run by other agencies.

Where this happens, you will be able to obtain birth control advice free but you will have to pay the standard prescription charge for supplies (that is, 20p for each prescription). Some local councils will continue to give totally free supplies.

HOW TO FIND OUT WHERE TO GO

You can find the address of your local family planning clinic in the telephone directory. It is best to ring first, or drop in to make an appointment. But some clinics will see you immediately. If you don't find it convenient to go to the clinic, try your family doctor. Other useful addresses are listed at the end of the chapter.

WHAT IF YOU CAN'T GET TO THE CLINIC?

If you are homebound because you are ill, or you have small children, or you live a long way from the clinic and have no transport, someone from the clinic may be able to visit you at your home. This is known as the 'domiciliary service'. It can only be arranged if you are referred to the service by a social worker or health visitor, but if you're in touch with one you can always ask to be referred.

WILL THEY ASK A LOT OF INTERFERING QUESTIONS?

They are not supposed to and they probably won't. If they do, you don't have to answer. The only thing they have to know is your name and address. They may also ask you your age, your occupation, your partner's occupation and your marital status, but you don't have to tell them if you don't want to.

IS YOUR HUSBAND'S CONSENT NEEDED?

It is still the policy of most clinics to ask for your husband's consent if you are having a coil fitted or an operation for sterilization. Their excuse is that the doctor must be protected from being sued by an irate husband who might demand compensation for loss of his ability to have children. However, there are no known cases to indicate that this is necessary. Early in 1973, Lord Aberdare, Minister of State for Health and Social Security, replying to a question from Baroness Wootton in the Lords, stated: 'There is no legal requirement either under English or Scottish law that the consent of the spouse must be obtained for the sterilization of the partner.' Some women simply sign their husband's name for them. More and more doctors are prepared to fit coils or sterilize without the husband's consent. If you're single, there's no problem.

What are the most effective forms of birth control?

The Pill

What is it?   Pills containing the hormones oestrogen and progestogen.

How it works   You take one pill each day – usually for twenty-one days followed by a seven-day break – and this stops you producing your monthly egg cell.

Advantages   Easy to use – it becomes a habit. You control your own fertility. It is almost 100-per-cent effective.

Disadvantages   You have to remember to take it every day. Some women suffer side effects, such as weight increase or headaches, although this can sometimes be helped by changing to another pill. The long-term effects aren't fully known.

Where to get it?   You need a prescription, which you can get from your family planning clinic or your family doctor.

The Coil (IUD)

What is it?   A small flexible coil or loop of plastic or metal which is inserted into the womb, without anaesthetic. If done skilfully, the insertion isn't painful.

How it works   Stops any fertilized egg from being implanted in the wall of the womb. No one knows exactly how.

Advantages   Once it's in you can forget about it except for yearly check-ups. You control your own fertility. It's usually very effective, though not quite as safe as the Pill.

Disadvantages	No good if you haven't been pregnant. (But see below: 'Copper-Seven coil'.) Can be uncomfortable at first and can cause irritation. In some women it causes backache and heavy menstrual and intermittent bleeding.
Where to get it?	It must be inserted by a doctor. You can get it from your local family planning clinic or family doctor.

Copper-Seven coil

What is it?	A small plastic intra-uterine device, shaped like a '7', with a copper tail.
How does it work?	It causes a chemical reaction which prevents conception.
Advantages	It can be used by women who haven't yet been pregnant and is as effective as a conventional coil. More comfortable, because it is smaller.
Disadvantages	The long-term effects of the absorption of copper by the body are not yet known. Can be very painful at first if you have never had a child. Has been known to slip out unnoticed, although this is rare.

The Cap

What is it?	A rubber cap or dome that fits over the entrance to the womb.
How it works	It prevents the male sperm from entering the womb.
Advantages	You shouldn't be able to feel it once it's in. You control it.
Disadvantages	You have to remember to put it in before you have intercourse. To be fully safe you must use spermicide cream with it, and it can be messy and awkward to insert. It's

possible to put it in wrongly, or to push it out of place. If you have intercourse more than once a night you should put more cream in. You have to leave it in for six hours after intercourse, and it's a bit of a performance taking it out: you have to wash it, dry it and powder it before you put it away.

Where to get it?	It must be fitted by a doctor. You can get it at your local family planning clinic or from your family doctor.

Sheath (*French letter or condom*)

What is it?	A thin covering of rubber which is fitted over the penis.
How it works	It prevents the sperm from reaching the womb.
Advantages	Anyone can buy it. Fairly straightforward to use. You know if the man's got one on. It offers some protection against venereal disease. If used properly, it can be quite effective.
Disadvantages	You have to rely on the man to use it. Some men resent having to wear it. Must be put on to an erect penis, so it can cause an unwelcome interruption. It can decrease sensitivity and lessen the enjoyment. Has been known to slip off. The man has to withdraw soon after ejaculation or it may leak. Now only considered properly effective if used with spermicidal pessaries.
Where to get it?	Most chemists, 'surgical supply' shops, family planning clinics.

Female Sterilization

What is it?	A surgical operation.
How does it work?	There are two methods. The first is called

laparotomy, which ties off the Fallopian tubes so that the eggs can't get to the womb. The second, laparoscopy, is a newer method which requires only two tiny cuts in the abdomen.

Advantages — Completely effective. Once it's done, there's nothing more to worry about. It doesn't interfere with your sex life.

Disadvantages — You can't change your mind: the operation isn't reversible. It's more complicated to arrange than other methods of contraception. Involves a stay in hospital of eight or nine days for a laparotomy, or forty-eight hours for a laparoscopy. Doctors will seldom operate on women who haven't had at least one child.

Where to get it? — You can arrange it through your family doctor or the doctor at your family planning clinic. The doctor will have to refer you to a hospital. It is then at the discretion of the surgeon at the hospital whether to sterilize you or not.

Male Sterilization (*Vasectomy*)

What is it? — A minor surgical operation.

How does it work? — Ties ducts from the testicles to prevent sperm being ejaculated.

Advantages — Completely effective. Doesn't affect the man's sex life or yours. If you have a steady relationship with him, you can let your own body function normally without any worries.

Disadvantages — You have to rely on the man to get it done. You only benefit if you have a steady relationship with him: not many men have vasectomies. The man can't change his mind about having children. Some men feel (wrongly) that it lessens their virility if they can't sire any more children. Doctors will seldom give vasectomies to men who haven't had at least one child.

Where to get it? The man can arrange it through his family doctor or family planning clinic.

NEW METHOD NOW ON TRIAL WITH THE FPA, WHICH MAY BE IN GENERAL USE WITHIN THE NEXT COUPLE OF YEARS

The 'before or after' pill

What is it? Pills which contain no oestrogen but a form of progestogen called 'clogestone acetate'.

How does it work? You can take it at any time from several hours before intercourse to ten hours afterwards. The effect lasts for ten hours and you can take it up to five times a week; after that you would have to use other methods of contraception as well. It prevents the egg from reaching the womb in a fertilized state.

Advantages Much smaller dose than the conventional pill. Fewer chances of side effects, and almost as effective. Ideal if you have sex irregularly or less than five times a week.

Disadvantages Long-term effects not known.

For further information and help

The Family Planning Association head office is at 27–35 Mortimer Street, London W1 (01 636 7866). Addresses of clinics in local telephone directories.

Brook Advisory Centres: there are five of them in London, three in Bristol, and one in Coventry, Birmingham, Cambridge, Liverpool and Edinburgh. Addresses in local telephone directories. The head office is at 233 Tottenham Court Road, London W1 (01 580 2991).

Abortion

The law still fails to recognize that it is every woman's right to control her own body. It does not allow a woman to have an abortion without the consent of two doctors. These doctors are usually men, they do not necessarily know what is best for the woman, and they themselves are not suffering from the unwanted pregnancy. Yet they make the decision. The woman cannot have an abortion just because she wants one.

Despite these legal obstacles, it *is* possible for most women to get an abortion if they know where to go for it. It helps if they are no more than twelve weeks pregnant and can spend *at least* £50 on the operation. Otherwise they will probably need to be very persistent and strong-willed if they are to avoid being depressed and discouraged. The more advanced the pregnancy, the harder it is to get an abortion: it is virtually impossible after six months.

Some facts and figures: about 150,000 legal abortions are carried out every year. Half of them are on the National Health and half are private; about half the women are single and half are married. More married women get National Health abortions than single women. By far the most common reason for abortion is risk to the woman's physical or mental health. The average time at which a pregnancy is ended is eleven weeks.

This section is divided into two parts. The first explains the relevant law and how it works in practice. The second tells you what to do if you think you are pregnant.

What the 1967 Abortion Act says

The Act says that you may get an abortion under the following conditions:

1. Two doctors must sign a form saying that they genuinely believe:
   (a) that continuing the pregnancy would involve a risk to your life or to the physical or mental health of you or any children you already have (taking into account your present and foreseeable circumstances); and that this risk would be greater than the risk involved in ending the pregnancy; *or*
   (b) that there is a substantial risk that if the child were born it would suffer a serious handicap from a physical or mental abnormality – as, for example, if you had German measles in the early stages of pregnancy.
2. The abortion must be carried out in a National Health hospital or in a clinic licensed by the Department of Health. This is so that the Government can control the way private abortions are handled – some clinics have had their licences taken away because they don't meet required standards.
3. If these conditions are not met, abortion is legal if it is carried out by one doctor who genuinely believes that it must be done immediately in order to save your life or prevent serious permanent injury to your physical or mental health.

How the Act works in practice

As you can see, the law gives you no automatic right to an abortion. It is left to the 'discretion' of the doctor, and doctors are free to interpret the law as they see fit. In fact, a doctor could now authorize *any* abortion, because statistics show that abortion is safer than childbirth (there are three deaths for every 100,000 abortions and eighteen deaths for every 100,000 births) – so condition 1(a) is automatically fulfilled. But a doctor who believes that abortion is morally wrong would not see things that way. So we are left with a ridiculous situation whereby a woman who wants an abortion is at the mercy of a doctor's personal prejudices and beliefs.

But if you have money you can almost always get an abortion. Some private clinics are very expensive (between £150 and £200), but you can get a relatively cheap abortion (between £51 and £70) through one of the non-profit-making agencies we have listed at the end of the section (pp. 148–9).

Getting an abortion on the National Health can be more difficult, for two reasons:

1. You may not be able to find a National Health doctor who approves of abortion and is prepared to sign the form. In some parts of the country, very few doctors will. In 1970, 17 per cent of abortions in Birmingham were on the National Health, as compared with 69 per cent in Liverpool and 75 per cent in Oxford.
2. There are often long waiting lists and you may not be able to get a hospital bed before your pregnancy is too far advanced.

The time factor is very important : When you are less than twelve weeks pregnant it is easier and a lot safer to get an abortion. It can be very difficult (though not impossible) if you are more than twenty weeks pregnant, even if you are prepared to pay. This is because the foetus is bigger, making the operation more complex and more open to risk.

What to do if you think you're pregnant (when you hadn't planned it)

1. Don't stop using contraceptives – you might be wrong.
2. When your period is two weeks overdue, have a pregnancy test (the test is not usually reliable until then). Don't wait any longer, hoping for the best. Abortion is simple and safe if it's done early. The sooner you find out whether you are pregnant, the longer you will have to decide what to do and to make the necessary arrangements. You can either go to your doctor for the test, or to a private pregnancy testing clinic.

Addresses of non-profit-making services are listed at the end of the section (pp. 148–9); commercial services (which charge about £3) are usually listed in the Yellow Pages of the telephone directory (under 'Pregnancy test services') and advertised in newspapers and magazines. Alternatively, you can buy a do-it-yourself kit, but these are not very reliable. A 'positive' result means you are pregnant; a 'negative' result usually means you're not.

3. If the result says you're not pregnant and your period still doesn't come, it may well have been wrong. It's best to have another test or see a doctor. If you miss two periods, you should definitely see a doctor. A positive result is very unlikely to be wrong.

4. If you find you are pregnant, don't panic or make any hasty decisions. Think about it carefully. If you are not absolutely sure what you want to do, try and talk it over with sympathetic people – perhaps with women who have had similar experiences. If you approach one of the organizations listed at the end of this section, they will help you make your decision: they won't push you into having an abortion if you are uncertain.

5. You don't have to have an abortion if you don't want one. If you are pregnant and single and you want to have the baby, you can contact One-Parent Families (address on p. 149). It will put you in touch with people who can help you while you are pregnant and after the baby is born.

6. You may want to have the child adopted: more about this on p. 231.

7. If you want an abortion, don't try and do it yourself. It can be very dangerous and it hardly ever works. 'Back-street' abortions, carried out by people who aren't doctors, are also dangerous.

8. If you want to try for a National Health abortion (that is, a free one) go to see your doctor. Try to get your own thoughts on the subject clear before you go, otherwise you may meet with hostile attitudes which could distress you or cause you to

change your mind for no good reason. (Don't be alarmed! Not all National Health doctors are uncooperative and yours may be very sympathetic.) If your doctor agrees to help you get an abortion, he will refer to you a gynaecologist for a second opinion. You may still have to wait some time before an abortion can be arranged. Remember that delay can be dangerous. If you are ten weeks pregnant and you don't have a National Health abortion lined up, it would be wiser to arrange a private abortion.

9. If you can't get a National Health abortion, or if you would rather pay and avoid the delay and complications you may encounter if you go through the National Health, go to one of the non-profit-making pregnancy advisory services. They may be able to help you get a National Health abortion even if you have been turned down; otherwise they will arrange a private abortion as cheaply as possible. They can usually help you out if you can't afford to pay, although they will ask you to try to raise the money first. Commercial pregnancy advisory services are in it to make money, so they charge a lot more. Addresses of non-profit-making services are listed at the end of this section (pp. 148–9).

10. If you are under 16 you can usually get an abortion through the National Health, although the doctor may insist on consulting your parents, even when you don't want them to know about it. If there is a Brook Advisory Centre in your area, try consulting them (address on p. 149).

11. If you are married, the doctor may ask for your husband's consent, but this may not be necessary, particularly if you have a private abortion. It is not required by law.

12. After you've had the abortion, make sure you have efficient contraception, so you don't run the same risk again – women often fail to do this. You should be able to get help from your doctor if you have a National Health abortion, or from the pregnancy advisory service (if it is a good one), or from your local family planning clinic. More about contraception on pp. 134–42.

13. It's wise to go for a medical check-up a few months after you

have had the abortion. If you later decide that you want to have a baby, make sure that your doctor knows that you have had an abortion, as this can – very occasionally – cause complications.

What are the different methods of abortion?

1. *Vacuum Aspiration.* This can be used if you are less than twelve weeks pregnant. The contents of the womb are gently sucked out. At present it is done with a general anaesthetic, although the method is used in other countries with a local anaesthetic, or with none at all.
2. *Dilation and Curettage* ('*D and C*'). This can be used if you are less than fourteen weeks pregnant. The womb is carefully 'scraped' clean. A general anaesthetic is used.
3. *Fluid Injection.* This can be used after you are fourteen weeks pregnant. Special fluid is injected into the womb and causes a miscarriage.
4. *Hysterotomy.* This can be used before or after you are fourteen weeks pregnant and involves a 'mini-Caesarean' abdominal operation with a general anaesthetic. Don't confuse it with a hysterectomy, which is the removal of the whole womb and which is not used for abortion. If you have a hysterotomy you will have to spend a few days in hospital. This method is not very popular, as the recovery period is longer and the risks greater.

NEW METHODS NOW ON TRIAL

1. *Out-patient vacuum abortion* ('*Karmen technique*'). This has been called the 'lunch-hour' abortion because it takes so little time. A new plastic suction tube is used, which reduces the risk of infection or damage to the mouth of the womb. The suction takes five minutes and only a local anaesthetic is needed. The patient can go home after a few hours' rest. The method is being tested by the National Health Service but is not yet widely available. It is also being used by the clinics run by the British Pregnancy Advisory Service.

Sterilization with abortion

It is quite common for women who have abortions under the National Health Service to be sterilized at the same time. This happened to half the married women who had National Health abortions in 1971. If you have several children already, the doctor may try to persuade you to agree to be sterilized before he signs the form authorizing the abortion. Don't be blackmailed into it. You are quite free to refuse if you are in any doubt at all. You can't be sterilized unless you give your consent.

It may be more dangerous to be aborted and sterilized at the same time than to have either operation separately. If you want to be sterilized you can arrange to have it done later when you have had time to think it over. With modern techniques, it involves only a very small cut and forty-eight hours in hospital.

However, if you are paying to have a private abortion and you definitely want to be sterilized, it is usually cheaper to have both done at the same time. The British Pregnancy Advisory Service charges £51 for an abortion, £75 for separate sterilization, and £90 to have both done together. This may be worth considering if you live in an area where it is difficult to get sterilization on the National Health, either because of doctors' attitudes or because there is a long waiting list.

(More about sterilization on pp. 139–41.)

Useful addresses

British Pregnancy Advisory Service, Guildhall Buildings, Navigation Street, Birmingham B2 4BT (021 643 1461). Branches in Leeds, Liverpool, Coventry and Brighton. Runs two clinics of its own. Free pregnancy testing and contraceptive advice. Abortion costs £10 for referral (including counselling and medical examination) and £41 for the operation.

London Pregnancy Advisory Service, 40 Margaret Street, London W1 (01 409 0281). Abortion costs £5 for counselling and £55 for the operation if you're less than twelve weeks pregnant, or £85 if you're between twelve and sixteen weeks pregnant. Pregnancy testing for patients only.

Release, 1 Elgin Avenue, London W9 (01 289 1123). No pregnancy testing, but they arrange abortions. Where appropriate, they'll try and put you in touch with sympathetic doctors and hospitals, to help you get a National Health abortion; otherwise they arrange private abortions at £80 if you're up to sixteen weeks pregnant or £100 if you're between sixteen and eighteen weeks pregnant. These prices can be reduced in special circumstances.

Brook Advisory Centres. The London headquarters is at 233 Tottenham Court Road, London W1 (01 580 2991). Other Brook centres in Coventry, Bristol, Birmingham, Cambridge, Liverpool and Edinburgh – addresses in local phone books. They charge £1·50 for a pregnancy test, but encourage you to become a patient so that you get contraceptive advice and counselling (which costs £5); they also arrange abortions, half of which are on the National Health and half private, costing between £55 and £70.

Marie Stopes Memorial Clinic, 108 Whitfield Street, London W1 (01 388 0662). Pregnancy testing costs £1·50. They arrange abortions costing £65 if you are less than twelve weeks pregnant and up to £120 if your pregnancy is further advanced.

The Family Planning Association. Headquarters at 27–35 Mortimer Street, London W1 (01 636 7866). Addresses of branches in local telephone directories. They charge £2·50 for a pregnancy test if you are not attending the clinic for contraceptive advice and £1·25 if you are. No abortion service.

One-Parent Families, 255 Kentish Town Road, London NW5 (01 267 1361). Formerly called the National Council for the Unmarried Mother and her Child. Practical help and counselling for single parents and single pregnant women.

Rape

Rape means being forced to have sexual intercourse against your will. As far as the law is concerned, 'sexual intercourse' simply means penetration: the sex act does not have to be completed.

If you are married it would be extremely difficult to prove to a court that your husband raped you, unless:

1. You have obtained a separation order from a magistrates' court which includes a 'non-cohabitation' clause (that is, a clause ending your legal duty to live with each other); or
2. You have made a legal agreement to separate and the agreement contains a 'non-molestation' clause.

However, if your husband forces you to have sexual intercourse against your will, he could be found guilty of assault. If you have started divorce proceedings but you are not yet divorced, you cannot claim that your husband raped you.

A boy under 14 cannot be guilty of rape in the eyes of the law because it is assumed that he is not capable of sexual intercourse.

The maximum penalty for rape is ten years.

If you want to prove that a man has raped you, you must prove that you did not give your consent. This would be true even if you were under 16, although then a court would more readily accept your claim that you didn't consent. If you did not resist the rape you can still claim that you did not consent if:

1. You allowed yourself to be raped because you were afraid of being hurt or killed.
2. You were incapable of defending yourself because the man plied you with drink or drugs with a view to overcoming your resistance. If you were incapable of resisting as a result of taking drink or drugs of your own free will, the attack will amount to indecent assault only.
3. The rape was carried out under false pretences. Examples from previous legal cases are:

(a) where a woman mistakenly thought that the man was her husband; or

(b) where she believed that the act was a medical operation.

In theory, your story does not need to be backed up by other evidence. In practice, it helps. You are more likely to be believed if you go straight to the police after the rape or if you are found in a distressed state by someone who can act as a witness. If it is just your story against the man's and there is no other witness and no obvious physical signs of a struggle, you may find that the police are unwilling to take any action against the man.

If the case goes to court and there is no evidence to back up your story, the judge will probably advise the jury not to convict. You can expect to be asked a lot of questions about your sex life, and it may be suggested – in defence of the man – that you have 'loose morals'. In other words you will have to contend with the common male attitude that a woman is fair game for sex and if she gets raped she probably asked for it and the man was doing her a favour.

Until such attitudes change, the only answer is for women to be trained in self-defence so that they can protect themselves from attack and do not have to rely on the law to defend them.

Indecent assault

Indecent assault is a sexual attack which does not amount to rape. It is usually easier to prove than rape. Again, you must prove that you didn't consent, although this does not apply to girls under 16.

The maximum penalty for indecent assault on a woman is two years; for indecent assault on a man, it is ten years. The reason for this discrepancy is that in law a man cannot be raped. The maximum penalty would only be used for a sexual attack on a man which in fact amounted to rape.

Lesbianism

There are no laws against lesbianism between women over 16. Male homosexuality, on the other hand, was strictly against the law until 1967, when it was made legal, but only if practised between two consenting men over 21 in private. The story goes that Queen Victoria, in whose reign male homosexuality was outlawed, could not believe that women indulged in such practices and therefore refused to consider a law against it. So it may be thanks to her that gay women are not penalized for their sexual preferences. However, this doesn't prevent them meeting discrimination in employment and housing. Anti-discrimination legislation might go some of the way towards improving that.

A man can divorce his wife for 'unreasonable behaviour' if he finds that she is lesbian.

Prostitution

Prostitution itself is not illegal. That is, it is not against the law for a woman over 16 to have sexual intercourse with a man in return for payment. Some marriages amount to little more than that.

But it *is* illegal to pick up a man in a street or public place for the purposes of prostitution. Call-girls, whose appointments are arranged by phone, cannot be touched by law, although those responsible for procuring girls for the business or living on their earnings can be prosecuted. Meanwhile, the call-girl's poorer sister who relies on casual pickups in Piccadilly or on Tooting Bec Common is likely to be hauled off to the magistrates' court if she is spotted by a policeman. What the eye doesn't see the heart doesn't grieve over.

A policeman can arrest a woman, without a warrant, if he reasonably suspects her of *both* of the following:

1. Being a 'common prostitute', that is, someone who has previously been cautioned for soliciting, but has persisted in doing so;
   and
2. Loitering or soliciting in a street or public place for the purposes of prostitution.

The first time a policeman sees you 'loitering or soliciting', he cannot arrest you, but he can caution you. The caution can be written down in the police records and quoted against you. If you are cautioned and you do not accept the accusation, you should apply to your nearest magistrates' court within fourteen days to have your record cleared. At the hearing, which is in private, the police have to prove that you were 'loitering or soliciting' at the time, and unless the court is satisfied that you were, it will order the caution to be struck from the record.

If the caution stays on your record, you are labelled a 'common prostitute' and a policeman can arrest you if he sees you 'loitering or soliciting' again. On a first arrest, the fine is likely to be small. But if you come before the court again and again, you may eventually be imprisoned. About 12 per cent of the prisoners in Holloway are there for charges connected with prostitution.

The laws against prostitution are often used by managers of hotels, cafés and restaurants as a pretext for not serving women late at night if they are unaccompanied by men.

It is *not* a crime for a man to hire a woman for prostitution. It is *not* a crime for a man to solicit a woman in a street or public place, for instance by 'kerb crawling'. However, it is an offence for a man to solicit another man, either on his own behalf or on behalf of a woman.

4. Marriage

Getting married or living together: the pros and cons

Obviously nothing we say will stop you doing whatever you feel like doing, but we thought it might help to point out some of the practical advantages and disadvantages of both. The 'unmarried' column assumes you are living with one man on a fairly permanent basis.

Advantages of being married	*Disadvantages of being unmarried*
Most people still do it this way. If you are a conformist by nature, you may find it simpler.	This is more unusual. There are social pressures towards getting married. And what do you call him? Man? Husband? Lover? There isn't a word which describes the relationship adequately and many couples end up referring to each other as 'husband' and 'wife', with the woman adopting the man's name.
If you have children, the law assumes that your husband is their father, and he is responsible for	If you want to claim maintenance from the father of your children, you must either take affiliation

Advantages of being married	Disadvantages of being unmarried
supporting them, even if you get divorced.	proceedings within three years of the birth, or prove that he has paid maintenance during that time.
If you divorce or separate, you can claim maintenance for yourself and your children.	If you separate, you can claim maintenance for the children but not for yourself.
Some landlords insist that couples should be married before they rent accommodation.	You may have to pretend that you are married in order to get accommodation, unless you can find a sympathetic landlord.
If you get divorced, you have certain rights to stay in the home until you are divorced and a claim on the property you have in common with your husband.	You have no legal right to occupy the home if it is in the man's name. If you separate, you will almost certainly have to leave.

Advantages of being married

Disadvantages of being unmarried

The tax position is more favourable if you are married. Your husband can claim a married man's tax allowance, and if you are working you get earned-income relief, which amounts to a single person's tax allowance. So between you, you can earn an extra £180 before tax. (You can't do this if you are very rich, but instead you can be taxed as two single people so you don't lose out.)

The man only gets a single person's tax allowance, unless you are looking after his children, in which case he can claim an allowance for you as an 'adult dependant' but then you would not be in a position to get earned-income relief.

You can opt out of paying National Insurance stamps, which could save you more than £1 a week. If you do this you can claim a pension on your husband's insurance.

You are responsible for paying your own National Insurance stamps. You cannot claim a pension on the man's insurance.

If you haven't been paying stamps you can get a maternity grant on your husband's insurance.

You can only get a maternity grant on your own insurance.

Even though you are single, you cannot claim supplementary benefit as a single person if you are found to be living with a man. You will have to rely on him to support you.

Advantages of being married	*Disadvantages of being unmarried*
If your husband dies, you inherit most or all of his property (if he has any).	Unless the man makes a will leaving his property to you, you may find you have no claim to it.
You are entitled to widow's benefits.	You get no widow's benefits.

Disadvantages of being married	*Advantages of being unmarried*
You have to pay £6 for a marriage licence.	You save £6.
In order to be unmarried, you have to go through a divorce.	If you want to separate, you don't need a divorce.
If you go out to work, you may find it difficult to get a suitable job or promotion because employers will assume that you are going to have children.	Employers do not automatically assume that you are going to leave to have children (although they may assume that you're going to get married).
Unless you have money (in which case you can buy most things), or unless you know a sympathetic doctor, you will probably need your husband's consent before you can get a coil fitted or have an abortion or sterilization.	Your body is your own. You will not need the man's consent in order to get a coil or have an abortion or sterilization.

Disadvantages of being married	*Advantages of being unmarried*
If you and your husband have a serious dispute over your children you will have to go to court to settle the matter.	If you have children, you have sole parental rights over them. The man cannot legally overrule any decisions you make concerning them.
If your earnings are high and your husband's are low, he could claim maintenance from you if you were separated.	The man could not claim maintenance from you if you separated.
Until you get a divorce, you cannot normally get your husband to leave your home, even if you own it.	If you own the home, you can throw the man out at any time.
You may have difficulty in getting hire purchase and credit facilities. Finance companies will usually ask for your husband's signature, even if you have a good independent income.	You may have less difficulty than a married woman in getting hire purchase and credit facilities, especially if you have a reasonable income.
Your income is treated as part of your husband's for tax purposes. You cannot easily conceal your earnings from him. Tax allowances for children and mortgage payments will normally go to him and he will get your tax rebates, unless you apply for a separate assessment.	You are taxed as a single person and you have complete control over your financial affairs. You can normally get a tax allowance for your children, unless you are receiving maintenance for them.

Disadvantages of being married	*Advantages of being unmarried*
If you have been paying full National Insurance stamps, you get a reduced rate of sickness and unemployment benefit. You cannot claim extra for your children (unless your husband is disabled and incapable of earning a living). If you rely on your husband's insurance, you cannot draw a pension until he retires and then you get less than a single person; and you are not entitled to any sickness or unemployment benefit.	You have full rights under the National Insurance scheme and get full sickness and unemployment benefit. If you have children, you can claim extra benefits for them.
You cannot claim supplementary benefit in your own right. Your husband has to claim the married couple's rate and you get less than a single person.	You can claim supplementary benefit in your own right and you are entitled to the full single person's rate, as long as they don't find out you are living with a man.

Getting married under 18

You can't get married until you are 16.

If you are under 18, you can't get married without your parents' consent. If you are a ward of court you will need the consent of the court. You will need the consent of both your parents except in the following circumstances:

1. Your parents are divorced or separated: in this case you will

need the consent of the parent who has been awarded custody of the children.

2. One of your parents has deserted the other: you will need the consent of the parent who has been deserted.

3. Someone other than your parents – such as the local authority – has been awarded custody of the children in your family: you will need the consent of whoever has custody.

4. You are adopted: you will need the consent of your adoptive parents.

5. One of your parents cannot give consent (e.g. because she or he cannot be traced or is mentally disabled): the Superintendent Registrar or the Church authority can let you get married with the consent of the other parent only. But if the consent of the other parent is not needed for another reason (because of divorce, for instance), you will need special permission from a higher authority – from the Registrar General if you are getting married in a registry office; or from the Master of Faculties, if you want a church wedding. Your Citizens' Advice Bureau will tell you where the nearest registry office is. Ask your local vicar how to contact the appropriate Church authorities.

6. If you have been married already and widowed, you can marry without your parents' consent, even if you're still under 18.

IF YOUR PARENTS REFUSE CONSENT,

you may apply to the magistrates' court, the county court or the high court for consent. It is easiest to apply to the magistrates' court. You can go along any morning at ten o'clock and tell the magistrates that you want to marry. A date will be fixed for your case to be heard and it will take place in private, although your parents can be present.

GRETNA GREEN

If you are 16 or over you can get married without your parents' consent anywhere in Scotland. Gretna Green is close to the border, which is why it has become so famous. At least one of you must stay in Scotland for fifteen days to meet the residence qualification, and you normally have to wait another seven days while the Registrar publishes notice of your intended marriage. You can save time by applying for a Sheriff's licence, but this is granted only in exceptional circumstances. If you want to know more there's a useful leaflet, *Marriage in Scotland*, available from the Scottish Office, Dover House, Whitehall, London SW1 (01 930 6151).

IF YOU LIE ABOUT YOUR AGE

in order to get married without your parents' consent, you may be prosecuted for making a false statement, but this will not invalidate the marriage (as long as you are 16 or over).

IF YOU MANAGE TO GET MARRIED WITHOUT YOUR PARENTS' CONSENT,

your marriage is valid anyway, provided you are 16 or over.

ONCE YOU ARE 18

you are free to marry without your parents' consent.

Outline of a married woman's rights

Changing your name

Most women adopt their husband's surname when they marry. In fact, there is nothing in law that says you have to (nor, incidentally, that you have to wear a wedding ring at any time). It is entirely up to you. You can keep your own name or you can combine it with your husband's in a double-barrelled name – although if this idea catches on in a big way one could imagine difficulties for future generations.

If you take your husband's name you can keep it after you get divorced and even after you remarry, if you want to.

You can change your name at any time, just by calling yourself by your new name. But there are times when you might need official-looking proof of your new name, to show your bank or the Passport Office, for instance. You can get this by swearing a statement before a Commissioner of Oaths. A solicitor can pre-

Afternoon Mrs Bloggs-Brown-Smith

pare the statement for you at a cost of between £5 and £10. It is known as a 'statutory declaration'. You can also change your name by Deed Poll, a more complex procedure. Some professional bodies require this as proof of a name change. You'll need your husband's written consent, 'unless good cause is shown to the contrary' and you must reveal your marital status. A man need not do so; he can even change his wife's name without her consent.

If you and your husband have children, they will be given his name and you won't be able to change that without his consent.

Sex

Your husband cannot normally be prosecuted for rape if he forces you to have sexual intercourse against your will, unless you are divorced or have a separation order which includes a 'non-cohabitation' clause – because, as far as the law is concerned, when you marry a man you consent to have sexual intercourse with him while you are married. But if he makes unreasonable sexual demands on you (or none at all, for that matter) you may be able to use this as grounds for divorce. (See pp. 150, 177.)

Violence

If your husband uses force or violence against you, you can take legal action to protect yourself. The most effective action is to obtain an 'injunction', that is a court order, ordering him not to molest you. If he then continues to be violent you can apply for an order that he leaves the home. At present you can only get such an order from the divorce courts if you have either started divorce proceedings or (if you have not been married three years) applied to the court for permission to start divorce proceedings. If your husband's behaviour improves, you need not continue the divorce proceedings, and your marriage can continue. The law should be changed so that women can obtain effective protection from their husbands without starting divorce action.

One way you may be able to do this now is by making a claim in the county court for compensation from your husband for the assaults he has made against you. As in the divorce courts, you could apply immediately for an injunction. At the time of writing this approach has not been tested, but you could ask your solicitor about it. (If you are unmarried and living with a man who assaults you, you can take similar legal action.)

For either method you will need a solicitor who is prepared to apply for emergency legal aid for you if your case is urgent. If it is *very* urgent you should be able to obtain your order on the same day as you see the solicitor or the following day. Normally, however, your husband must be given two days' warning that you intend to apply to the court, so it takes at least a few days longer. (On how to get a solicitor see p. 299.)

It is also possible to prosecute your husband for assault in the magistrates' court, but this usually takes longer and will be more difficult unless the police will take action against your husband for you. Usually they are unwilling to intervene in what they call 'domestic quarrels'.

You can sue your husband to obtain compensation if he causes you loss or damage, and he can do the same to you. This happens most often when a married couple have been in a car accident together and the one who was passenger sues to get compensation under the driver's insurance policy.

FURTHER INFORMATION

Women's Aid, 369 Chiswick High Road, London W4, gives advice and assistance to wives who are beaten by their husbands. And see p.168.

The family home and other possessions

Since 1882, married women have been allowed to own property. But while you are married you have no right to a share of any of your husband's property. You can only claim a share when you get divorced. If your husband buys a house, you would be better off if it were purchased in both your names and not in his name alone. But whether it is in your name or not, you have a right to stay in the home for as long as your marriage lasts, and possibly longer. A married woman's rights to the family home are explained in detail on pp. 240–50.

If you and your husband disagree about who owns what, you have a legal right to the following:

1. Anything you own at the date of your marriage and anything you buy with your money during the marriage.
2. Anything your husband buys and gives to you or puts in your name, such as a house or a car, unless he can prove that he didn't give it to you. If he disputed your claim, you would have to present some proof that he gave it to you, such as an entry in a diary, a note that went with the gift, or evidence from someone else who saw him give it to you.
3. Any money, stocks or shares that have been deposited into a bank in your name – or into a joint account with your husband, in which case you may be entitled to half.
4. You would normally be joint owner of anything purchased from a joint bank account or other pooled resources.

You would not have a right to money paid by your husband as a guarantee against your overdraft, or as a surety for a mortgage you are paying.

Your husband does not usually have a right to money, stocks or shares you have deposited into a bank in his name, except where you are being maintained by him and he is receiving an income from your property with your knowledge and consent.

Money matters

As a married woman, you have a right to your own income and your own bank account. But when it comes to tax, your income is treated as though it belonged to your husband, unless you apply for separate assessment (more about that on p. 57).

During the time that you are married, you have no right to any part of your husband's income and capital, beyond the fact that he has a duty to maintain you. You can only claim a share when you get divorced.

BANK ACCOUNTS

On the whole, it's best to have a joint bank account with your husband if you are dependent on him; and best to have your own bank account if you have an independent income. If you have your own bank account, the money in it belongs to you. If you have a joint bank account and you and your husband disagree about who has a right to the money in it, your claim will depend on the following factors:
– If you have been paying in sums from time to time, you will normally be entitled to half the money in the account, even if you've paid in less than half. Likewise, your husband will be entitled to half, even if you have paid in more than him.
– If you haven't paid anything into the account and you have simply been drawing out money to cover household expenses, it could be decided that your husband had opened the account as a convenient method of managing his household affairs and had not

intended to give half the money to you – in which case you would not be entitled to any of the money.

– If you have paid all the money into the account and your husband contributed nothing, it will probably be decided that all the money belongs to you.

HOUSEKEEPING MONEY

There was a time when anything a married woman bought or saved out of her housekeeping money actually belonged to her husband. Back in 1949, a woman called Mrs Hoddenott won some money on a football pool which she had paid for with savings from her housekeeping money. She bought some furniture with the winnings and it was later decided in court that her husband owned that furniture. But the law was changed in 1964. You now have a right to *half* of anything you save, buy, or win out of your housekeeping money, unless you and your husband agree to the contrary. This ruling does not apply to money your husband gives you for other purposes, such as a dress allowance, nor does it apply to money you give him (which is all his).

NATIONAL INSURANCE

As a married woman you can opt out of paying National Insurance contributions, as explained on pp. 66–8.

Children

You and your husband have equal custody of your children. If you have a dispute over them, the matter will have to be decided in court. The court's decision will rest on what is best for the welfare of the children. More about children on pp. 203–39.

Entering into contracts

You have as much right as a single woman to make contracts where and when you please (although this wasn't always so).

However, you will find, in practice, that the people you are most likely to want to make contracts with, such as hire purchase companies and landlords, still ask for your husband's signature. See p. 265 for more details.

If your husband *does* sign a contract for you, he is responsible for paying any debts that you might incur as a result.

If you come to an agreement with your husband in the normal course of domestic events – say for example that he promised to pay you a certain amount of housekeeping money each week – the agreement probably won't be legally binding. The only way you could make it legally binding would be to draw up a contract (you would need a solicitor's advice), and this might make it possible to sue for breach of contract.

Leaving the country

You can get a passport without your husband's consent, even if you were previously on his passport. If you are on your husband's passport, you must submit his passport with your application form to the Passport Office. If you can't get hold of it, you must give the Passport Office your husband's name and last known address and they will have to write to him and ask for it.

You can put your children on your passport, or get them separate passports without your husband's consent. More about that on pp. 207–8.

'Domicile'

'Domicile' does not have anything to do with citizenship or nationality: it is a legal term which implies that a person intends to settle permanently in a particular country. It only becomes important if you want to take legal action, as it determines where the case can be tried. Before the law was changed in 1973, a married woman automatically had the same 'domicile' as her husband, even if she was living in another country. Therefore, a woman living in England could not start divorce proceedings against her husband if he was living abroad, except in special circumstances.

A married woman now has a right to her own domicile. She can start divorce proceedings in England or Wales if she has her permanent home there or if she has lived there for one year immediately before she starts proceedings – no matter where her husband is.

Citizenship

If you are not a citizen of the United Kingdom and you marry a man who is, you can apply for UK citizenship. But if you are a UK citizen and you marry a foreigner, he does not have the same right. If he is not entitled to stay in the country, you will either have to stay here without him, or leave in order to be with him. More details of immigration rules on pp. 276–84.

Further information

Women's Aid, 369 Chiswick High Road, London W4, gives advice and assistance to women who are beaten by their husbands.

A pamphlet explaining the law as it affects battered women is available from the NCCL, 186 King's Cross Road London WC1.

5. Divorce and Separation

How to go about getting a divorce or separation

If you want to be legally separated from your husband, the two
most common ways of doing it are:

1. BY GETTING A DIVORCE

This ends the marriage altogether so that you and your husband become single people again. See p. 171.

2. BY GETTING A SEPARATION ORDER FROM A MAGIS-
TRATES' COURT

This does not end the marriage, but it means that you can
make firm arrangements for maintenance and custody of the
children. See p. 187.

Which to choose

There is no point in going to a magistrates' court for a separation
order unless: (a) you don't want to end the marriage because you

think that there is a chance of a reconciliation; or (b) you are waiting to get a divorce but in the meantime you need money, or you and your husband cannot reach an agreement about who should look after the children.

Proceedings in a magistrates' court can be just as lengthy as divorce proceedings, and more complicated. They are still based on the old-fashioned grounds that were needed for getting a divorce before the Divorce Reform Act was passed: for example, in a magistrates' court you would have to prove that your husband was guilty of 'persistent cruelty' where you would only have to prove 'unreasonable behaviour' in a divorce court.

The amount you are likely to get in maintenance from a magistrates' court is usually less than the amount you would get in a divorce court.

The powers of a magistrate are limited: he cannot make any arrangements concerning your home, or award a lump-sum payment. He can only order weekly payments of maintenance.

In contrast, divorce proceedings are usually fairly straightforward these days and divorce courts have far wider powers to make financial and other arrangements. So unless you need money immediately or believe that you and your husband can settle your differences, don't bother with a separation order, but start divorce proceedings. All in all, there are five different ways of becoming legally separated from your husband. The others are:

3. YOU CAN COME TO A VOLUNTARY AGREEMENT WITH YOUR HUSBAND

and get a solicitor to draw up a legal document so that the terms of your agreement can be enforced in a court of law. This has the same effect as a separation order, but it means you don't have to go to court. Obviously this is only appropriate if you and your husband are on reasonably good terms. It is often used by couples who are waiting to get a divorce on the basis of a two-year separation; or who have agreed on a trial separation. See p. 195.

4. YOU CAN GET A JUDICIAL SEPARATION

This means going through the same proceedings as you would if you were getting a divorce, but it does not end the marriage. It is rarely done these days except by people who have religious objections to divorce. See p. 195.

5. YOU MAY BE ABLE TO HAVE THE MARRIAGE ANNULLED

This has the same effect as a divorce but it requires proof that your marriage is not valid. This would only be appropriate in certain circumstances, which are described on p. 196.

Of course, it could happen the other way round

Your husband could start proceedings against you (although men seldom, if ever, apply for separation orders, since they are rarely in a position to claim money from their wives). We hope the information given here will be equally useful if you are on the receiving end, but for the sake of simplicity we have written it as though you were taking legal action against your husband. It would apply in reverse if he were taking action against you.

Divorce

When can you apply?

As a general rule, you can't get a divorce until you have been married for three years. But you may be able to get one sooner if you have suffered 'exceptional hardship' because of the marriage, or if your husband is 'exceptionally depraved'. When the judge makes his decision about this, he must consider the welfare of your children and whether there is any possibility of a reconciliation.

You can apply even if you are still living with your husband.

What do you have to prove?

You must prove to the court that your marriage has broken down *'irretrievably'* for one of five reasons:

1. You and your husband both want a divorce and you have been living apart for at least two years.
2. You have been living apart for five years and you want a divorce, even if your husband doesn't.
3. Your husband has deserted you for at least two years.
4. Your husband has committed adultery and you find it intolerable to live with him.
5. Your husband has behaved in a way that makes it unreasonable to expect you to live with him.

Living apart for two years

This is the easiest way to get a divorce. If you and your husband agree to live apart for two years you don't have to present any other reason to the court. Your husband must give his consent by filling in a special form and sending it to the court. He can withdraw his consent at any time up to the granting of the divorce – so can you.

If you are getting a divorce this way, you may be able to do it without a solicitor, as you will see if you read the section on 'Do-it-yourself divorce' (p. 197).

'Living apart' means living in separate households. It is just possible to claim a divorce if you and your husband have been living under the same roof. This is explained under the heading of 'Desertion' (p. 174).

The two years of living apart are supposed to be continuous, but if you have lived together occasionally during that time for a total of not more than six months, you can still get a divorce after you have lived apart for a total of two years. So if you tried a reconciliation and it lasted three months, you can apply for a divorce two years and three months after the date when you first started living apart.

The judge can postpone the final granting of the divorce if he thinks that adequate financial provision has not been made for you (or your husband).

Living apart for five years

This is the simplest way of getting a divorce if your husband does not give his consent. (And it's the simplest way for him to divorce you if you don't consent.) When the Divorce Reform Act was passed in 1969, it was this provision that led to its being called the Casanova's Charter by some who feared the wholesale desertion of ageing and blameless wives by randy and irresponsible husbands. Their fears seem to have been unfounded – nothing of the sort has happened. And besides, the Act offers some protection:

1. A judge can refuse to grant a divorce which has been sought under the five-year ruling if he thinks it would cause grave hardship (financial or otherwise) to the wife (or husband) who refused consent. In deciding this, the judge must consider how the husband and wife have behaved and what would be in the best interests of the children.

2. A judge can grant a decree nisi (p. 180) but refuse to make it absolute if he thinks that adequate financial provision has not been made for the wife (or husband). He might do this if the husband has refused to pay maintenance to the wife, or if the wife would suffer from losing her pension rights under her husband's insurance. In a case reported in *The Times* (4 October 1972) a man failed to get a divorce after five years' separation because the judge considered it would cause grave financial hardship to the wife:

Mr Kenneth George Julian, a retired Assistant Chief Constable of Cornwall, was refused a divorce decree yesterday because it would cause financial hardship to his wife.

It is believed to be the first time under the new divorce law that a decree has been refused in such circumstances, though several wives have unsuccessfully opposed decrees on the ground of hardship.

Mr Justice Cusack said in the Family Division of the High Court that the wife, Mrs Kathleen Victoria Julian, aged 58, of St Nicholas Street, Bodmin, Cornwall, would receive £790 a year police widow's pension if her husband died first. But she could not have the pension if they were divorced.

Mr Julian, aged 61, of Southbourne Road, St Austell, Cornwall, was paying her £61·50 a month maintenance and was willing to increase this by £4 a week and also provide an annuity of £215. He wishes to marry a woman of 46.

Mr Julian was living with his sister. He was in bad health and had had two strokes. Mrs Julian was also in bad health and was unfit for work.

The judge said: 'There will be a very substantial monetary gap between the provision which her husband can now make for her and the financial benefit she receives if the marriage remains. Dissolving the marriage will result in grave financial hardship and I dismiss the petition.'

Desertion

This means you can apply for a divorce if:

1. Your husband has left you; *and*
2. he has stayed away for at least two years; *and*
3. he has done so intentionally.

YOU CAN ALSO GET A DIVORCE FOR DESERTION UNDER THE FOLLOWING CIRCUMSTANCES

1. You go on living under the same roof with your husband, but he refuses to have anything to do with you. In one case, a wife withdrew to a separate bedroom which she kept locked, refused to cook for her husband or do any household duties for him and only communicated with him by notes: it was decided that she had deserted him. But in another case, a wife refused to have any sex with her husband and hardly ever spoke to him, but occasionally cooked him a meal and did some household chores: it was decided that although it was an unhappy household, it was one household rather than two and therefore it was *not* a case of desertion.

   or

2. You split up because you could not agree on where to live. If

this is so, the one who has acted 'unreasonably' can be divorced for desertion. It used to be the case that the husband had the right to say where the home should be and if the wife disagreed she was guilty of desertion. This is still true today, but only if the husband is the breadwinner and the wife isn't working. If you and your husband both work, you have equal rights to say where your home should be. So unless one of you has obviously acted more unreasonably than the other, the law does not make it clear how the divorce should be granted and it will be left to the judge to decide on the facts of the particular case.

In fact, desertion is rarely used as a reason for applying for a divorce, except where a wife has been hoping her husband might return. If your husband deserts you and you don't want to wait two years, you can probably divorce him for 'unreasonable behaviour' as described on p. 176.

YOU WILL NOT BE ABLE TO GET A DIVORCE FOR DESERTION IN THE FOLLOWING CIRCUMSTANCES

1. Your husband left you because you behaved unreasonably. (A fuller explanation of this is given under the heading 'Unreasonable behaviour', p. 176.)
2. Your husband has been imprisoned or mentally ill and therefore had no choice about deserting you.
3. Your husband made a genuine offer to return and you refused.
4. You and your husband have lived together for a total of six months or more since the time he deserted you. You are allowed up to six months' attempted reconciliation, as explained under the heading 'Living apart for two years' (p. 172).
5. You have sexual intercourse with another man and the court decides that this was the reason why your husband deserted you: or if you have intercourse with another man after your husband has deserted you – since this ends his duty to return to you.
6. You and your husband have been legally separated. In this case you will be able to get a divorce under the two-year ruling.

Adultery

You can get a divorce for this reason if you can prove to the court

1. *That your husband had sexual intercourse with another woman.*
   This is normally done by the husband and the woman involved
   making statements admitting their adultery. Alternatively,
   there should be evidence of a familiar relationship between
   them, indicating that they were likely to have intercourse.
   Proof that they have spent a night in the same bedroom is
   normally taken as evidence of adultery, although the judge
   may want some additional proof that your husband's adultery
   has made it intolerable for you to live with him. Direct
   evidence from an eye witness is not necessary.
   and
2. *That you find it intolerable to live with your husband.* Usually, all
   you have to do is tell the court that you find it intolerable to live
   with him, but you may be asked to give reasons. If you go on
   sleeping with your husband for a long time after you discover
   that he has slept with another woman, you will not be able to
   get a divorce on the ground of adultery. But you are allowed
   up to six months' attempted reconciliation, as explained under
   the heading 'Living apart for two years' (p. 172).

Unreasonable behaviour

This part of the law is very vague and it would be impossible to
list all the kinds of behaviour that might be called unreasonable.
Each case must be decided on its own particular facts, but the
following guidelines may be useful:

1. According to the law, the behaviour complained of must be
   'grave and weighty'.
2. Your husband's behaviour would be 'unreasonable' if it were
   clear that he knew that it would result in your leaving him, and
   that any normal woman in your position would have done the
   same.
3. Physical or mental cruelty, if sufficiently 'grave and weighty',
   would be unreasonable. You can claim physical cruelty by

saying that he has knocked you around with kicks and blows; but the odd blow struck in a temper may not be considered unreasonable. Persistent nagging, insults, slights or unkindness might amount to mental cruelty. If your husband completely ignored you, that might be counted as mental cruelty.

... grave and weighty behaviour ...

4. Sodomy or bestiality would be considered unreasonable; so would:
5. Mentally unbalanced behaviour;
6. Drunkenness (depending on how often it happened and what effect it had on him);
7. Unreasonable sexual demands;
8. Refusing to have children – by insisting on coitus interruptus or contraceptives, or by having a vasectomy without your consent;
9. Refusing to have sexual intercourse.

Here are two typical accounts by women of their husbands' behaviour, which would be accepted as 'unreasonable' by the court.

My husband stopped being interested in me sexually or any other way. I became suspicious and when I questioned him he admitted he had another woman. He said he was in love with her but didn't want to leave me and the children. He suggested I might find another man.

He used to come home from work, spruce himself up and go out again. He would come back at 1 or 2 o'clock in the morning. This happened several times a week.

My husband became very cold towards me. When I suggested we might make love, he said I had to give him time. Once he said if I was desperate I should go on the streets. He rarely talked to me, only if he had to. He said his work was more important to him than I was. He didn't see that I had anything to complain about, since he provided me with a home and regular housekeeping. I became more and more depressed and eventually I went to my doctor and discussed the situation with him. He suggested marriage guidance but when I put it to my husband he just laughed and said I should go on my own as I was the one who needed help.

To give you an idea of what does not *amount to unreasonable behaviour in the eyes of the law, the case of Buchler v. Buchler (1947) is still cited as an example. The judge pronounced:*

It may no doubt be galling – or in some sense of the word humiliating – for the wife to find that the husband prefers the company of his men-friends, his Club, his newspapers, his games, his hobbies or indeed his own society, to association with her, and a husband may have similar grievances regarding his wife. But this may be called the reasonable wear and tear of married life.

How do you get a divorce?

FIND A SOLICITOR

You will almost certainly need one, unless the divorce is very straightforward. (See p. 197 for Do-it-yourself divorce.) If you don't know how to get hold of a solicitor, ask your local Citizens' Advice Bureau (address in the telephone directory) or go to the magistrates' court and ask the officials there to tell you where you can find one. Read the section on 'Going to a solicitor' (p. 298).

APPLY FOR LEGAL AID

Divorce is an expensive business, but if you qualify for legal aid, you will either get it free, or you will pay only a part of the cost.

Get your solicitor to help you fill in the legal aid form. You will probably be interviewed by an official from the Supplementary Benefits Commission and asked for evidence of your income. If you are not working; if you are earning less than £25 a week; or if you have dependent children and other heavy expenses, you may be eligible. It can take up to three months for them to decide whether or not to grant you legal aid. Read the section on 'Getting legal aid' (p. 301).

IF YOU CAN'T GET LEGAL AID

and your husband agrees to the divorce and is not putting up any defence, it will probably cost between £80 and £150. But if there are complications over maintenance and custody of children it could cost a great deal more. If your husband is defending the divorce, it may be very expensive indeed. Make sure that your solicitor gives you an estimate of the cost before you start and tells you if anything happens to put the price up during the proceedings. If you apply for a divorce, and get one, on the grounds of adultery, desertion, or unreasonable behaviour, your husband will have to pay your legal costs.

THE DIVORCE PETITION IS DRAWN UP

by your solicitor, or by a barrister if the case is more complicated. Copies are sent to the court, to your husband and, if the case involves adultery, to the other woman. You must also fill in a form saying what arrangements you have made for the custody, maintenance and education of your children. Your solicitor will help you with this.

YOUR HUSBAND REPLIES

by filling in a form of 'acknowledgement of service'. At this stage he must say whether he agrees to the divorce and whether he agrees with the arrangements made for your children.

IF HE DOES NOT DEFEND THE DIVORCE,

a date is fixed for the case to be heard and the whole business can be over within three months. In court, you will have to give evidence to support your reasons for seeking the divorce and you may need witnesses, especially if the case involves adultery or unreasonable behaviour. You will be asked to explain what arrangements have been made for the children. Most undefended divorce cases are over very quickly – they take between five and fifteen minutes to be heard. *N.B. If you are divorcing by mutual consent after two years' separation and you have no children under 16 or in full-time education or training, you can now get a 'postal divorce' without going to court. See p. 202.*

IF THE DIVORCE IS DEFENDED,

the whole procedure is a lot longer and more complicated. Some divorces are defended to start with, while disagreements over children and property are being sorted out. Very few continue to a defended hearing, which could last for several days and cost more than most people can afford, unless they were getting legal aid.

THE COURT GRANTS A DECREE NISI

if it is satisfied that your reasons for wanting a divorce are justified. Disagreements over children or property can be settled afterwards 'in chambers', which means privately before a judge. A decree nisi cannot be made absolute until the court is satisfied that necessary arrangements have been made for the welfare of the children; and, if the divorce is brought after two years' or five years' separation, that adequate financial provision has been made for the wife (or husband). (See p. 184.)

FINALLY, THE DECREE IS MADE ABSOLUTE

This means that the marriage is over and you are both single people again. A decree absolute is normally granted six weeks after the decree nisi, but if there are complications over children or financial arrangements, it could take longer. Your solicitor will tell you if there are.

WILL THERE BE ANY PUBLICITY?

If the divorce is undefended, the newspapers can only publish the fact that the decree has been granted; the names of the people directly involved (husband, wife, and co-respondent in adultery cases); and the legal grounds for granting the divorce ('adultery', 'unreasonable behaviour', 'two years' separation', etc.). The press can only publish further details of the case if the divorce is defended.

How can you stop your husband divorcing you?

It isn't easy. You would have to show that your marriage had not broken down 'irretrievably' by proving that the reason presented as grounds for divorce was not true. If your husband is divorcing you on the grounds of adultery, unreasonable behaviour or desertion, you may be able to prove that these are not true. But if he applies for a divorce after five years' separation there is nothing you can do about it, unless you can prove that you would suffer grave hardship as a result. (In practice, this means financial hardship.) One example of a woman who did this successfully is given on pp. 173–4.

How to get a divorce if you have married a man from abroad

IF YOU GOT MARRIED UNDER LAWS THAT PERMIT POLYGAMY

(i.e. marriage where the husband can have more than one wife), your marriage may not be recognized by the English courts. The legal position is very complicated and you should consult a solicitor.

IF YOUR HUSBAND LIVES ABROAD

before the law was changed in 1973 a woman could not get a divorce in Britain if her husband was permanently resident ('domiciled') in another country. However, if your permanent home is in Britain you can now get a divorce here, no matter where your husband is living.

IF YOU GET A DIVORCE ABROAD

the decree may not be recognized under English law. The reasons are too complex to explain here. If you have been granted a divorce abroad and you want to remarry in England, take the divorce document to your registry office and the Registrar will advise you whether or not it is valid. If you are in difficulties, get further advice from a solicitor.

Arrangements for your children after divorce

This is explained in the section on children (p. 209).

Division of property after divorce

This is explained in the section on property (pp. 243, 248).

Getting maintenance when you divorce

Your husband will probably have to pay money to help maintain

There... that should look after your maintenance problems, m'dear

MISS-DIVORCEE

any children of the family. He may also have to pay money to maintain you.

What is maintenance?

Maintenance takes the form of regular payments of money, and the amount you get will depend on the financial circumstances of you and your husband. You and your husband have equal responsibility to support each other and your children. So it is just possible that he could claim maintenance from you. This would only happen if you were earning a good wage and he had a good reason for not being able to support himself. The situation is very unlikely to occur, and we have assumed throughout this section that you are in a position to claim maintenance from him.

When can you claim maintenance?

You can ask for maintenance to be paid as a temporary arrangement while your divorce is going through. Then, when the case has been heard and the decree nisi granted, you can claim maintenance as part of a permanent settlement.

Maintenance during divorce proceedings

When your solicitor files your divorce petition you can include in it a request for maintenance to be paid from the date of filing the petition until the date when the divorce is granted. If your husband does not agree, your request will be heard by the Court Registrar after you have filed the petition. He will consider any evidence submitted by you and your husband – this is usually submitted in the form of affidavits drawn up by your respective solicitors. If he accepts that your request is reasonable, he will then make an order for maintenance.

HOW MUCH WILL YOU GET?

The law simply states that you should be given as much maintenance as the court thinks reasonable. In practice, this tends to be less than you would get after the divorce. However, when the final order is made after the divorce, you may get a lump sum to cover the expenses you have incurred during divorce proceedings; or the final order of maintenance may be backdated. So you may eventually be compensated if the interim order is not sufficient.

Final order of maintenance after divorce

Once your divorce has been granted, the court has far wider powers to make financial provision for you and your children. It can make orders for:

1. Periodical payments (i.e. maintenance).
2. Secured periodical payments: this means setting up a trust fund so that payments can be made out of it which are not dependent on your husband's future income and which can continue after his death.
3. Payment of lump sums.
4. Arrangements about who should live in the family home, or how it should be divided between you. This is explained in detail on pp. 240-50.

Unsecured payments will normally last from the time when you make the application for maintenance until the death of you or your husband. Secured payments will last until your own death. But if you remarry all maintenance payments to you will stop. The only exception is where the court has ordered a lump sum to be paid in instalments: if you remarry before the instalments have finished, the full sum must still be paid.

PROVISION FOR CHILDREN

The court can also order periodical payments, secured periodical payments, lump sums and property settlements for any 'child of the family'. This means any child born to you and your husband or adopted by you, and any other child who has been treated by both of you as a child of the family, except a foster child.

The court can order payments before or after the divorce. It can even order them if divorce proceedings are dismissed. Payments will normally last until the child leaves school. The court may order payments to continue beyond that if the child goes on to college, training or an apprenticeship.

HOW MUCH WILL YOU GET?

Arrangements about the division of family property are made at the same time as arrangements about maintenance. If you are awarded generous maintenance payments, you can normally expect to get less in the way of property, and vice versa.

The court is supposed to take certain factors into consideration before it decides how much maintenance to award. These are:

1. The income, earning capacity, property and other financial resources which you and your husband are likely to have in the foreseeable future.
2. The financial needs, obligations and responsibilities which you and your husband have or are likely to have in the foreseeable future. 'Needs' might include your expenses for education. 'Obligations' might be unpaid debts, hire purchase payments, the support of your children by a previous marriage, or the support of your husband's wife and children by a previous marriage. 'Responsibilities' might include the moral obligation of your husband to support a woman he is living with but hasn't yet married.
3. The standard of living of the family before the marriage broke down. It is a general rule that your standard of living should be maintained at the same standard as your husband's.
4. How old you and your husband were when you got married and how long the marriage lasted. If you were divorced by your husband after many years, you might have trouble finding a job, so you could expect to get a higher rate of maintenance than if you had been divorced when you were young, after a short marriage, when you could be expected to fend for yourself, as the following case illustrates:

Sir George Baker, President of the Family Division of the High

...and remember to maintain your ex wife at the same standard of living as yourself

Court, cut the maintenance awarded by magistrates to a 21-year-old wife deserted after five months of marriage from £3 to 10p. He said: 'In these days of Women's Lib there is no reason why a wife whose marriage has not lasted long and has no child, should have a bread ticket for life.' He added that the wife 'had not lost anything by the cessation of cohabitation'. [28 February 1973]

5. Any physical or mental disability that either of you may have.
6. The amount that you and your husband have each contributed to the welfare of your family. If you have been looking after the home and caring for your family, this would be counted as a contribution – on which basis you might also be able to claim a lump-sum payment or a property settlement.
7. The importance to you and your husband of any benefit that would be lost on divorce. For instance, you might lose your right to a widow's pension under your husband's occupational pension scheme. You can be compensated for this loss if your husband gives you a lump sum to provide you with an income after retirement. Get your solicitor's advice about this.
8. The way that you and your husband have behaved. Although 'irretrievable breakdown of marriage' is now the only ground

on which anyone can get a divorce, if the judge considers you to be 'guilty' of 'gross conduct' and your husband comparatively blameless, he may award you less maintenance than if you appeared to be 'innocent'.

No matter how carefully the court considers all these matters, what happens when most marriages break up is that the income available is simply not enough to support two families, and the husband, wife and children all suffer as a result.

If you remarry

you will no longer be able to claim any maintenance for yourself, but your former husband should continue to support his children.

An important thing to remember:

if a divorce court orders your husband to pay maintenance to you, ask for the order to be *registered with the magistrates' court*. Your solicitor will explain how it is done. It means that your husband pays his money to the magistrates' court and they forward it to you by post: if he fails to pay, you can then take legal action against him by going to the magistrates' court, as explained on pp. 192–4.

Getting a separation order from a magistrates' court: maintenance, custody and 'non-cohabitation'

What is a separation order?

Applying for a separation order means asking a magistrates' court to make an order saying that your husband must pay maintenance for you and your children; and that you are to have custody of your children. You can also ask for the order to include a 'non-cohabitation' clause, which ends your duty to share accommodation with your husband. But magistrates are often reluctant to grant this, as explained below (p. 190).

What do you have to prove?

To get a separation order you must prove to the court one of the following facts:

1. Your husband has deserted you. Unlike the divorce procedure, you can apply to the magistrates' court at any time: you don't have to wait until he has deserted you for two years, or until you have been married for three years. A fuller explanation of the legal meaning of 'desertion' is on p. 174.
2. He has been guilty of persistent cruelty to you or the children. You must prove that you (or they) have suffered physical or mental injury as a result of his cruelty, or that you were likely to do so. One act of cruelty would not be sufficient, although several acts of cruelty in one day might be.
3. He has been convicted in court of assault or indecency towards you or any of the children.
4. He has had sexual intercourse with another woman.
5. He had sexual intercourse with you when he knew he had venereal disease, and did not tell you.
6. He is a habitual drunkard or drug addict, in a way that makes him dangerous, incapable of managing his affairs, or intolerable to live with.
7. He has forced you to practise prostitution.
8. He has refused to pay sufficient maintenance for you and the children.

If you are accusing your husband of adultery, he can defend himself by showing that

1. you knew all about it and forgave him; or
2. you agreed to it; or
3. you encouraged it by 'wilful neglect or misconduct' – e.g. by refusing to have sexual intercourse with him or by having a lesbian relationship; or
4. you went on living with him for more than three months after you discovered his adultery. If you live with him for a shorter period than that, it will be counted as attempted reconciliation and you will still be able to apply for a separation order on the grounds of his adultery.

When can you apply?

As a general rule you should apply for a separation order within six months of the cause of your complaint. You must apply within six months of the time when you first discovered your husband's adultery; and within six months of one act of cruelty if there were others before that. If your husband has deserted you or refuses to maintain you, you can apply at any time.

You can apply while you are still living with your husband: this may help if you want to leave him but can't until you are sure you have some money coming in.

How to get a separation order

GET A SOLICITOR

You will almost certainly need one. If you don't know how to get hold of one, ask your local Citizens' Advice Bureau or inquire at the magistrates' court (addresses of both these places are in the telephone directory). Read the section on 'Going to a solicitor' (pp. 298–300).

APPLY FOR LEGAL AID

If you are not working; if you are earning less than £20 a week; or if you have dependent children and other heavy expenses, you will probably be eligible for it. Get your solicitor to help you fill in the legal aid form. Read the section on 'Getting legal aid' (pp. 301–5).

GO TO THE MAGISTRATES' COURT AND APPLY FOR A SUMMONS AGAINST YOUR HUSBAND

You can do this any morning without an appointment, if you arrive at about 9.45 a.m. You don't need a solicitor at this stage, but if you already have one, she or he may give you a letter addressed to the Clerk of the Court, explaining what you want. If you don't have a solicitor, the officer at the court will help you with your application. The magistrate will hear the application in private and may ask you one or two questions connected with your complaint.

A DATE WILL BE FIXED FOR THE CASE TO BE HEARD

once your application has been accepted. Your husband will be sent a summons, telling him to appear in court on that day. You are expected to be there too.

AT THE HEARING,

you and your husband will be able to produce evidence and call witnesses to prove your case. What often happens is that the case is not finished at the first hearing, but another date is fixed, some weeks ahead.

FINALLY, AN ORDER IS MADE BY THE COURT

The court has power to order any of the following:

1. *Non-cohabitation.* If the court includes a 'non-cohabitation' clause in the order, it means that you are no longer obliged to live with your husband. If he then forces you to have sexual intercourse with him, he can be prosecuted for rape. Courts are often unwilling to include non-cohabitation clauses, in case there is some hope of reconciliation, and they will only do so if you seem to need protection from your husband.
2. *Custody of the children.* The court will order that either you or your husband has custody of the children. The parent who has custody lives with the children and looks after them.
3. *Access to the children.* The parent who does not have custody is usually allowed to see the children at certain times. The court normally allows this, unless that parent is considered to be a danger to the children.
4. *Maintenance.* Your husband will be ordered to pay a certain amount each week to help support you and your children. If the case is not settled in one hearing, and you are in urgent

need, the court may make an 'interim order', which can last for three months.

How much maintenance will you get?

There is no legal limit, but magistrates rarely order as much maintenance as you would obtain in the divorce court. They are supposed to award a sum which would enable the wife and children to have the same standard of living as the husband, but magistrates still tend to assume that a man needs more to live on than a woman. And then, of course, there is often the problem that couples do not have enough money to run two households.

MAINTENANCE FOR THE CHILDREN ONLY

If you have no grounds for applying for a separation order – for instance if you have simply decided that you want to live apart and your husband hasn't committed any of the matrimonial offences listed above – then you can apply to the court for custody of the children and maintenance for the children, but not maintenance for yourself. You do not have to prove that your husband has done anything wrong. The court will consider what is in the best interests of the children and may ask for a report from a probation officer or social worker before it reaches a decision.

How long does the maintenance order last?

Maintenance for the children normally lasts until their 16th birthday, or until they leave school. The court may order payments to continue beyond that if they go on to college, training or an apprenticeship.

If the maintenance order is granted while you are living apart from your husband and you start living with him again, the order will cease to have effect immediately. The only exception is where arrangements have been made to maintain a child who has been placed in the care of a 'third party', such as the local council – in this case, payments still have to be made to support the child.

If you remarry, you can no longer claim maintenance for yourself, but your former husband must continue to support his own children.

How is the maintenance paid?

Your husband pays the maintenance to the court, and the court sends it on to you by post.

What happens if the man stops paying maintenance?

This section applies to married and single women who are claiming maintenance from the fathers of their children (see p. 204).

A lot of men stop paying maintenance after a while. If this happens to you there are certain steps you can take to get the money you are owed.

What to do if the man is paying maintenance to the magistrates' court

(He will be doing this if the magistrates' court ordered the payments in the first place; or if a divorce court ordered the payments and you had them registered with the magistrates' court. The court will forward the payments to you by post, if they arrive.)

Go to the magistrates' court and apply for an 'arrears of maintenance summons'. This means that the man has to appear in court and explain why he hasn't paid. You can't get legal aid at this stage, but all you need do is go along to the court any weekday morning and explain what you want. The court officials will help you. If the man still doesn't pay up, you can apply for an 'attachment of earnings' order. This means that maintenance is deducted from his wages before he gets his take-home pay. It's a good solution if the man has a steady job. If he hasn't, the payments will probably lapse again when he goes out of work. It will then be very difficult and time-consuming trying to get your money.

What normally happens in a situation like this is that you wait each week to receive your money from the court. If it doesn't turn up, and you have no other money, you have to go to the Social Security office and claim supplementary benefit. (Details about supplementary benefit on p. 113.)

This is a very unsatisfactory situation. Everything happens on a week-to-week basis: one week the maintenance may turn up, the next week it may not. Each week that it doesn't turn up you have to make a special trip to the Social Security office to get enough money to live on. You may not be able to get supplementary benefit immediately – you may have to wait overnight or over a weekend without any money.

But there is one way of avoiding it. The magistrates' clerk (who deals with the administration of maintenance orders) may let you sign over your maintenance payments to the Department of Health and Social Services. This means that the Social Security office becomes responsible for collecting the payments from the man and gives you a supplementary benefit order book. You will be able to cash the orders each week regardless of whether the man has paid up.

Unfortunately, you can't do this unless the Social Security officials agree to it. They are often unwilling to put themselves to the extra trouble, and they will almost certainly refuse if your maintenance payments are higher than you would get on supplementary benefit. But if you think it would make life easier for you, it is well worth asking them to do it and trying to persuade them to take over the responsibility.

A man can eventually be arrested and prosecuted if he fails to pay maintenance over a long period of time. If convicted, he may be imprisoned for up to three months or fined up to £100. Men who fail to pay maintenance are the only 'debtors' who can still be put in prison. It seems absurd that this form of punishment survives long after the idea of imprisoning debtors has been abandoned as ineffective and unjust. It would not be necessary if all mothers had a right to an adequate, independent income from the state.

What to do if the man is paying maintenance directly to you

(He will be doing this if the divorce court ordered the payments and you didn't have them registered with the magistrates' court; or if he arranged to pay maintenance without going to court.)

If the divorce court ordered the payments, you will have to go back to the same court to take legal action against the man. This is rather more complicated than going to the magistrates' court and you should get advice from a solicitor.

If the man arranged to pay maintenance by a legal agreement, as explained on page 195, consult the solicitor that drew up the agreement.

If you simply made an agreement between you, with no legal backing, then all you can do is start divorce or separation proceedings.

What if you don't want to claim maintenance?

(This section applies to both married and single women.)

If the father of your child has a reasonable income and is reliable, you may get more money from him than if you were getting supplementary benefit. If the payments arrive regularly, you will be spared the ordeal of having to squeeze your day-to-day living expenses out of the Social Security office. However, if the father has a low or unsteady income, or if he is unreliable, he probably won't keep up the maintenance payments, and, because of the uncertainty, it can be even worse than relying totally on supplementary benefit. You may in any case prefer to remain independent from him and not look to him for any part of your income.

You do *not* have to claim maintenance from the father. Instead, you can claim supplementary benefit and your refusal to pursue the man for maintenance should *not* endanger your right to full benefit.

The Social Security officials will do all they can to get the father to pay maintenance – because if he does, they will be able to pay you less. When you go to claim supplementary benefit, they will question you about him. If you are not married, they may ask you a lot of personal questions to try to establish his identity. Remember, you do not have to tell them who he is or where he is and you still have a right to claim benefit. If you have no other money, you should be given the full amount for a single person, plus allowances for the children.

If you don't tell the Social Security officials who the man is, they are supposed to try to find out for themselves. Once they know who he is, they will probably try to persuade you to take legal action against him to make him pay. Don't let them intimidate you: you are quite free to say 'no' if you don't want to. However, the Social Security officials may decide to take legal action themselves. This would mean that they would be responsible for collecting the maintenance and they should still pay the supplementary benefit to you.

Separation by legal agreement

If you want to arrange a separation by voluntary, legal agreement, you will need a solicitor. Chapter 11 tells you how to get one (pp. 298–300). Your solicitor will explain the procedure to you and advise you what arrangement would be in your best interests. Make sure he explains your tax position in regard to maintenance payments as this could make a considerable difference to their value (as shown on p. 55).

Your agreement can cover maintenance payments, arrangements about looking after the children and living in the family home, and the division of your belongings.

If your husband doesn't abide by the agreement, inform your solicitor, who will take steps to ensure that he does.

Judicial separation

This is very rare nowadays and is only useful if you have religious objections to divorce, or if you have not yet been married three years so cannot take divorce proceedings. You may obtain a decree of judicial separation even if you are not domiciled in this country. You apply for it in the same way as you would apply for a divorce. The only differences are:

– You can apply at any time – you don't have to wait until you have been married three years.

– At the end of it you are officially separated but the marriage still exists.

Getting your marriage annulled

This has the same effect as a divorce: it ends the marriage. To get an annulment you must prove that your marriage is not valid. You can do this by establishing one of the following facts:

1. You are too closely related to your husband to be legally married to him. Under the Marriage Act, a woman cannot marry her father, son, uncle, nephew or brother.

2. One of you was under 16 when you married.

3. The marriage ceremony did not comply with the requirements of the Marriage Act of 1949. This may not mean that the marriage is invalid, unless you both knew about it at the time. Even then it may not: for example if you married when you were under 18 without your parents' consent, the marriage would be valid.

4. One of you was already married to someone else.

5. You are both of the same sex.

6. You have not been able to consummate the marriage: this means not having ordinary sexual intercourse.

7. One of you entered into a polygamous marriage abroad while domiciled in England or Wales.

8. One of you refused to consummate the marriage: you will have to show that whoever refused made a definite decision, not just excuses.

9. One of you was mentally unbalanced when you got married, to the extent of being unfitted to marriage or subject to regular attacks of insanity.

10. The one who is not applying for the annulment was suffering

from a contagious form of venereal disease at the time of the marriage and the other did not know.

11. You were pregnant by another man when you got married.

   (You can't get an annulment for reasons 6–11 if your husband can satisfy the court that you knew there were grounds for claiming one, but led him to believe you wouldn't do so; and that it would be unjust to him if you did. Apply within 3 years of the marriage if you want an annulment under reasons 8–11.)

12. One of you did not consent to the marriage. This could be for one of the following reasons:

You were incapable of understanding that a marriage had taken place – for instance: you thought it was a betrothal ceremony; or you were mentally unbalanced and didn't realize you were getting married.

. . . You mistook the identity . . .

You mistook the identity of the other person.
You were forced to marry against your consent, by threats or violence.

Do-it-yourself divorce

It is possible to conduct your own divorce, although it is still very rare in British courts. A solicitor can charge up to £100 for a straightforward divorce. If you do it yourself it will cost only £12.

So if you are not eligible for legal aid, you could save a lot of money.

It is not a good idea to embark on a do-it-yourself divorce unless you are getting the simplest kind of divorce, namely one claiming 'irretrievable breakdown' after two years' separation; and unless arrangements for maintenance and custody of the children are completely straightforward. If there is any possibility of a disagreement between you and your husband and you are not represented by a solicitor, you may end up with a very bad deal.

Here is a brief description of what to do to get an undefended divorce after two years' separation.

1. Get two copies of the petition form marked 'Wife's petition – two years' separation' from the Law Stationers, 237 Long Lane, London SE1; or Chancery Lane, London EC4; 6p each. 'Notes to Forms of Petition' accompany each form explaining how to answer the questions. If you have children you will also need the form 'Statement: Arrangements for Children', which is available from the same place.

2. Take the completed forms and your marriage certificate to the court at Somerset House if you live in London; or to your nearest divorce county court if you live outside London. Get the address from the telephone directory under county court or ask your Citizens' Advice Bureau where it is. You pay a £12 'filing' fee and you are given a reference number.

3. The court sends your husband a copy of the petition and an 'Acknowledgement of Service' form which he has to complete and return to the court. You will be sent a copy.

4. When you get the copy of your husband's 'Acknowledgement of Service' form, go to the court and fill in a 'Directions for Trial' form. Then apply for a hearing – you will be given instructions on how to do this. *N.B. If you are divorcing by mutual consent after two years' separation and you have no children under 16 or in full-time education or training, you can now get a 'postal divorce' without going to court. See p. 202.*

5. After four or five weeks you will receive a 'Notice of Hearing' which tells you when the case is to be heard.

6. At the hearing you will have to go into the witness box when your case is called. The judge will have the forms you and your husband have filled in. In theory all you need do is tell the judge your name, address and factual details of the marriage; that you and your husband have lived apart for two years; and that you want a divorce. It might be a good idea to take along a friend or relative who has seen you regularly during those two years, to give evidence if necessary.

7. This should all be over in a matter of minutes. The judge grants a decree nisi, saying that the marriage will be ended within six weeks 'unless sufficient cause be shown to the court'. In six weeks' time you need to send another form to Somerset House applying for your decree absolute, which will be sent to you in the post. This means that the divorce is complete and you and your husband are single people again.

Anyone with a little time to spare and a reasonable amount of intelligence should be able to do this kind of divorce. You will find it easier if the clerk of the court and the judge are sympathetic. To give you an idea of what it can be like, we quote from a report in the *Guardian* (28 February 1972) by Jane Routh. She conducted her own divorce with the co-operation of her husband on the ground of 'irretrievable breakdown' after two years' separation . . .

I was to conduct the case in the court of a small North Country town.

From the Law Stationers, the petition forms cost 5p. It would be difficult to buy the wrong ones – mine were marked 'Wife's petition – two years' separation', and equally difficult to complete them incorrectly – 'Notes to Forms of Petition' accompany each form, explaining in detail how each question should be answered.

I took my two copies of the completed form and my marriage certificate to the local County Court offices. No one had filed their own petition in that court before. There was momentary confusion until the clerks realised they simply had far less paperwork themselves than if a solicitor had sent them my forms. The clerk of the court (a woman) most helpfully explained the whole procedure to me. I gave her a cheque for £12, then the court took over. The petition was served on my husband, who acknowledged service within eight days. The court sent me a photo-copy of this.

I was then able to apply for a hearing. On the 'Request for Directions for Trial' form, I estimated that the case would take ten minutes. Four weeks later, the court sent me my 'Notice of Hearing' and another form asking for a list of witnesses and names of my solicitors and barrister. 'None'.

There were almost two months to wait until the case would be heard, and I had nothing more to do. A couple of weeks before the hearing, I asked the clerk if I could listen to some undefended cases. I sat through a whole morning of these. . .

On the morning of my own case . . . my father sent a message that he was coming . . . Mine was the seventh on the list of cases called for 10.30, but after the first case (of $2\frac{1}{2}$ minutes) the clerk signalled to me that mine would be heard third. I was unable to assess much of what was happening: the business consisted mainly of mumbles and shuffled papers.

The clerk called my and my husband's names. I went to the witness box, thrusting handbag and books and papers on my father, who went into the witnesses' waiting room with them. I affirmed. I waited. Nothing happened, so I began to announce who I was. The judge looked up, and stopped me:

'Are you conducting this case yourself?'

'Yes, I am, your Honour.'

'Have you any previous legal experience?'

'No, I have not, your Honour.'

I had not expected this: I had understood that it would be perfectly straightforward. The clerk had treated it as a matter of course. There followed an angered peroration about solicitors, the profession, and divorce by computer, culminating in : 'Why had you no solicitor?'

. . . cowardly, I said something about not having £100. The judge said that there was legal aid for such cases. I said I was not eligible for legal aid. In that case, I was told, I could afford a solicitor.

'Even if one is not eligible for legal aid, it is not always possible to put one's hands on that amount of money.'

'Oh, so you have made enquiries, then?'

'Yes, your Honour.'

'Have you taken statements?'

'No, I have not, your Honour.'

At this point the clerk turned and advised the judge that the case rested on 'clause D' (separation), in other words that I would not be citing adultery. The judge looked at his book. I felt so defeated that I had no vision of what to do next. I remained standing in the witness box.

'Have you called any witnesses?'

'No, I have not, your Honour.'

'I won't hear this case without a witness.'

I thought of reapplying for another hearing, and the time that would take. Then I thought of my father, and said: 'While I did not inform the court on the appropriate form that I should be calling any witnesses, there is someone in the witness room at the moment who could act as a witness.' (How quickly one learns the pedantry.)

'You are under oath now, anyway. What have you to say?'

I went through the information that I had put on the form of petition as appeared to be the practice in the other cases I had heard, adding nothing by way of evidence about unhappiness, brutality, and so on, but simply relying on a statement about the period of separation. I ended with 'and I ask your Honour to grant a decree nisi to this marriage'.

'Yes, all that is on the form. Call the witness.' I wanted to tell my father that I was sorry, that I didn't want to involve him in my problems, that I had tried to do it on my own. He took the oath. Silence. I asked the judge if I should question the witness, and was told I might. For a moment, my mind was completely blank, then I asked my father who he was, and to tell the court his relationship to me. (Deprecating smile from the judge.) I asked Dad about the dates of my marriage and separation, and whether, to the best of his knowledge, we had lived together since then.

At this point, the judge intervened to ask father whether he was in a position to know if we *had* lived together.

'Yes, sir, I visit my daughter regularly.'

'Is the mother living?'

'Yes, we both visit our daughter regularly.'

'So there are strong family ties?'

'Yes, sir, we are a close family.'

This *seemed* to make all the difference. I could not thank my father: he went out, and I was motioned back into the witness box. The judge waved what I recognised as my husband's acknowledgment of service, and began to say that the court would have had the form if . . . but the clerk nodded to him. Of course they had the form. He did not ask me to identify the respondent's signature, as is the usual practice, but informed me that nothing my husband said disagreed with my account. He asked no questions about maintenance or property, although I did have ready some documentary evidence to show what arrangements we had made about our house.

'I suppose I shall have to grant your request.'

Postal Divorce

If you divorce by mutual consent on the ground of two years' separation, and you have no children under 16 or in full-time education or training, you can now get a 'postal divorce' which means you don't have to go to court. Your solicitor, if you have one, will arrange this for you and all you have to do is make a sworn statement, giving the facts of the case. If you are conducting your own 'do-it-yourself' divorce, follow the instructions on p. 198, but when you go to the court (see para. 4) ask for your case to be put on the 'Special Procedure list'. You will be given a special 'Directions for Trial' form and another form which you must fill in and have sworn before a Commissioner of Oaths (costs 50p) or before the clerk of the divorce court (free). Hand in the form to the court; you will be told when it is to go before the judge; and you will be notified by post when your divorce is granted.

Useful things to read

The Divorce Reform Act 1969: An Explanatory Guide, published for the National Citizens' Advice Bureaux by the National Council of Social Service, 3p plus 3p postage from NCSS, 26 Bedford Square, London WC1 3HU. A short and clear explanation of the new divorce laws.

Getting a Divorce by Edith Rudinger, 60p from the Consumers' Association, 14 Buckingham Street, London WC2 6DS. A more detailed explanation of the law, the grounds for divorce, the proceedings, and financial provision.

Proceedings for Divorce, a booklet produced by the Divorce Registry, available from Somerset House, London WC2.

6. Children

Your rights as a mother

If you are not married

You are the legal guardian of your children. You automatically have custody of them, which means you have a right to make all the decisions about their upbringing and are responsible for looking after them on a day-to-day basis.

You can only lose your rights over the child if you have it adopted by someone else (more about adoption on p. 231); or if you abandon it, neglect it, or treat it in a way that is unacceptable to the local council, so that it is taken into care (more about that on p. 211).

The fact that your child is illegitimate does not affect its rights in any way. However, if you want to make the child legitimate, you can do this by marrying the father; by adopting the the child yourself; or by adopting the child jointly with your husband (if the man you marry is not the child's father).

The child will be given your last name unless the father signs the particulars of the birth that you give to the registrar; or unless he signs a formal declaration confirming that the child is his.

The father is responsible for supporting the child if he agrees to do so voluntarily; or if you take 'affiliation proceedings' against him (see below).

If you don't agree to allow the father of your child or children to visit them, he can apply to the magistrates' court for 'right of access', which means the right to spend a certain amount of time with the children (say, one day a week and every other weekend). The court will probably rule that he should be allowed to see them unless he has such a bad character that it would be dangerous to let him near them. The father can also apply to court for custody of the children, but it is most unlikely that the court would take them away from you and give them to him: this would only happen if the father could prove that you were incapable of looking after them.

WHAT IF YOU DON'T WANT TO ACKNOWLEDGE THE FATHER?

It can be very difficult for a man to establish that he is the father of your child. He would have to take the matter to court and prove:
– that you accepted payments or gifts from him shortly after the birth of the child; or
– that you have acknowledged that he was the father in some other way, in a letter, for example, or by admitting it to people whom he could call as witnesses.

A blood test can only prove that a man is *not* the father of a child: it cannot prove that he is the father.

CLAIMING MAINTENANCE FROM THE FATHER

You must take 'affiliation proceedings' against the father of your child if he refuses to accept responsibility and you want him to support the child financially. This means going to a magistrates' court and proving that he really *is* the father.

You can apply for an affiliation order while you are pregnant, or within three years of the child's birth. You can apply after three years if you can prove that the man has paid money towards the maintenance of the child during the year after it was born. If the man leaves the country and later comes back, you can apply up to three years after his return. You cannot apply if you are married to another man and living with him. You can apply if you are separated from your husband.

What to do

1. Go to your local magistrates' court and apply for a summons. You can turn up at 10 o'clock on any weekday morning and explain to the court officer what you want to do. He will help you with your application and it will be heard in private by the magistrate. A date is then fixed for the hearing and the father is sent a summons through the post, telling him to appear in court on a certain day.
2. Find a solicitor and apply for legal aid. Most women who take affiliation proceedings get legal aid very easily. You can ask one of the officials at the court, or your local Citizens' Advice Bureau, to help you contact a solicitor and fill in the legal aid forms. There is more information about this on pp. 298–308.
3. At the hearing you will probably have to give evidence, unless the man admits to the court that he is the father. Your evidence must be backed up, for example by another witness who has heard the man admit that he is the father; or by letters the man has written to you; or by proof that he has already paid money towards the child's maintenance.

If the court decides that the man is the father, it can order him to make weekly payments to you for the maintenance and education of the child; and extra money to offset the expense of the birth. Payments can be backdated to the day of the birth if you made your application within two months of that day. The father has to pay the money to the court, and the court sends the money to you each week through the post.

Alternatively, the court may order the payments to be transferred – either to the local council, if your child has been taken into care; or to the Supplementary Benefits Commission ('Social Security'), if you are receiving regular payments of supplementary benefit.

If you marry, the father must continue to pay maintenance for the child. But if the child is adopted by anyone else but you alone, he no longer has to pay.

WHAT HAPPENS IF THE FATHER STOPS PAYING MAINTENANCE?

You may find that the father does not make his maintenance payments regularly. One in ten illegitimate children are covered by affiliation orders, and in half of those cases the fathers pay up irregularly or not at all.

If this happens to you, you can go to the magistrates' court and apply for an 'arrears of maintenance' summons. If that doesn't work you can apply for an 'attachment of earnings' order. If that doesn't work, you can ask your local Social Security office to take over responsibility for collecting the maintenance and give you a supplementary benefit order book so that you can cash the orders each week, whether or not the maintenance arrives. All this is explained under the heading 'What happens if the man stops paying maintenance?' (p. 192).

WHAT IF YOU DON'T WANT TO CLAIM MAINTENANCE FROM THE MAN?

See p. 194.

If you are married

Until 1973, the legal guardian of a legitimate child was still the father. This meant that he had a right to take all the major decisions about the way his child was brought up. If the mother disagreed, she could only challenge his decision by going to court and applying for custody of the child.

But in 1973 the Guardianship Act was passed, which gave the mother the same legal rights and authority over her child as the father and established that the rights and authority of both parents 'shall be equal and exercisable by either without the other'. When the Act comes into force, which it is expected to do in 1974, you, the mother, will be able to make major decisions affecting your child in the father's absence and without his consent. He will be able to do the same without your consent. If you disagree, either of you will be able to apply to the court to have the matter settled there. The court's decision need not entail the awarding of custody to either parent.

You and your husband are equally responsible for supporting your children and you are both equally liable to be prosecuted if you fail to look after them properly, or treat them cruelly, or damage their physical or mental health.

IF YOU AND YOUR HUSBAND SEPARATE OR DISAGREE OVER THE CHILDREN,

either one of you can apply to a magistrates' court or county court for custody of the children. You will need a solicitor for this, so read pp. 298–305. The court will give equal consideration to both your claims, but will base its decision on what it thinks would be best for the children. In practice, children usually go to the mother, especially if they are young. The parent who is not given custody of the children is normally allowed to spend a certain amount of time with them. The court will also make arrangements for the children to be financially supported, as explained on p. 191.

IF YOUR HUSBAND ILL-TREATS YOUR CHILDREN,

you can apply for a separation order or a divorce because of his 'unreasonable behaviour'. At the same time, you can apply for custody and maintenance for the children.

TAKING YOUR CHILDREN OUT OF THE COUNTRY

Until the Guardianship Act comes into force, the situation is this: you can put your children on your passport or get them separate passports without the father's consent. But if you have a British visitor's passport, you can only do this if a court has awarded you custody of the children. If the father of the children writes to the Passport Office and says that he objects to your taking the children out of the country, they will accept his objection and refuse to issue passports to you for the children. They will not accept a similar objection from you. This is because the father is still the legal guardian of the children. But, if a court has awarded you custody of the children, the situation is reversed: the Passport Office will not accept the father's objection, and they will accept yours if you write to them saying you do not want the father to take the children out of the country.

When the Guardianship Act is passed : it is not yet certain how the Passport Office will interpret the Act – whether they will accept objections from both parents or from neither. What is most likely is that both parents will have equal rights to take the children out of the country (unless one has been awarded custody), and where there is a disagreement the matter will have to be settled in court.

(Details about a married woman's passport rights are on p. 167.)

MAKING YOUR CHILDREN WARDS OF COURT

If you think your husband may take your children away from you against your will – particularly if you think he may take them out of the country – and there is no other way of stopping him, you can apply to have them made wards of court. Go straight to a solicitor and insist that he takes out a summons immediately. This is a lot more effective than going to the police or to a magistrates' court. If the first solicitor you see cannot do it, get him to put you in touch with one who can. You can also apply for legal aid – the solicitor will help you. You should only resort to this in an emergency. It means that the court takes over custody of the children and awards the right of 'care and control' to one parent. Once the wheels are set in motion the children can be made wards of court. If the court considers there is a real risk that the children will be taken away from the applicant they will issue a 'Home

Office letter'. The Home Office then arranges for a watch to be kept on all ports and airports.

If you are getting divorced

IF YOU AND YOUR HUSBAND AGREE

about who should keep the children after the divorce, there will be no need to fight it out in court. When the divorce petition is first presented to the court, you must fill in a form explaining what arrangements have been made for the children (for instance, what plans you have made for their education, and how they will divide their time between your husband and you). The judge must approve these arrangements before he grants the divorce. If he does not approve – which would be unusual – the matter will have to be settled at a private hearing 'in chambers' after the divorce hearing. You may have to make alternative arrangements.

IF YOU DO NOT AGREE WITH YOUR HUSBAND

about who should keep the children, the court will decide who is going to have custody. You must make an application for custody when you file the divorce petition, or when you acknowledge that a petition has been filed by your husband. This is a complicated matter and you should certainly have a solicitor to deal with it for you and present your case to the court.

Normally, the court rules that children should stay where they are until the divorce is over, unless there are urgent reasons why they should be moved.

HOW DOES A COURT DECIDE WHO SHOULD HAVE CUSTODY OF THE CHILDREN?

1. A social worker attached to the court will probably investigate the situation. She will visit the homes of you and your husband and talk to you both and to the children, if they are old enough. She will then make a report to the court.

2. If the matter isn't settled before the divorce hearing, there will be another hearing afterwards, in private before the judge.
3. The judge must decide what is in the best interests of the children. This should have nothing to do with who caused the breakdown of the marriage. If the children are small, they will normally go to live with the mother, but this is not a hard and fast rule.
4. You are more likely to get custody of the children if:
   – You are living with them at the time when the court makes its decision about custody.
   – You are living in the family home, or you have established a good home for them somewhere else.
   – You are living in conventional circumstances.
5. You are less likely to get custody if:
   – You are not living with the children at the time of the custody decision.
   – You are living in more cramped conditions than your husband.
   – You are living in a way that might be considered haphazard or unconventional, or sharing with other people in a communal household.

Normally, the judge grants custody and 'care and control' of the children to one parent. 'Custody' means the right to take long-term decisions affecting their lives (such as what schools they should go to and what religion they should follow). 'Care and control' means the day-to-day responsibility of looking after them. However, the judge may grant joint custody to both parents and care and control to one; or custody to the father and care and control to the mother.

Arrangements about care and custody of the children are sometimes dealt with after the divorce and sometimes before, but if there is any disagreement, they are not dealt with at the divorce hearing.

Divorce is explained in detail on pp. 171–82.

Further information (for single mothers)

One-Parent Families, 255 Kentish Town Road, London NW5 (01 267 1361).

Gingerbread, 9 Poland Street, London W1 (01 734 9014): some practical help and moral support for single parents.

How your child could be taken into care

(This section applies to married and single parents)

Having your child taken into care means that the social services department of your local council takes over all your responsibilities as a parent. If this happens to a child of yours, she or he may be allowed to stay at home, or may have to move to accommodation approved by the council, such as a hostel or a 'community home'. You and the father still have to pay money to support the child. There are three ways that this can happen.

1. You can ask the council to take your child into care, perhaps because you are ill or homeless, or because you feel unable to cope. If the council considers that it would be in the best interests of the child, it takes over responsibility for the child until you ask for it to be returned to you. Under this arrangement, the council has no power to keep the child against your wishes.
2. The council can decide to take your child into care because you appear to have abandoned it or to be incapable of looking after it properly. The council must write you a letter telling you what it intends to do. If you consent in writing, the council takes over all your duties as a parent and you have no further rights over the child. The same happens if you do not reply and the council cannot find out where you are within the space of a year: in which case, it concludes that you have abandoned the child.

If you object, you should write to the social services department of the council and tell them so. They will then have to take the matter to court, and you will have a chance to put your case to the court. You can probably get legal aid for this so you can have a solicitor to represent you. Ask your Citizens' Advice Bureau about legal aid, and read the section on pp. 301–5.

3. A court may decide that your child is in need of 'care and control' and make a care order placing the child in the care of the local council. Care orders are compulsory: they do not require the parent's consent. They are used as a last resort when all other measures have failed. They are usually made because the child has done something wrong and because the court considers that the parents are not looking after and controlling the child properly. The kind of behaviour by a child which may lead a court to make a care order would be:
   – conviction for a number of criminal offences;
   – persistently playing truant from school, in the case of children under 16;
   – mixing with 'bad company';
   – taking drugs;
   – sleeping around, in the case of girls only.

If a child is under 16 when a care order is made, the order lasts until the 18th birthday. If the child is 16 or over, it will last until the 19th birthday. It can be ended sooner if the child or the council makes an application for it to be discharged, and that is accepted by the court. A parent cannot apply for a discharge.

Your child may be allowed to stay at home after a care order is passed. If your child is sent away to a hostel or community home, she or he can be visited by you and may be allowed home at weekends. You and the father will still have to pay maintenance for the child.

(More about care orders, from the child's point of view, on p. 238.)

Nurseries and other child-care facilities

If you have children under school age, you may not be able to look after them all day every day; or you may not want to. Instead you may be able to arrange for other people to look after them. In this section we describe the different child-care facilities that are likely to be available to you.

If you want to find out about child-care facilities in your area, contact the social services department of your local council. For information about nursery education, contact your local education authority. Addresses and phone numbers are listed in the telephone directory under the name of the council.

Day nurseries run by local councils

These are the only state-run nurseries which cater for children of women who have full-time jobs. They are run by the social services departments of local councils, and they are usually open between 8 a.m. and 6 p.m., including school holidays. They take children from 6 weeks old to school age. They are not free, but the amount you pay depends on your income. It could vary from nothing at all to over £8 a week. Standards vary considerably. Since they are not run by local education authorities, very few have any trained teachers on the staff. Instead, they have trained nurses and nursery nurses. Some try to provide good educational facilities, but many are overworked and under-staffed.

CAN ANY CHILD GO TO ONE OF THESE DAY NURSERIES?

No. Day nurseries have to give priority to children from 'deprived backgrounds' – which means children of single parents who have to go out to work; children whose mothers are ill; and children who live in poor housing conditions. They also have to give priority to children of teachers if there is a shortage of teachers in the area. Places are limited, so you will find it almost impossible to get a place for your child unless you fit into one of these categories. It helps if you have a recommendation from a doctor, health visitor or social worker.

The official attitude towards full-time care for under-fives is summed up in the Plowden Report:

We do not believe that full time nursery places should be provided, even for children who might tolerate separation without harm, except for exceptionally good reasons. We have no reason to suppose that working mothers as a group care any less about the well-being of their children than mothers who do not work ... but some mothers who are not obliged to work may work full time regardless of their children's welfare. It is no business of the educational service to encourage these mothers to do so. It is true, unfortunately, that the refusal of full time nursery places for their children may prompt some mothers to make unsuitable arrangements for their children's care during working hours. All the same, we consider that mothers who cannot satisfy the authorities that they have exceptionally good reasons for working should have low priority for full time nurseries for their children.

In view of this restrictive policy it is hardly surprising that there are only 5 day-nursery places for every 1,000 pre-school children. Numbers have declined since the war – from 903 nurseries in 1949 to 453 in 1970. A recent survey carried out by the British Humanist Association showed that London boroughs provided day-nursery places for only 1½ per cent of children under 5.

Nursery schools and classes

These are run by local education authorities and staffed by qualified teachers, to provide education for children aged between 3 and 5. Most are part-time, from 9 a.m. until midday or from midday until 3 p.m. A few are from 9 a.m. until 3 p.m., but these are of little use to mothers who have full-time jobs and no one to look after the children for them after school hours and in the holidays. All are free of charge.

Nursery classes are attached to primary schools. Sometimes the only way to find out about classes in your area is to ask each primary school what it provides.

Nursery education is still very scarce and there are long waiting lists for most schools and classes. It may be worth finding out about the ones in your area while your child is still a baby: you may be able to put her or his name on the waiting list. If that doesn't work, try talking to the teacher in charge of the nursery school or class. She or he can usually decide whether to accept children, regardless of the number of applicants.

The Labour government seems committed to extending nursery education. The situation would be greatly improved if it were extended to all children between 3 and 5 whose mothers wanted them to attend. In 1970 only 4 per cent of children of 3 and 4 received nursery schooling, compared with 33½ per cent in 1908. Britain's record is poor compared with France, which provides nursery education for 50 per cent of its 3-year-olds and for 80 per cent of its 4-year-olds.

Private nursery schools

These have to be registered with the social services department of the local council. Their opening hours vary – some are part-time and more like play groups; others are full-time and cater for working mothers. Prices vary from about £5 to over £8 a week. Standards also vary: some have trained teachers and others don't. In order to be registered they have to meet certain standards of accommodation, safety and record-keeping. They do not have to meet specified educational standards.

Pre-school play groups

Play groups are usually run by mothers who want to give their children a chance to play creatively with other children. They are not much use for mothers who work full-time, as they normally run from 9.30 a.m. until midday; some are open for two or three mornings a week, others every morning. Prices vary – from 5p to 25p per session. There is often a rota of mothers to help the play-group leader.

Many play groups are affiliated to the Pre-School Playgroups Association, which exists to promote play groups and public interest in them, to maintain high standards, and to advise people who want to set up new groups. Its headquarters are at Alford House, Aveline Street, London SE11; and at 304 Maryhill Road, Glasgow NW.

Play groups have to be registered with the social services

department of the local council, and in order to be accepted for registration they must meet standards of safety and accommodation. Local councils often help play groups by providing grants or accommodation. Many Adult Education Centres provide courses for people who want to train as play-group supervisors – although it is possible to start a play group without being trained.

Baby-minders

Baby-minders are people who look after children in their own homes as a means of income. They are still the most common form of child care used by working mothers. Prices vary (although £3 a week is fairly common) and so do standards. Some baby-minders are excellent, but others just do it because they need the money when they don't really have the facilities for the children to play.

Baby-minders are legally obliged to register with the local council, so that the council can check that their homes are safe, particularly against fire risk, and that they are not looking after too many children at once. But many baby-minders avoid registering so that they can take more children than the council would allow. It's advisable to check first that the baby-minder you are considering leaving your child with has registered with the council. Contact the social services department.

A baby-minder who fails to register could, after due warning, be taken to court and fined – unless she is a close relative of the children she is looking after; or unless she is looking after children for no more than two hours a day. It would help if councils provided grants so that baby-minders could improve their premises and provide equipment, but so far nothing like that has happened although there are a few pilot schemes to train baby-minders.

'One o'clock clubs', occasional crèches, etc.

'One o'clock clubs' are usually run in parks where there is a play hut available. The idea is that mothers bring their children along between 1 and 3 in the afternoon. Mothers have to stay, but play equipment is provided. The clubs are supervised and the service is free. Some councils run 'Mother and Toddler Clubs' and 'Pram Clubs' along the same lines – in parks or community centres. Sometimes maternity and child welfare centres run crèches once or twice a week for a few hours at a low charge or free. Details of all these facilities from the social services department of your local council.

Factory nurseries

There are about sixty factory nurseries in Britain – most of them in the north, where employers depend on married women workers. They are financed by the employer, although mothers are often charged a fee. There are serious snags to this kind of child care, as it means the mother must take the child to work with her, and home again in the evening when they are both tired, with no time to do shopping on her own. When she changes jobs, she loses her child's place in the nursery. Some factory nurseries forbid mothers to see their children during the day. It might be a better idea if employers provided the funds for nurseries, but let them be run by the workers, perhaps through a trade union committee.

After-school and holiday care for school-aged children

One of the biggest worries for women who go out to work is what to do with their children from the time school ends to the time they get home from work, and during the school holidays. There's always enough talk about 'latch-key' children turning delinquent to make working women feel guilty, but there's seldom any constructive help available for them.

At present only a few councils provide play centres: these are open until about 6.30 p.m. in the term time, and they are open all day, from about 9.00 a.m., in the holidays. Some give the children a light tea in the term time and a midday meal in the holidays. The children are supervised and entertained. Play centres are usually found in big cities. In London there are about 160 open during term time and 80 open during the holidays. If there isn't one in your area, you could get together with other women and ask the council to set one up. It is time the Government recognized that a large proportion of mothers are a permanent part of the work force, and provided child-care facilities to suit the situation.

Combined day nursery and nursery school

One of the greatest drawbacks of state-run facilities for children under school age is the division of responsibility between two government departments: the Department of Education is responsible for nursery schools and the Department of Health and Social Security is responsible for child care (that is, day nurseries, baby-minders, etc.). The two rarely co-ordinate their activities. The result is that children of working mothers cannot have pre-school education and mothers who want to send their children to nursery schools cannot have them looked after for a full day.

However, there are a few exceptions, such as the Hillfields Nursery Centre in Coventry, a combined nursery and nursery school. It opened in June 1971 and cost £65,000. It caters for a total of 140 children aged from a few weeks to five years. It is open from 7 a.m. to 6 p.m. Mothers can leave their children for as long as they need to. They pay according to how long the children stay there, and those who can't afford the charges pay a minimal amount or nothing at all.

The centre has a head teacher, a deputy head, and another qualified teacher, plus one senior and twelve nursery assistants with nursing qualifications. It is under the administration of the local Director of Education, with the active participation of the health and social services departments.

It's a pity there aren't more centres which cater for all children on a flexible basis. Mrs Thatcher's White Paper doesn't consider the possibility, but it should not be beyond the scope of any local council with the imagination to combine the resources of its education, health and social services departments.

Education

What the law says

YOU MUST SEND YOUR CHILDREN TO SCHOOL

If you have children aged between 5 and 16, you must see that they receive 'efficient, full-time education suitable to [their] age, ability and aptitude'. Your local education authority is obliged to provide this education. What this means in practice for over 90 per cent of children in Britain is that their parents send them to the local state school, where they get whatever's going in the way of education.

What happens if your children play truant, or you fail to send them to school regularly?

Your local education authority (LEA) will probably send you an 'attendance order', which orders you to send your child to a certain school regularly. If you fail to obey, you – or more likely, your husband – will be summoned to court and may be fined. If this happens, you stand a chance of avoiding conviction if you can prove one of the following to the court:

1. The child was unable to go to school because of illness or some other unavoidable reason (this must have been something that affected the child, not the parent).
2. The child was away from school on days set apart for religious observance by the religion that you follow.
3. The school was not within walking distance and the LEA failed to make suitable arrangements for transport.

TRANSPORT

If your child's school is more than walking distance from your home, the LEA is obliged to provide free transport or to pay travelling expenses there and back. 'Walking distance' means 2 miles for a child under 8 and 3 miles for a child over 8, measured by the 'nearest available route'. It makes no difference if the route is unsafe for a child or unfit for wheeled transport.

POWERS OF THE TEACHERS

Once your child is at school, within school hours, the teachers take over your rights and obligations as a parent and they are therefore allowed to exercise reasonable discipline over the child. The LEA has full responsibility for children while they are at school, and if your child comes to any harm you may be able to sue for damages (you will need a solicitor for this; see pp. 298–308). If a child is sent home early, it is the duty of the school to see that she or he arrives safely.

In theory, teachers have no control over what your child does or wears outside school hours (and this includes homework). In practice, however, teachers can often make children conform by reprimanding or punishing them in school.

PUNISHMENT

Most LEAs make their own rules about corporal punishment, and schools are supposed to keep records of all corporal punishments that are given to the children. In practice, the records are rarely complete and few parents know that they exist. It is worth finding out what punishments are allowed in your child's school. A teacher who gives out punishments that are more severe than the rules allow should be reported to the headmaster or to the LEA. The Inner London Education Authority, for example, does not allow corporal punishment in primary schools.

If the teacher uses more than reasonable discipline – for instance, by beating a child over the head – she or he can be prosecuted by you for criminal assault: report the matter to the LEA or get advice from a solicitor (see pp. 298–301). Sometimes, of course, parents want teachers to be stricter than they are. But parents cannot insist on corporal punishment.

A child under 16 cannot be expelled from a state school, but can be suspended for a limited period or transferred to another school. A child over school-leaving age (16) who is suspended for two weeks can be expelled when the two weeks are up. If your child is suspended or expelled you have a right to appeal against the decision to the school governors or managers.

RELIGION

All state schools and voluntary schools (that is, most schools where you don't pay fees) have to begin each day with 'collective worship' and must provide a certain amount of religious instruction. If you do not approve of this sort of thing, you can arrange for your child to be withdrawn from morning prayers and religious instruction. (Unfortunately, it seems that a child cannot make a personal decision about this.)

Dear God, please save me from Morning Prayers and Religious Instruction

Getting financial help from the local education authority

Some LEAs are more generous than others. Some will pay for a child to be sent to boarding school if the schools in the area are not suitable. If you are eligible for supplementary benefit (and you can find out whether you are by reading pp. 113–21), you should also be eligible for grants to help buy school uniform or ordinary school wear, school maintenance grants to help support children over 16 who are still at school, and free school meals. You can get information about these benefits from your local education authority or Social Security office.

Discrimination against girls in schools

If you have a daughter at school you may notice that she is treated differently from the boys of her age. This happens in innumerable ways. Here are some examples of the sort of thing that can happen:

1. At the infant level, girls are encouraged to play with dolls and the 'wendy house' while boys play with the more adventurous and mechanical toys.
2. In many primary schools, girls have to share a smaller playground with the infants, while the larger playground is mapped out for football and monopolized by the boys.
3. Early reading books show father going out to work, taking all the family decisions and giving the children treats, while mother breeds and cooks and cleans – thus endlessly reinforcing the traditional sex roles.
4. Textbooks deal with subjects from a totally male viewpoint: history, for example, appears to revolve around male rulers, soldiers and adventurers, while the contribution of women to a very different aspect of history is almost totally ignored.
5. Girls are made to do needlework and cookery while boys do woodwork and metalwork.
6. Laboratory facilities for girls are often limited, and they are encouraged to take biology or general science, while physics and chemistry – and the best laboratory facilities – are reserved for the boys.

In evidence presented to the House of Lords Select Committee on the Anti-Discrimination Bill, a deputy chief education officer described two schools with different policies towards girls' education and showed how this affects the girls' choice of sixth-form subjects and further education:

SCHOOL A

Mixed grammar school recruiting predominantly from council housing estate in urban area of high unemployment. Bias academic – little technical work encouraged. School has too few science laboratories for existing intake and some laboratories are earmarked exclusively for boys. At 13 + pupils are given 'options' but girls are offered different (limited) options from boys unless they specifically press for science or technical subjects. Headmaster does not favour higher education for girls other than teacher training.

Headmaster considers he has a duty to give preference to boys because of their vulnerability in the unstable employment market in the region, but he is now being persuaded by the education service to alter his attitude and timetabling.

VI form numbers 1964–1969 = 228

	Boys	Girls
Arts	48	58
Sciences	94	17
Mixed courses	11	
Entering universities	74	27
„ colleges of education	20	36
„ colleges of technology	17	7
Direct entry to industry	44	3

SCHOOL B

Mixed grammar school 40 miles from School A. Mining area. Unemployment situation the same.

Headmaster believes in completely free options. School has outgrown its resources – more pupils than room available. Both boys and girls therefore use nearby Technical College laboratories and workshops. Electronics VIth form includes girls. Project Technology work however limited to boys because girls timetabled for housecraft simultaneously. There is no other discrimination in timetabling.

Comment. More girls read maths and science for 'A' level than at School A. More girls go on to university and technical college than at School A. The VIth form is evenly balanced between girls and boys, i.e. fewer girls drop out at the 16 + level than at School A.

Discrimination against girls at school affects their attitudes and aspirations generally, their chances of getting to college or university, their choice of career and their patterns of employment: in fact, their whole future.

There is a good case for arguing that, by allowing this sort of discrimination, the local education authority is in breach of the 1944 Education Act. The Act says that every LEA should provide schools 'to afford all pupils opportunities for education . . . as may be desirable in view of their different ages, abilities and aptitudes'. It would be difficult to prove that a girl's 'age, ability, and aptitude' are any different from a boy's.

How can a parent make changes?

A lot of parents feel helpless to make any changes in their children's education – often because their own childhood has left them with a strong aversion to school and an exaggerated sense of the head teacher's authority.

As a parent you of course have every right to make your objections known to the teachers and to suggest changes. This can have a considerable effect inside the school, although it may be some time before you or your children are aware of it. If complaining to the teachers makes no difference, you can complain to the school governors or managers (by writing to them at the school); then appeal to the local education authority; then, if all else fails, appeal to the Secretary of State for Education.

But there is a limit to what can be achieved by complaining through the official channels. Two causes of the shortcomings of the present state education system are: (1) the Government does not give it enough money; and (2) most schools are isolated from the activities of the neighbourhood. The first is a matter of local and national politics. The second can be tackled at the level of the individual school – by parents becoming more closely involved with the work of the school and helping to shape policy through the parent-teacher associations. So, rather than writing a letter of complaint, you may find it more effective to get together with the teachers and other parents and work with them to make changes within the school.

Alternative schooling

If you don't want your children to 'go to school' in the conventional sense of the word, there are ways of getting round the Education Act. For instance:

FREE SCHOOLS

These are a new and growing phenomenon. Two of the most well-known are the Scotland Road Free School in Liverpool and the Islington Free School in London. They represent an ideal which is very different from the traditional concept of education: children are given a lot more freedom than in ordinary schools to decide what and how they are going to learn. They are encouraged to learn spontaneously, developing their knowledge and personalities without the strictures of authority.

The most useful information on the subject is given in a booklet produced by the Islington school: *How to Set Up a Free School* by Alison Truefitt, price 25p, or more if you can afford it (address on p. 227). She explains in the booklet how alternative education can be kept within the law:

At present, the most obvious slots for free schools are either inde-

pendent status or 'otherwise' status. Section 114 of the 1944 Education
Act defines an independent school as a 'school at which full-time
education is provided for five or more pupils of compulsory school
age (whether or not such education is also provided for pupils under
or over that age)', and it also defines a 'school' in general as an
'institution'. Section 36 of the Act says 'It shall be the duty of the
parents of every child of compulsory school age to cause him to receive
efficient full-time education suitable to his age, ability and aptitude,
either by regular attendance at a school or otherwise'. The key words
'institution', 'education', 'full-time', 'suitable' and 'otherwise' are
not further defined by the Act.

EDUCATION AT HOME

It is possible to satisfy the local education authority that you are
providing your children with 'full-time, efficient education'
etc. by teaching them at home. It helps if you have teaching qualifications or can provide them with a 'tutor' who has. Alison
Truefitt describes one successful experiment by a mother in
Ealing, West London, a graduate with a teaching diploma who,
unusually, had taught in every kind of state school, from infants to
grammar:

Her daughter, now seven, and the youngest, took a violent and
unaccountable dislike to her state primary school. In fact she developed
a severe school phobia, being sick every morning and so on. When after
being ill at home for some time the daughter was due back for the
last two weeks of term; and when, seeing the sickness coming on
again, her mother said suddenly 'you needn't go back to school at all
this term', the child recovered almost visibly.

The child is now extremely happy at home, and starting to read
and take an interest in things again, which she had dropped while at
school. The mother insists that the child is not in fact withdrawn or
particularly shy: 'she talks all the time when we have her friends
round here', just that she hated the huge size of the school she was
at . . .

The LEA have made no inquiries about what the child is doing
[in the way of lessons]. The mother says she does 'very little sitting
down and teaching her. Certainly nothing regular'. It is interesting
that the Ealing LEA are allowing this situation to continue, though

they have 'suggested' that mother and child attend a child guidance clinic, which they are doing in the hope that this will prevent the LEA climbing further on their backs. However, it is unlikely the authority would have taken so liberal a view if they had not been dealing with a professional teacher who clearly knew the ropes.

(Since this was written, the child returned, of her own free will, to a different school in the same area.)

Further information

Advisory Centre for Education, 32 Trumpington Street, Cambridge CB2 1QY (Cambridge 51456): for information in most aspects of education. You have to pay a fee.
Islington Free School, 57 White Lion Street, London N1 (01 837 6379): for a booklet on how to set up a free school (price 25p, or more if you can afford it).

Adoption

Some facts and figures about adoption

In 1971, 48 per cent of adoptions were cases where children were adopted by their own parents or relatives; 42 per cent were by non-relatives, arranged through adoption agencies; 10 per cent were by non-relatives, placed directly by the mother or arranged through private individuals.

If you want to adopt a child

You can adopt a child through one of many registered adoption agencies. These are either local councils, welfare organizations or voluntary societies. You may be able to adopt privately if you already know the child or its family; if you are related to the child; or if you have made contact with the child through a 'third party', such as a doctor, social worker or a friend. However, adoption through a 'third party' may soon be restricted by law. A complete list of adoption agencies is available from the Association of British Adoption Agencies (address on p. 234).

YOU HAVE TO BE VERY CAREFULLY VETTED

if you adopt through an agency. They will want to discuss the matter with you at great length and find out all about you before they decide whether you are a fit person to adopt. You are more likely to be accepted if you fulfil all of the following conditions:

1. You are married. If you are living with a man but not married to him, you cannot adopt as a couple. You may be able to adopt if you are single, but this is a lot more difficult.
2. You are under 40. The age limit for a man is usually higher. If you are in your late thirties, you are more likely to be accepted if you already have children. You must be at least 25 if you are not related to the child and at least 21 if you are.
3. You have a good home and an adequate income to support the child.
4. You are in good physical and mental health and have a satisfactory mental history.

5. You are prepared to adopt a child who is non-white, disabled, or who is no longer a small baby. There is a very long waiting list of parents wanting to adopt healthy white Anglo-Saxon babies and it is getting increasingly difficult to adopt new-born racially mixed babies. Meanwhile, there are a great many older children and children who are non-white or physically or mentally disabled, who cannot find adoptive parents.

6. The agency (if it is a good one) must be satisfied that you can 'genuinely accept another person's child as your own'.

RELIGION?

It used to be very difficult for non-religious people to adopt. Some adoption societies still insist on adoptive parents following a certain religion, but there are now more local councils handling adoption than voluntary agencies, and councils are forbidden by law to make religious stipulations.

HOW LONG WILL IT TAKE?

Prepare yourself for a long wait. It could take two years or more before you are given a child.

HOW MUCH?

The buying and selling of children is not allowed these days. So it would be illegal for you to accept or offer any money in the course of the adoption, except by paying a fee to an agency. Local councils do not normally charge for arranging adoptions.

WHAT ABOUT THE NATURAL PARENTS?

You cannot adopt without the consent of the natural mother (and father, if the child is legitimate), except in certain circumstances, which are explained further on in this section. The natural parents are no longer shrouded in secrecy as they used to be: it is common practice for the adoption agency to talk quite openly

about them and give you detailed information about the child
and its background. You will know the mother's name because
you will see the child's birth certificate. But you can, if you choose,
conceal your identity from the natural parents.

ONCE YOU HAVE BEEN ACCEPTED AS A POSSIBLE ADOPTIVE PARENT,

you must look after the child for three months before the court
can make the adoption order. You must make sure that the social
services department of your local council is informed in writing
that you are looking after the child with a view to adoption (unless
either you or your husband is a parent of the child). You will be
visited by a social worker from the council and the court will also
appoint a 'guardian ad litem' (usually a social worker or probation officer) to be responsible for the child during those three
months, to interview all the people concerned with the adoption,
and to report to the court on whether the adoption arrangements
are suitable.

After three months, if all goes well, you have to go to court for
the legal adoption to take place. Adoption proceedings normally
take place in the county court or juvenile court. They are heard in
private before the judge. (Some judges are fond of delivering a
lecture at this point.) You can choose to be identified by a serial
number rather than by name if you don't want the natural parents
to know who you are. If the court is not entirely satisfied that you
are ready to adopt the child – for instance, if you don't have
proper accommodation – it can make an interim order allowing
you to keep the child for up to two years, in the hope that you will
be able to improve your circumstances during that time. You must
make a fresh application to the Registrar of the county court for a
permanent adoption order *at least* two months before the interim
order comes to an end.

When the adoption order is granted, you take over full rights and
responsibilities as the child's parent. The natural parents no
longer have any rights over the child. To replace the original
birth certificate, you can get a copy of the entry in the Adoption

Register, which gives the date of the adoption order and the name of the court that made it. Alternatively, you can use the short form of birth certificate which simply shows the child's place and date of birth, sex and adoptive name.

CAN THE CHILD FIND OUT ABOUT ITS NATURAL PARENTS?

If an adopted child wants to see a copy of the original birth certificate, she or he can do so only by applying for permission to the court which made the adoption order. Courts rarely grant permission. However, a person adopted in Scotland can, once over 17, get a copy of the birth certificate without going to court.

Having your child adopted

If you do this, it is important to understand that you will lose all contact with the child and all your rights as its mother. Obviously it is something you must think about very carefully before you make your decision. Try and talk it over with sympathetic people and don't be afraid to change your mind, even if it's right at the last moment.

You can arrange an adoption by contacting one of the adoption agencies. The social services department of your local council may be able to arrange the adoption; otherwise it can put you in touch with an agency that will. If you are not completely satisfied with the first agency you approach, it is worth visiting several until you find a good one.

The agency will want to talk the matter over with you very carefully and at length, to make sure that you really want to have the child adopted and that the adoption will be in the best interests of the child. You will be given a form which explains in simple words what a legal adoption is, and points out that the child may be sent abroad. Before your baby can be placed with an adoptive parent you will be asked to sign the form, stating that you understand exactly what it means.

You must give the agency full details of your background and the baby's; the baby is given a medical examination, and you will need a certificate which states that it is healthy and free from any physical or mental defect. It would be illegal for you to give or take any money from a person who might adopt your child.

You can make certain demands about the way you want the baby to be brought up, for instance that you want it to be brought up in a certain religion, or with other children in the family. You can usually arrange to meet the prospective parents if you want to.

ADOPTION PROCEDURE

During the three-month period when your child lives with the people who want to adopt it, before the adoption order is made, you will be visited by the 'guardian ad litem' appointed by the court to supervise the adoption. She will have visited the adoptive parents and checked that everything is going smoothly. She will explain the procedure to you again and if you still want the child to be adopted, you will be asked to sign the final consent form, which is then presented to the court.

You will probably not have to go to court to give your consent, but if you have to be interviewed by the court for any reason and you don't want to see the adoptive parents, ask to be interviewed separately.

You must give your consent in writing before the adoption order can be made. If you are married, your husband must also give his consent. If you are single, the father's consent is not necessary, but if he is paying maintenance, the court should tell him that the baby might be adopted and give him a chance to make his views known.

If the father wanted to apply for custody of the child, he would have to do so before the adoption order is made and he would have to satisfy the court that he could take care of the child. If custody were granted to the father, the child would not be adopted by anyone else and he would take over full rights and responsibilities towards the child.

You can withdraw your consent any time you want to, right up to the day of the final court hearing. Don't sign anything unless you are absolutely convinced that you are doing the right thing. You may withhold your consent indefinitely. However . . .

The court can make an adoption order without your consent if it is satisfied that:

1. You have persistently failed to fulfil your duties as a parent;
   or
2. You have abandoned, neglected or persistently ill-treated the child;
   or
3. You cannot be found;
   or
4. Your refusal to consent is 'unreasonable';
   or
5. You are incapable of giving your consent, for instance because of mental illness.

The court can make an order without the married father's consent for the same reasons.

If you give your consent at first and then decide that you don't want your child to be adopted, your new decision will be accepted unless it can be shown to be totally unreasonable. If the court is considering granting an adoption order without your consent, it must tell you its reasons and give you a chance to apply for legal aid and get a solicitor to represent you in court. If the adoption order goes through without your consent, you should get a solicitor and lodge an appeal *immediately* (read pp. 298–305 on how to get a solicitor and apply for legal aid).

When could your refusal to consent be called 'unreasonable'? This could happen only in exceptional circumstances. However, the law is loosely defined and it would be possible for a court to make an unsatisfactory judgement. In a recent case, certain principles were laid down for deciding whether refusal to consent was 'unreasonable', including: 'A reasonable parent gives great weight to what is better for the child.' So one factor contributing to a court's decision that you were 'unreasonable' might be that you refused to let your child go to a home which could provide a better life in the material sense.

Adopting your illegitimate child jointly with your husband

In 1971, over 11,000 children were adopted by one or both of their natural parents. In most of these cases, the child was born to a single woman who then married and made the adoption jointly with her husband. This makes the child legitimate and gives the man full parental rights and responsibilities towards the child. If you are considering doing this it's important to realize that as the single mother of an illegitimate child you have *sole* parental rights and responsibilities. If you marry and the child lives with you both as one of the family, your husband becomes responsible for the childs maintenance. If you later divorce, he could claim custody of the child, although this would normally be granted to you.

How the law may be changed

A report was published in October 1972 by the Home Office Departmental Committee on the Adoption of Children, which made the following recommendations:

1. The minimum age for all adopters should be 21.
2. Adoption through a 'third party' (that is, a private individual who is not the child's mother) should no longer be allowed.
3. Adoption by relatives of the child and by the mother jointly with her husband should no longer be allowed except in exceptional circumstances; and it should first be considered whether or not it would be more appropriate for them to be made guardians of the child.

Further information

Association of British Adoption Agencies, 4 Southampton Row, London WC1 (01 242 8951): for general advice on adoption and a list of all adoption agencies.

Adoption Resource Exchange, 39 Brixton Road, London SW9 (01 735 8941): deals with the adoption of children with special needs.

Independent Adoption Society, 160 Peckham Rye, London SE22 (01 693 4155): for adoption without religious specifications.
How to Adopt: a Consumers' Association publication, from 14 Buckingham Street, London WC2 (01 839 1222).

Fostering

Fostering is quite different from adoption. Its purpose is to provide homes for children while keeping them in touch with their parents, to enable families to reunite when possible. All fostering arrangements are supervised by the social services department of the local council.

If you want your child to be fostered

You can make your own arrangements if you know someone who is prepared to foster the child, but that person must inform the council. Otherwise, you can approach the social services department of your local council and ask them to arrange fostering. They will decide what they think is best for the child. If they agree to arrange fostering, you will be able to visit your child at the foster home. You will be expected to pay a certain amount of money each week, depending on how much you can afford.

You generally have a right to take the child back to live with you whenever you want. However, this may not be so easy if the child has been with foster parents for a long time and you are planning to take her or him permanently out of the country, as the following case (from *The Times*, 26 February 1973) illustrates:

In December 1972, it was decided in the Family Division of the High Court that a Ghanaian girl, now nearly ten, should remain with the English foster parents with whom she had lived since she was three months old, rather than return to Ghana with her parents. The court's main findings were: (1) The parents for nine years had delegated all parental responsibility and had told untruths about the extent of their contact with the child and about their financial support. (2) The foster parents had been good parents, and had lavished loving care and affection on her. (3) The child had a firm view that she did not want to leave them and go to Ghana. Sir George Baker, President of the court, said 'By nurture, she is wholly English': if the child remained there was no reason to anticipate that anything would go wrong. She would remain in all probability an ordinary English girl, save for her colour. And there were more and more English children in this country who were coloured.

If you become a foster mother

On a day-to-day basis you have the normal rights and responsibilities of a parent, but you have only very limited rights to make long-term decisions concerning the child.

You will look after the child on a temporary basis – which may mean for the whole of its non-adult life, or just for a few weeks while the natural mother is in hospital.

You must return the child to its parents whenever they want you to (unless the local council has taken over the parents' responsibilities by means of a care order). The only way you can postpone this is by making the child a ward of court (more about that on p. 208). The matter is then decided between you, the council, the natural parents and the court.

You must make sure that the local council knows that you are fostering a child. You must give them details of the name, sex, date and place of birth of the child and its natural parents.

What normally happens is that the council approaches a woman and asks her to be a foster mother. If you want to be a foster mother, you can approach the council. The social services department must inspect your home to see that it satisfies certain requirements. You will be paid a weekly sum – this varies considerably from one area to another.

Leaving home when you're under 18

If you're a girl it's a lot more difficult for you to leave home under 18 than it is for a boy. Your freedom of action is restricted by a set of rules which do not apply to boys of your age: they seem to be based on the assumption that if a boy has sex or leads a wild life, that's normal, but if a girl does the same she is set on the path to disgrace and ruin.

What could happen if you leave home?

It's not actually illegal for you to leave home, but you are still a 'minor', which means that you are meant to do what your parents say. So a great deal depends on your parents' attitude. If they don't object to your leaving and you manage to keep out of trouble, then you will probably be left alone. But if they do object and they ask the police to find you: or if you do something that brings you to the notice of the police or the social services department of your local council, and they decide you are in need of 'care and protection', then you may find yourself in court, even though you haven't broken the law. What may happen in court is explained below.

The law says you can be taken to court because you are in need of 'care' for a number of different reasons, for instance:

Your parents think you are beyond their control.

You are not going to school regularly (only if you're under 16).

The police or your parents think you are in 'moral danger'. In practice, this means having sexual intercourse or being likely to have it when you are under 16 (the age of consent); and even if you are 16 or 17 and legally entitled to have sex, you may be thought to be in 'moral danger' because you are sleeping around, going to clubs late at night, living in a mixed flat or commune, involved in prostitution or taking drugs, sleeping rough outside, or doing anything equally unconventional.

If you are taken to court, you can apply for legal aid to pay for a solicitor to represent you. This could be a great help. Get information about it from your Citizens' Advice Bureau or tell the court officials that you want legal aid. (Legal aid is explained on pp. 301-8.)

If the court decides that you are in need of 'care and control'

one of the following things could happen:

1. Your parents might have to promise the court to take care of you and exercise proper control over you.
2. The court may pass a supervision order, appointing a social worker to keep an eye on you for a certain period.
3. The court may pass a care order, placing you in the care of the local council (this cannot happen if you are 17 or over). It means that the social services department of the council takes over all responsibility for you and decides whether you should live at home, in a hostel or in a 'community home'. If a care order is passed when you are under 16 it will last until you are 18. If it is passed when you are 16 it will last until you are 19.

If you are placed in the care of the council, you can apply for the care order to be ended at any time: you can get legal aid for this, and the solicitor will tell you what to do. If the court agrees to end the care order, it will either let you go completely free, or substitute a supervision order. If the court refuses to end the order you can't apply again for another three months.

(More about care orders, from the parents' point of view, on pp. 211-12.)

If you have been sleeping with a man, he may be prosecuted

Again this is only likely to happen if your parents object to your leaving home or if you are in trouble with the police for some other reason. The reasons why the man may be taken to court are explained in the section on sex (p. 132).

How to avoid trouble when you leave home

You will be less likely to end up in court if you can give the appearance of leading a respectable life – sharing suitable accommodation with a girl friend, holding down a regular job, and mixing with people who look respectable in the eyes of the police and the court – and if you can somehow avoid your parents making a complaint to the police. Things will be a lot more difficult if you are under school-leaving age, as you probably won't have any income, and if you leave school to get a job, this may be a reason for taking you to court.

Once you are 18, you can live where you like.

Where to get help

Many of the bigger towns and cities now have youth advisory centres, which may be able to help you. Your local Citizens' Advice Bureau should know the address. There is also a growing number of 'alternative' help and information centres: the best way to finding the address of the one nearest you is to write or phone to BIT, 146 Great Western Road, London W11 (01 229 8219).

7. Housing

Married women: your right to the family home

FIRST OF ALL, MAKE SURE THAT THE HOME IS IN YOUR
NAME AS WELL AS YOUR HUSBAND'S

Whether you buy or rent your home, you should see that it is in
both your names, for reasons that we will go into below. If it isn't,
you can have it transferred to joint names. Your landlord (if you
rent) may object. but it is worth insisting. If you think of marriage
as an equal partnership, you should look upon this as your right,

not just as a safeguard against future hazards – even if you are not paying an equal amount towards it.

Should you and your husband ever split up, your right to stay in the home will be far more secure if it is in joint names. But you will, of course, be equally responsible for keeping up mortgage or rent payments if they fall into arrears.

Where the home is privately owned

YOU HAVE AN ABSOLUTE RIGHT TO STAY IN THE HOME,

whether it is in your name, his name, or joint names, until you actually get a divorce. If your husband tries to throw you out or forces you to leave, you can get a court order saying that he must let you stay. If you want to do this, get a solicitor and apply for legal aid, as explained on pp. 298–305.

YOUR HUSBAND HAS AN EQUAL RIGHT TO STAY IN THE HOME,

even if you are the sole owner. You would only be able to get him out if he were violent or molested you or your children and you applied for a court order (see p. 207). You would probably need medical evidence that your husband's continued presence would endanger the physical or mental health of you or your children (for instance, because he was committing incest). This procedure is unusual and is only used as a last resort.

IF THE HOME IS IN YOUR HUSBAND'S NAME,

he can sell it without your permission. However, there are certain steps you can take to prevent him from doing this. You can *register your right of occupation*, either with Her Majesty's Land Registry, or at the Land Charges Registry: your Citizens' Advice Bureau will be able to tell you how to do this, or else you can go straight to a solicitor. You can do this at any time while you are living in the home. If you have left the home you will need to make an application to the court first and should seek legal advice. It is wise to register your rights as a matter of course without waiting to see if your marriage runs into difficulties; and if your relationship with your husband becomes unstable you should do it immediately. Your husband will not know that you have done it, although it would be possible for him to find out if he made inquiries.

Once you have registered your right of occupation, your husband cannot sell the house without your consent, until you get a divorce and other arrangements are made by the court, as explained on p. 245. However, the house can still be sold by the mortgage company if mortgage payments are not kept up.

WHO OWNS WHAT DURING THE MARRIAGE?

Before 1882, a married woman had no right to own property: everything she had belonged to her husband. Since then, married women have been allowed to own property and, as the law stands now, husband and wife each have a right to own separate property.

Too often, this means that the husband, still the main bread-winner in most marriages, owns most of the family's property; while the wife, who stays at home to look after children or has a lower earning capacity if she does go out to work, owns little or nothing. However, it is becoming more common practice among young couples to buy their homes in joint names.

If you get divorced, you can then claim a share of the family property which is larger than you actually *own*, because it will be based on your needs, your contribution as a wife and mother and various other considerations. But the law does not recognize that you have a right to a share in the property while the marriage is still in existence, unless it is jointly owned. (But see p. 249 for how the law may be changed.) However, there is one exception . . .

Claiming a share of the family home and property during marriage

If the family home and property is in your husband's name you may be able to establish a share in it by applying to court for a calculation of your share, under Section 17 of the Married Women's Property Act. You can also use this section of the Act if the home and property is in both your names but your husband does not agree that you are entitled to your share. You will need a solicitor and you should apply for legal aid (read pp. 298–305).

When working out your share, the court first considers whose name the property is in. As a general rule, the home will belong to your husband if it is in his name, to you if it is in your name and to you both equally if it is in joint names. But this rule can be altered by the following considerations:

– How much money did you each put into the purchase of the house and the repaying of the mortgage?

– When you bought the home, did you intend it to be a joint purchase? In deciding this, the court considers whether the down-payment came from a bank or building society where the account was in joint names or in one name only; and whether you looked for the house together and made the decisions jointly, or whether one of you made all the arrangements.

The proceedings will take several months, possibly even a year. It helps if you can produce your own financial records, with details of your earnings, expenditure and income tax.

You can take these proceedings either during marriage or within three years of the divorce. But if you're getting divorced, it's probably better to claim a share of the property as part of the divorce proceedings, under the Matrimonial Causes Act, 1973; it's usually quicker and you are likely to get more. A solicitor will advise you on this.

IF YOU GET DIVORCED

You and your husband may come to a private agreement, before the divorce, over the division of your property: if so, you must tell the court what you have arranged. The court will not discuss the matter any further unless it thinks the arrangements are unfair to either one of you. If you and your husband can't agree, the matter will have to be decided by the court after the divorce, at a private hearing before the judge.

What share of property are you entitled to when you get divorced?

There are no straight answers to that question. The relevant divorce law is very complicated and a lot of it is new, so judges are constantly making decisions that alter its meaning. As a result, married women can never be sure exactly what their rights are in this respect. Judges still seem to believe that a woman's contribution to the home as wife and mother is less valuable than the man's contribution as breadwinner; and that men need

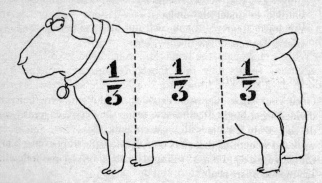

more to live on than women. In the light of recent court decisions, the most a woman can expect after divorce (when the family home is in her husband's name) is usually one third of the total value of the joint income and capital of herself and her husband.

When the court decides what your share in the property should be, it takes the same factors into consideration as it does when it decides how much maintenance should be paid; these are described in the section on maintenance (pp. 182–94). If you are awarded generous maintenance payments you can normally expect less in the way of property, and vice versa.

When the court is deciding what your share of the property should be, they consider two main factors:

1. First, how much you are automatically entitled to. This is determined by the calculations described above (p. 243): such things as whose name is the home in? how much have

each of you paid towards the down-payment and the mortgage? when you bought it, did you intend it to be a joint purchase? You will also be entitled to a share if you have made major improvements to the home which have added to its value – such as building, painting and decorating.

2. Then the court considers your contribution to the home in non-financial terms. This usually means your contribution as wife and mother. How highly this is valued depends on the judge. You may get more this way than you are automatically entitled to under the financial calculations described in the previous paragraph, but, as we said earlier, the most a judge is normally prepared to give a wife is one third.

What arrangements can be made to divide the property?

Once your share has been established, the property must be divided accordingly. If you and your husband cannot agree how to do this, your lawyers will negotiate with each other and try to work out something that suits both of you as far as possible. Then the judge makes the final ruling. Normally one of the following arrangements are made:

1. The property must be sold, so that you can divide the proceeds.
2. The home is transferred from your husband to you, in which case you own it outright. This is unusual, except where the husband is very rich, or where there is a large mortgage.
3. You are allowed to stay in the home with your children until they grow up: after that you may either sell it and divide the proceeds; buy your husband's share; or return the home to him.
4. Your husband pays you a sum of money for your share of the home, and you go to live elsewhere; or vice versa.

If the home is in joint names and the divorce settlement does not include any arrangement that one of you should have sole rights to live there, then you are both legally entitled to go on living there, unless you can prove to a court that your former husband's presence endangers the physical or mental health of you or your children.

If you have nowhere to live after the divorce

If the divorce settlement leaves you with nowhere to live, you can apply to the court for permission to stay on in the family home. If you have custody of the children it is quite likely that permission will be granted.

An example of a High Court decision on the division of property and maintenance after divorce

Mr and Mrs Harnett married in 1954. They had two daughters aged 11 and 8. In 1970 Mr Harnett divorced his wife because she had an affair with another man.

The family home was in Mr Harnett's name. It was worth £22,000, as its market value was £27,000 and there was a mortgage of £5,000. Mr Harnett had an income of £1,880 a year.

After the divorce, Mrs Harnett bought a house of her own. It cost £10,850 and she owed mortgages of £9,650. Mrs Harnett earned £2,124 a year.

Mrs Harnett claimed a share in the value of the family home. She said she had made a substantial contribution to it in money's worth, by her work as a wife and mother during sixteen years of marriage. She also asked the court to make an order that her husband should pay her a lump sum or transfer the house to her for her use.

Mr Harnett was only prepared to pay £4 a week maintenance for each of his daughters. He refused to pay anything to his wife because she had caused the breakdown of the marriage.

The judge decided that a wife's behaviour should only be taken into account in a decision like this if it was obvious that she had set out to destroy the marriage, while her husband was blameless. Mrs Harnett's behaviour had not been that outrageous and the judge decided to ignore it.

The judge ruled that the wife should be entitled to approximately one third of the joint income and capital of husband and wife (although if the husband were rich, the wife might get a smaller proportion); if the wife were awarded high maintenance payments, then she should get less in the way of a lump-sum payment and share of property; and vice versa.

The judge considered Mrs Harnett's claim that she had contributed to the home in money's worth by her work as a wife and mother: he decided that this did not *entitle* her to a share in the home, since housework did not improve the value of the property. He said that Mrs Harnett's contribution as a wife and mother should be taken into account only in deciding how much maintenance she should have.

The judge ordered Mr Harnett to pay £10 a week maintenance to Mrs Harnett for each of the daughters. He also ordered him to give Mrs Harnett £12,500 to pay off the mortgages on her house and provide her with £1,500 cash. He ordered Mrs Harnett to make a legal settlement so that her new house would provide a home for herself and her children until they were 25 or married; and its value would then be equally divided between herself and Mr Harnett.

The judge thought this arrangement was fair, as Mrs Harnett was receiving £1,500 cash plus a half-share in the value of her new house which amounted to £5,500. The total value of her award was £7,000, which was approximately one third of the value of the family home.

Where the home is rented

As a general rule, you have a right to live in the family home, even if the tenancy is in your husband's name, until you actually get divorced.

IF YOU GET DIVORCED

You can go on living in the home under one of the following circumstances.

1. The tenancy was in your name in the first place.
2. You come to an agreement with your husband to transfer the tenancy to you.
3. You are living in private accommodation and the divorce court orders the landlord to transfer the tenancy to your name. If you want this done, get your solicitor to ask the court to order the transfer as part of the divorce settlement. The court does not have to agree to this, but it probably will if you have custody of the children. Then the landlord is obliged to obey. If you leave it until after the divorce, you will have no way of getting the tenancy transferred, unless your husband has left the home and the landlord agrees to do it. Many landlords are reluctant to transfer tenancies: they would rather evict you. However, if you don't get the matter settled during the divorce proceedings and you are living in unfurnished accommodation, the best thing to do is pay the rent and say nothing. Once the landlord has accepted rent from you, he will find it extremely difficult to evict you. If you are living in furnished accommodation the landlord can ask you to leave anyway (see p. 256).
4. You are living in a council house or flat, and the council transfers the tenancy to you. The court cannot order this: the matter is left to the discretion of the council. If you have custody of the children, the council will probably agree to it, and if it doesn't, it has a duty to find you somewhere else to live. But you will have to *ask* the council to transfer the tenancy, and insist on your rights, otherwise you may find it does nothing to help you. Contact the housing department. You will find the address in the telephone directory under the name of your local council.

If the tenancy is in both your names and the divorce court does not order that it should be transferred to one of you, you and your husband both have a right to go on living there. You can only get him out by proving that his continued presence in the home endangers the physical or mental health of you or your children. Here is an example of one divorced woman who succeeded in getting her husband evicted.

W. and H. married in 1950 and had two sons: one was now married and living in his own home; the other, aged 14, was living with his parents in the house they jointly rented from the council.

In July W. obtained an undefended divorce on the grounds of her husband's unreasonable behaviour. She was given custody of her 14-year-old son.

H. continued to live in the house. In November 1972, W. applied through her solicitor to the county court to get a court order to make her husband leave the home. Her application was refused. She appealed to the Court of Appeal. This time she succeeded. But the court said that in cases where a joint tenancy gave husband and wife equal rights to occupy the house, a court order would only be granted where 'it was both imperative and inescapable'. The evidence which decided the court to grant an order in this case consisted of statements from a doctor that the husband's continuing presence in the home was likely to undermine the mental well-being of the wife and the son, and that unless something was done, both the wife and the son would become psychiatric invalids.

If your husband dies

Details about wills and inheritance are on p. 108.

How the law concerning family property may be changed

The Law Commission has been looking into ways of making the legal position regarding family property more favourable to the wife. It has produced a report which takes the view that marriage is a form of partnership to which both husband and wife contribute in ways that are different but equally important. It sums up what is considered to be the prevailing view:

We are no longer content with the system whereby a wife's rights in family assets depend on the whim of her husband or on the discretion of the judge. We demand definite property rights, not possible discretionary benefits.

It has put forward two main proposals to improve the situation:

1. *Co-ownership of the matrimonial home*. This means that unless husband and wife agree to the contrary, they will both be equal owners of the home, simply because they are married. It will not depend on who bought the home or in whose name. The Commission also made certain proposals dealing with ownership of household goods. It suggests that whoever occupies the home should have the right to use all the household goods.

2. *Community of matrimonial property*. This means that husband and wife are free to buy and sell their own things during the marriage, but when the marriage ends, whether by death or divorce, everything they bought during the marriage is shared equally between them. This would be done by calculating the total value of their property and compensating whoever has less, either in money or by transferring particular items. The Commission suggests that certain things might be excluded – such as property owned by the husband or wife before the marriage and property received as a gift or inheritance during marriage.

What are your rights if you have set up home with a man who is not your husband?

Where the home is privately owned

If the home is in both your names, you have equal rights to it. If you separate and cannot agree about who should go on living there or how the property should be divided, you can apply to a court to have the matter decided. You will need a solicitor for this and you should apply for legal aid (see pp. 298–305).

If the home is in your name alone, you have full rights to it and you can ask the man to leave at any time. If he refuses to leave, you can have him evicted.

If the home is in the man's name, you have no rights at all. If you separate, you will not be able to stay there, even if you have children. You will not be entitled to a share of the property, even after you have been together for a long period of time. But there is one exception. If you actually agreed to marry the man when the house was bought, and you paid a considerable amount towards it, you may be entitled to a share in it if you take proceedings under Section 17 of the Married Woman's Property Act. (If the property is in your name, the man might establish a share in it by the same means.) The proceedings are explained on pp. 242–3.

Here is an example.

A woman and man had been living together for a long period of time. They had a child but decided to have it adopted. The year after that they raised a mortgage and bought a plot of land together, which they registered in the man's name. They intended to build a house there so that they could live in it when the man got a divorce and was free to marry again. They both saw the architect and they built the house together. The woman did a lot of the manual work – more than most women would normally do.

They both had other work, and each week they put their earnings into a box. Later, the money was transferred to a Trustee Savings Bank in the woman's name so that the man's wife would not find out. For a time they both made mortgage repayments. But when the bungalow was finished, they separated. The man lived there for a while and made further mortgage repayments. He then sold it for nearly £2,000.

If the case had been decided twenty or thirty years ago, the woman would have had no claim to the property at all. In fact, the court treated the situation as if the man and woman were an engaged couple, and considered whether they had intended it to be a joint purchase. It decided that, although the woman had only contributed one twelfth of the money towards the home, she should in the circumstances be entitled to one third of the proceeds from the sale.

Where the home is rented

If the tenancy agreement is in your name, you can of course stay, and you can throw the man out any time;

otherwise
If the home is rented from the council: councils rarely give joint
tenancies to unmarried couples. If you've been living in a council
house or flat and the tenancy is in the man's name, you will
probably have to leave. But if you have children, insist that the
council provides you with somewhere else to live: it has a duty to
house homeless families.

Here are two cases from the records of the Catholic Housing
Aid Society to show what has happened to women in this situation:

A woman with five children had been living in a council flat with a
man who was not her husband. The tenancy was in his name. They
had been living together for a long time but over the past few years
their relationship had deteriorated. The man had made a number of
physical attacks on the woman. She had twice summonsed him for
assault. The second time he was given a short prison sentence. She
approached the CHAS when he came out of prison and attacked her
for a third time.

The council Housing Department firmly refused to transfer the
tenancy from the man's name to the woman's: they said they had no
proof that the relationship had ended and, besides, the man had always
been a reasonable tenant and had paid the rent regularly. (All this
time the man was not living in the council flat, but was keeping a
second home somewhere else.) The Housing Manager refused to
change his mind even after several meetings with the CHAS on the
woman's behalf.

At one stage, the man built up a small arrears of rent and the Manager said he would therefore evict him. Wheels were set in motion for
this, but they were stopped when the man appeared at the Housing
Department and paid the rent he was owing. Eventually, the woman
was offered a place to live by a voluntary housing association.

A woman with one child had been living in council accommodation
with a man who was not her husband: the tenancy was in his name.
Very soon after they had moved in, their relationship broke down and
the man, who now had a new girl-friend, asked the woman to leave
and became quite violent when she refused. He would not let her use
the kitchen or the bathroom and made her live in one small box-room.
She had to collect water from friends down the road and eat out.

After a long time, the council agreed to grant a joint tenancy and threatened to evict the man if he refused to let the woman share the house.

If the home is rented from a private landlord:

there is nothing much you can do unless the man agrees to leave. If he does, you may be able to persuade the landlord to transfer the tenancy to your name. However, landlords are reluctant to do this as a rule. They would rather evict. They are more likely to agree if the tenancy is in both your names. Whether you are living in furnished or unfurnished accommodation, the thing to do is to pay the rent and say nothing. Once the landlord has accepted rent from you he will find it more difficult to evict you, particularly if you are living in unfurnished accommodation, and you are prepared to fight for your rights.

If the man you are living with dies

and he has not left anything to you in a will, you will not inherit anything. There are special rules which determine how a person's property should be distributed when there isn't a will, but they take no account of a 'common-law' wife. It is therefore important that the man should make a will if he wants to leave anything to you.

Finding a place to live – rented accommodation

Renting from a private landlord

You don't have to be a woman to have problems finding a place to live these days. The only thing that helps is money – unless you happen to have a close friendship with an estate agent or a property owner.

But if you are single with young children or if you are pregnant, you will probably find it especially difficult. You can't very easily conceal young children, but if you are pregnant your best bet is to hide the fact from all prospective landlords. Once you get a place, the landlord may try to evict you if he finds out, but there are ways of putting this off for several months (or altogether, if your place is unfurnished), as you will see if you read the 'Quick guide for tenants' on pp. 255–60.

Renting from the council

You can find out about this from the housing department of your local council. Councils will normally only house families and old people. A single woman with children counts as a family. A pregnant woman does not, although some councils will house homeless women if they are far advanced in their pregnancy. If you are eligible for council housing and you put your name down on the list, they may eventually provide you with a permanent home. It could mean waiting years and years, but some councils have fewer housing problems than others, and it is always worth putting your name on the list. The address of the housing department is in the telephone directory under the name of the council.

If you are actually homeless and you have children (whether you are married or not) the council has a *duty* to house you. This usually means living in low-standard 'half-way' housing but they may eventually find you somewhere more permanent. Don't be too optimistic about it, though!

If you have to go into half-way housing, you may run the risk of having your children taken away from you and placed in the care of the council (more about this on p. 211). If the council will not house you and your children together, you may be better off trying to find private accommodation, or approaching an organization like Shelter or the Catholic Housing Aid Society (addresses below).

Further information

Catholic Housing Aid Society, 189a Old Brompton Road, London

SW5 (01 373 7276): helps homeless people find homes, with special department for single parents.
Shelter Housing Aid Centre, 189a Old Brompton Road, London SW5 (01 373 7276): helps to house homeless families.

Quick guide for tenants

(This guide only applies if you are renting from a private landlord.)

Once you've found a place to live, the next problem is making sure you can stay there. Some landlords will try anything to squeeze money out of you or force you to leave. It helps to know what your rights are and where to go for help.

Is your place furnished or unfurnished?

It's important to know this because if it's unfurnished you will be in a much stronger position if you have any trouble with your landlord – details below. The position may not in fact be clear.

For example, the place may be described as 'furnished' when you take it but if it contains only a few sticks of furniture, it may be 'unfurnished' as far as the law is concerned. If in doubt, get free legal advice from a solicitor, as explained on pp. 302–3.

Furnished accommodation

WHAT TO DO IF THE RENT IS TOO HIGH

Apply to your nearest Rent Tribunal for a rent reduction. The address is in the telephone directory. The procedure is explained on pp. 313–14. The tribunal will fix a 'fair rent', which may be lower than the rent you have been paying. Once the rent has been fixed, the landlord cannot legally increase it without making a new application to the Rent Tribunal. Some landlords do, though, so if you have just moved into a place, it is worth checking the register at the tribunal office to see whether you are paying more than the fixed rent. If you are, you may be able to recover the extra amount by going to the Rent Tribunal. But beware – if you go to the Rent Tribunal your landlord may serve you with a notice to quit.

WHAT TO DO IF THE LANDLORD WANTS TO GET YOU OUT *

If you have signed a lease for a fixed period and the time is up, the law cannot protect you. You will have to leave. If you have a weekly, monthly or yearly tenancy agreement, the landlord must give you a formal notice to quit which says that you must leave within a certain period of time. This is where you can use delaying tactics; contact your Rent Tribunal before the notice expires and make an application to have a fair rent fixed. This will give you the right to stay for up to another six months. If you want to stay even longer, you can make another application to the tribunal before the six-month period comes to an end, so long as on your first application you were allowed to stay for the full six-month period. If your landlord objects, it is then up to the tribunal to

*In March 1974, the Labour government announced that it would give tenants of furnished accommodation security of tenure.

decide whether you should be allowed to stay any longer. If your time runs out and the tribunal does not give you the right to stay any longer, the landlord must get a court order before he can evict you, and that usually takes a long time. At this stage you should get advice from a solicitor. The least you can do is get the court to stop the eviction order from taking effect for twenty-eight days. Hopefully, this will give you a chance to look for somewhere else to live.

Unfurnished accommodation

WHAT TO DO IF THE RENT IS TOO HIGH

Apply to the Rent Officer to have a 'fair rent' fixed. But beware: there is always a chance that the Rent Officer will put the rent up, not down. Before you appeal, check the rent register at your local Rent Office (address in the telephone directory): it will show you what is considered a reasonable rent for accommodation like yours. The landlord can always apply to the Rent Officer himself, proposing a higher rent. If he does, you have a chance to argue against his proposal.

If you appeal to the Rent Officer, he will come and see the place and then try to get you and your landlord to agree to a rent that you both think fair. If he fails, he will refer the question to the Rent Assessment Committee. The procedure is described in more detail on pp. 314–15. Once a 'fair rent' has been registered, the landlord cannot put the rent up for at least five years, unless he makes large improvements to the property. If you've just moved in, it's worth checking the register in the Rent Office to see whether a fair rent has already been fixed. If it has and the landlord is charging you more, you can probably recover the extra rent. The most effective way of doing this is by deducting it from future rent.

This does not apply if you are a council tenant, or a member of a housing association or trust; or if your place is classed as 'luxury accommodation'. (Check with the housing department of your local council to find out if this is so.)

WHAT TO DO IF THE LANDLORD WANTS YOU OUT

You have an almost unlimited right to stay. Your landlord cannot evict you without a court order. The court will only grant an order in a few very limited circumstances, such as non-payment of rent. There is one exception: if the landlord lived there before you did and, when you signed the tenancy agreement, he gave you written notice that he might want to return, and he later decides that he wants the place for himself or a member of his family, you will probably have to get out. In any case, don't be intimidated by the landlord, and if he takes you to court, make sure you have legal advice (p. 302).

It is also worth knowing . . .

'KEY MONEY' IS ILLEGAL

If your landlord made you pay a large sum of money just for the privilege of taking over the tenancy, he is in fact breaking the law. The same applies if he charged an unreasonable amount for 'fixtures and fittings'. If you have paid key money you may be able to get it back by suing the landlord. You will need a solicitor for this. If you report him to the housing department of your local council, they should prosecute him.

YOUR LANDLORD IS ALSO BREAKING THE LAW

if he tries to evict you without a court order, or harasses you (for instance, by changing the lock, cutting off power supplies or charging you for unnecessary repairs with the intention of making you leave). If he does, tell the housing department of your local council. They will write him a letter, which may have the desired effect, and they have a duty to prosecute if your landlord continues to break the law, but they are rarely prepared to do so. It may be worth going to a solicitor and taking the landlord to court yourself.

IF YOUR LANDLORD SUCCEEDS IN EVICTING YOU
WITHOUT A COURT ORDER

go straight to a solicitor (see p. 299 for how to do this). If you take
the matter straight to court you will get an order enabling you to
go back, but if you delay it may be more difficult.

TENANTS' ASSOCIATIONS

are one of the best means of fighting a difficult landlord. Get
together with other people who pay rent to the same landlord so
that you can support one another by collective action – for
instance by refusing to pay a rent increase, or by making a joint
demand for necessary repairs.

If you live in a council house or flat

You will not encounter the same landlord problems as private
tenants – although councils do put the rent up and do evict
tenants for non-payment of rent. As a general rule, you will be
allowed to stay as long as you pay the rent. If you can't afford to
pay the rent, read on . . .

How to get help with your rent and rates

If you can't afford to pay your rent or rates (whether you rent
from a private landlord or from the council) you can get financial
help in the following ways. But the most important thing is that
you must ask for it. No one is going to call round and offer it to you.

1. The council gives *rent rebates* to council tenants and *rent
   allowances* to other tenants. The amount you get will depend
   on your income and it is calculated on a very complicated
   basis. To give you an idea: if you are single with one dependent
   child, your total weekly income is £13·25, and your rent is £5
   a week, you will get a rent rebate or allowance of £3 a week.

You can find out more about it from the housing department or the treasurer's department of your local council.

2. The council will give you a *rate rebate* if your income falls below a certain level. This is organized in much the same way as rent allowances and rebates.

3. If you are claiming supplementary benefit, the Social Security will pay your rent and rates. But if they think the amount is unreasonably high they will only pay a portion of it.

Mortgages

Can single women get mortgages?

The short answer is yes – some women can. Building societies are getting rather more enlightened in their attitudes these days and few will admit to discriminating against women. We 'tested' twenty-five of the larger societies, masquerading as house hunters in the Reading area. Twenty-one claimed they would offer mortgages to single women on the same terms as they would to single men. The exceptions were the Burnley Building Society the Leicester Temperance and the Leicester Permanent, who said they might require a guarantor (male, no doubt) 'on occasions'. The Leicester Permanent said it wanted a guarantor for all women under 30. The Leeds and Holbeck Society said they would not consider women under any circumstances because of 'quota restrictions'. A pamphlet on *Hints for Home-buyers* from the Building Societies Association confesses: 'Problems can arise where young unmarried women are concerned'.

Decisions about who should get mortgages and on what terms are normally left to the discretion of local branch managers, so policy varies from one region to another. A woman who would easily get a mortgage in London might have more difficulty in the north of England. And although building societies protest that they don't refuse mortgages to women because of their sex, they might find several other good reasons for turning them down.

A *Money Which?* report on mortgages (December 1971) says:

All building societies in our survey claim that they treat single women in a steady job on the same basis as men. This seemed to be confirmed by the experiences of one of our investigators . . . However, they are likely to be particularly helpful if she is older – say, over 30 – and in a professional type of job like teaching or nursing.

Local authorities seem to treat single women in the same way as building societies.

Insurance companies are rather choosier. About 65 per cent claim to treat single women on the same basis as men, but 10 per cent will not consider them at all. The rest (about 25 per cent) will consider giving them a mortgage only in special circumstances – single women over 30 or 35 with, say, professional qualifications or high earnings.

The main problem for women is that mortgage companies are less likely to lend to women with low earnings than to men, and women almost invariably have the lower-paid jobs. Even when we have anti-discrimination legislation, it will probably still be legal for mortgage companies to discriminate against women.

What about married women?

How much mortgage companies are prepared to lend depends on the income of each person who wants to borrow. But where married couples are concerned, they are unwilling to take the wife's earnings very seriously. Generally they are prepared to take account of her earnings only if she is past child-bearing age or has a professional type of job to which she can easily return after having children. Even then they usually take only half her earnings into account.

So assuming you and your husband both earned £1,200 a year, the *maximum* mortgage you could normally expect to raise would be £5,400; that is, three times the total of all your husband's yearly income and half yours. However, *Money Which?* reports that a young couple who approached ten building societies and two London borough councils finally got the best terms from the Greater London Council, which was prepared to take almost all the wife's earnings into account. It is obviously worth shopping around to get the most favourable terms.

Our policy is only to take your husband's income into account, Mrs Thing

What sort of mortgages are available?

There are all sorts of different deals you can make to raise money for a house. Here are the main types of mortgage:

1. *Building society repayment mortgage.* This is the most common type of mortgage. You borrow a sum of money and pay it back over the years, with interest. The maximum time allowed is usually twenty-five years. In the end you spend about twice as much as you originally borrowed. The money you pay for interest is tax-free and you tend to pay this off first, so that the mortgage costs you less in the early years.

   Building societies normally lend up to 80 per cent of what they reckon to be the value of the house, but you can get more with a 'mortgage indemnity policy', and this means paying a bit extra. Some of the bigger societies will lend only to people who have been saving with them for at least a few months. Some give less favourable terms if you are buying a house that was built before the war; or if you are buying a flat or 'maisonette'.

The most you could expect to borrow would be three times your yearly income.

2. *Local council repayment mortgage.* This is the same as above, except that you get it from the local council in the area where your new house is. A few councils will lend to people living in their area, no matter where the house they are buying happens to be.

   Local councils are more likely than building societies to lend you money if you want to buy a flat or 'maisonette', or an older house. It is easier to get a 90 or 100 per cent mortgage from a council without having to pay for a 'mortgage indemnity policy'. *Money Which?* says: 'About one third of the local authorities in our sample would lend only £5,000 or less – the rest up to between £7,000 and £10,000.' Councils sometimes let young people pay money back over thirty or thirty-five years.

3. *Option mortgage, from a building society or local council.* This is the best for people who pay little or no tax: the Government subsidizes the loan and you pay less money each month at a lower interest rate. You don't really benefit from an option mortgage if you are paying enough tax to get full income tax relief. You can switch to an ordinary repayment mortgage later on if your income goes up.

4. *Endowment mortgage.* You buy a life insurance policy from an insurance company and get the loan either from the insurance company or from a building society. There are two varieties: with-profits and without-profits. If you have a with-profits endowment mortgage, you get a sum of money when you finish the payments. It costs more in monthly payments and it's only a good idea if you pay a higher rate of tax – say, if you earn over £5,000 a year. Without-profits endowment mortgages are less expensive than the with-profits variety and generally more expensive than mortgages from building societies or local councils. The main advantage of both varieties is that if a couple buys a house and the husband dies, the mortgage is paid off by the insurance policy, and the house belongs to the wife, without her making any more payments.

If you want to get a mortgage, it's important to shop around until you find the best deal. Don't be discouraged if you are turned down or offered unfavourable terms by a number of companies.

Useful things to read

Buying a House by L. E. Vickers, published by Penguin, 25p, gives a full description of almost everything a potential house buyer needs to know (although it lacks a feminist analysis!).

Money Which? (December 1971) gives a complete breakdown of all the facts and figures on mortgages. It may be available in your local library; otherwise write to the Consumers' Association, 14 Buckingham Street, London WC2 6DS.

The Legal Side of Buying a House, also from the Consumers' Association, is about just that, and is available, price £1·25, from some bookshops or from the CA headquarters.

Saving and Home Buying, price 20p, for a detailed breakdown of the costs of home buying and moving, from the Building Societies Association, 14 Park Street, London W1Y 4AL.

8. Women as Consumers

Whether we like it or not, it is a fact that in most households the women get lumbered with most of the shopping. So we have included this chapter which outlines your rights as a consumer. Most of what is said applies to men too.

Buying by 'HP'

When people talk about buying by 'HP', they may be referring to one of *four* different ways of paying for something by instalments: hire purchase, credit sale, conditional sale, or personal loan from a finance company. They all differ slightly in the way they are defined by law and the protection they offer to the buyer, but they all have certain things in common:

1. You pay for the goods gradually, after you have taken possession of them.
2. You normally have to put down a deposit first.
3. You usually end up paying more than you would if you had paid it all at once.
4. If you can't keep up payments, you may have to return the goods, or you may be taken to court.

Getting a man's signature

When you buy something by HP you have to sign an agreement. Most companies that organize HP payments seem to think that women – particularly married women – are a bad risk. So if you are married, they will probably ask you to provide your husband's signature. If you are single, they may ask you to provide the signature of a male guarantor (a guarantor is someone who takes responsibility for paying your debts in full if you don't pay them). If you think this is inconvenient, unnecessary, or downright insulting, it is worth making a fuss about it and explaining that you are perfectly capable of taking responsibility for the agreement on your own. If you are earning a steady wage, tell them so. They may back down – particularly if you convince them that you have an independent income. If they don't, you can try to

find somewhere else to buy what you want, or you can give up and provide the necessary signature. Unfortunately, there is nothing in law to prevent companies from discriminating against women like this. They are free to refuse credit whenever they like.

Money Which? recently asked its readers if they had any experience of women being refused credit without a male guarantor. Here are excerpts from two typical replies:

I have experienced a certain amount of annoyance and frustration when asking for 'terms' for some articles, usually in the furniture and electrical shops who will not allow me to sign an agreement as I am a woman and therefore not considered to be credit-worthy ... Some shops will allow me to sign such an agreement if I will return to the shop with my husband to sign also. I point out that I am a woman earning over £1,500 p.a. but most shops are not interested ... I have asked friends who have experienced the same impasse, the separated woman and divorcee has to ask a male to back them up too. This backing, although really only a formality, is a bit of an imposition and does apparently tie the male to act as guarantor should the lady default.

At the beginning of August I saw a coat I liked in a Birmingham store ... As I was not carrying my cheque-book the very helpful assistant suggested I had a credit sale, it wouldn't cost any more during their August-only offer and I had sufficient cash with me for the initial payment. Being the naïve type (my husband and I have never previously had any hire-purchase or credit-sale agreement) I expected to sign my name and take the coat home, having duly presented my Barclaycard and Lloyds Bank card as guarantee of credit-worthiness. At the office I was asked to fill in a form which included the name of a friend (for reference only) and given another form to take for my husband to sign. As I was buying the coat by Bankers Order from my own earnings I could see no reason, on thinking it over, why he should have to do this ...

The different ways of paying by instalment

1. *Hire Purchase:* if you buy something under a hire purchase agreement, you do not actually *own* it until you have paid the last instalment. This puts the company you have bought it from in a particularly powerful position, but you are quite well protected under the Hire Purchase Act, if the sum involved is less than £2,000. (Details below.)
2. *Conditional Sale:* this is almost exactly the same as a hire purchase agreement and gives you the same protection under the Hire Purchase Act. The company owns the goods until you have fulfilled certain conditions, which normally include paying most or all of the instalments.

3. *Credit Sale:* this way, the goods become yours as soon as you sign the agreement. You have limited protection under the Hire Purchase Act, if the sum involved is between £30 and £2,000.
4. *Personal Loan from a Finance Company:* this method is becoming more and more common. Two separate deals are involved: you buy from the seller and borrow from the finance company. It may seem to be the same as a hire purchase deal, but it isn't. You are not protected under the Hire Purchase Act.
5. *Trading Checks.* You get a 'trading check' (which is like a money voucher and issued by a finance company), either from the shop where you want to buy, or directly from the finance company. You use the check to buy the goods and then pay for the check by instalments. You can only use it in shops which have an arrangement to use trading checks. You are not protected by the Hire Purchase Act.

Read any agreement very carefully,

especially the small print. If you don't understand it, don't sign. Get help first from your Citizens' Advice Bureau.

Can you cancel an agreement once you have signed it?

You can if it is a hire purchase, conditional sale or credit sale agreement, within the limits of the Hire Purchase Act; and if you signed the agreement at home. If so, you should be sent a copy of the agreement within seven days of signing it and within the following three days you can notify the seller that you want to cancel. You should return the goods and refuse delivery of any that haven't yet arrived. If you have paid a deposit, you should get it back in full.

What if you can't keep up the payments?

UNDER A HIRE PURCHASE OR CONDITIONAL SALE AGREEMENT:

If you have paid less than one third of the total price, the company which owns the goods can come and take them away. If you have paid more than one third and the total sum is less than £2,000, the goods can't be taken away unless *you* formally end the agreement and allow them to be taken away; or the company gets a court order.

If you end the agreement, the company will take the goods away and you will still have to pay any back instalments you have missed. If the amount you have paid does not add up to one half of the total price, you have to make up that difference as well. If the company gets a court order you can reclaim all the money you have paid so far. So it may be better to wait and let them take you to court – the judge may settle the matter in a way that is more favourable to you. Get a solicitor and apply for legal aid (pp. 298–305).

UNDER ANY OTHER CREDIT AGREEMENT:

You own the goods, so nobody can take them away. You should come to an arrangement with the company to sell them if you want to raise money to pay off the debt. Otherwise, the company you owe the money to will have to take you to court if it wants to recover the debt.

General shopping

Making a down-payment

It is important to find out whether you are making a part-payment or a deposit. If you make a *part-payment*, this is part of the agreed price and you can claim some or all of it back if the sale falls through. If you make a *deposit* this is a separate agreement which is supposed to reassure the seller that you are serious about wanting to buy. Unless you agree in the first place that it is in part-payment and recoverable, you may not be able to claim it back if the sale falls through.

If goods are wrongly described

The seller is breaking the law. If you buy something that turns out to be different from its description (on the packet or in the brochure, for instance) you can demand your money back. If you don't get it, consult your Citizens' Advice Bureau or go to a solicitor (pp. 298–301).

This applies to price tags too. It is illegal to indicate that goods are cheaper than they actually are. If a shopkeeper says that goods are cut-price, they must have been sold at the higher price for twenty-eight consecutive days during the past six months. But there's nothing to stop him claiming that his goods are cheaper than his competitors', or that they are a special cheap line.

Safety of goods

Some goods have to meet certain standards of safety laid down by law. These are: paraffin heaters, inflammable nightdress material, children's cots, electric blankets and toys. The amount of celluloid is restricted in all toys except ping-pong balls, and the amount of lead and arsenic is restricted in paint used for toys. If you buy anything which you find is dangerous, complain to the Public Health Inspector or the weights and measures department of your local authority.

Faulty goods

If you buy something which is faulty, you can usually claim compensation from the person who sold it to you. A new law was passed in 1973 called the Supply of Goods Act, which gives the buyer considerable protection. It says that anything which is sold must be of a 'merchantable' quality, and goes on to define the word as follows: 'An article sold must be as fit for the purpose for which articles of that kind are commonly bought, as is reasonable to expect, having regard to the description applied to it, and the price paid (if this is relevant) and any other factors.' So if you buy something which does not come up to these standards, you can claim compensation. An article in *The Times* (6 September 1973) explains:

It is worth looking at some of the many cases where the courts have decided that an article has not been of merchantable quality:

A pair of pants containing an excess of sulphite; a bun with a stone in it instead of a raisin; pet food which contains a chemical toxic only to mink, although not to other animals; a water bottle which bursts; a catapult which breaks and injures a child. All these items have been declared 'not merchantable'.

A multiplicity of minor faults can also entitle the buyer to send the article back: a car or washing machine which keeps going wrong, not from any major defect, but suffering from a series of minor troubles, one after the other . . .

The acid test is, 'would the average person have bought the article if he had known its true condition?'

You will probably not be able to claim compensation if:

1. The seller specifically points out a particular defect to you.
2. You examined the article before buying it.
3. You bought something at an auction (unless the article does not fit the description in the sales catalogue).
4. You bought something, such as a second-hand car, from a private person in answer to a newspaper advertisement. Here you can only claim compensation if it does not fit the description which the seller gives you.

THE SELLER CAN COMPENSATE YOU IN ONE OF SEVERAL WAYS:

1. By repairing the article so that the fault is corrected and its value, appearance and usefulness are not affected.

2. By replacing the article with a similar one which isn't faulty.
3. By replacing it with a different article. You don't have to accept this if you don't want to.
4. By letting you keep it and refunding part of the purchase price, depending on how serious the fault is. If he doesn't offer you enough, you don't have to accept this as compensation.
5. By giving you your money back.
6. By giving you a credit note. If you are given a credit note, read it carefully. It may not be valid beyond a certain date. If there is no date on it, it is valid for six years. You can refuse a credit note if you are returning faulty goods, but not if you have simply changed your mind and there is nothing wrong with them.

IF YOU ARE NOT SATISFIED

with the compensation offered to you, you may be able to take the seller to court (or the manufacturer, if he is responsible under a guarantee). If you have a claim for less than £75, you can have it settled by the Registrar of the county court without using a solicitor. It will cost you nothing except the price of issuing a summons, which is £4. This is a new procedure, introduced in 1973 and designed to help people with small claims. Get details about it from your Citizens' Advice Bureau. If your claim is for more than £75, you will need a solicitor if you want to take the matter to court. This can be very expensive. Before you embark on it, make sure you get advice from a solicitor under the 'green form procedure' described on page 302, or from your Citizens' Advice Bureau.

If you buy something which has a manufacturer's guarantee

Read the wording carefully. You may have to sign it and send it back before it has any effect or it may apply immediately. If you don't accept a manufacturer's guarantee, you can still claim compensation for faulty goods as described in the previous section.

If you take something to be repaired and don't collect it

If you take something to be repaired, serviced or cleaned and you don't collect it, the person you left it with can eventually dispose of it, *if*:

1. He has a sign prominently displayed in his shop which says that goods are accepted for treatment (that is, cleaning or repair, etc.) under the terms of the Disposal of Uncollected Goods Act.
2. He tells you that the article is ready for collection, and how much it will cost.
3. He tells you that it will be sold if you don't pay within twelve months.
4. He sends you a registered letter saying that the article is to be sold, fourteen days before he plans to sell it.

If he tells you the lowest price he is prepared to accept, he can then sell to anyone. If not, he must sell it by public auction. When he has deducted his charges, you can claim the rest of the proceeds.

If you are sent goods you haven't ordered and you don't want

The person who sent them has six months to collect them: if he doesn't, they automatically become yours. Alternatively, you can write (any time within five months after they arrive) saying that you didn't order them and giving your name and an address where they can be collected: if he doesn't collect them within thirty days of receiving your letter, they become yours. (This is laid down in the Unsolicited Goods Act, 1971.)

Cutting off the gas or electricity

THE GAS BOARD

can cut off your supply if you haven't paid your bill within twenty-eight days, but it must give you written notice seven days beforehand and twenty-four hours' notice if a Gas Board official has to come into your home to remove pipes.

THE ELECTRICITY BOARD

must give you twenty-one days' notice, then after a further seven days, it must send you written notice saying that if you don't pay your bill the supply will be cut off. Unless it has to force entry into your home, it need not give twenty-four hours' notice before an official comes to disconnect the supply.

IF YOU CAN'T AFFORD TO PAY YOUR BILL

and you are threatened with having the supply cut off, go to your local Social Security office and explain what has happened. They may be able to pay the bill for you (p. 113).

IF THE WORST COMES TO THE WORST

an official will call at your home to cut off the supply. At this point a convincing sob-story can stay execution. Or you can pretend to be out. A social worker from the social services department of the council may intervene on your behalf if there are children in the house. If the official can't get in, he will have to get a warrant from a magistrates' court. In order to get a warrant he will have to satisfy the magistrate that you have been given twenty-four hours' notice and that all the preliminary proceedings have been carried out as the law requires; and give information under oath explaining why the warrant is necessary. But in the case of an emergency, the Gas or Electricity Board can get an entry warrant simply by convincing the magistrate that life or property is at risk. Once the supply is cut off, you will have to pay to get it reconnected.

IF YOUR HOME IS ENTERED BY FORCE,

the Gas or Electricity Board must repair any damage they do, or pay you compensation. If they force entry while you are away, they should leave your home as securely locked as it was when they arrived.

9. Women and Immigration

The immigration laws are extremely complicated and open to widely different interpretations. They discriminate against men and women alike. We are not attempting here to give a full account of the law, but to give a few basic guidelines and draw attention to the aspects that have particular significance for women.

The Home Office appears to be unaware that women immigrants exist except as wives and dependants – as a random quotation from the 1973 Immigration Rules will illustrate:

> Where the passenger is a citizen of the United Kingdom and Colonies, holding a United Kingdom passport, and presents a special voucher issued to him by a British Government representative overseas ... he is to be admitted for settlement, as are his dependants if they have obtained entry certificates for that purpose ...

But despite the impression given by the Home Office, women should be allowed to enter Britain independently, under the same conditions as men.

Conditions for entering Britain

Briefly, the following rules apply. You can enter the country without restrictions if you are a 'patrial'. This category includes citizens of the UK and Colonies who were born, adopted, registered or naturalized in Britain, or have a grandparent who was born here. If you are a Commonwealth citizen with one grandparent born here, you are not a patrial, but you will be treated as one until the Home Secretary changes his mind: as this rule has only recently been introduced, he is unlikely to do so for a while.

All other people are subject to immigration control. There are three main categories and each is treated in a slightly different way:

1. Commonwealth citizens.
2. Citizens of the Common Market.
3. Other non-Commonwealth citizens.

Citizens of the Common Market are virtually free to come and go as they please. But the rest are considerably restricted – black people most of all. They cannot enter without a special entry voucher, visa or work permit, and these are often very hard to come by.

Here are a few general points worth noting:

1. If you are uncertain about your right to enter or settle in Britain, don't automatically believe what the Home Office tells you. They may not have considered all the facts that could be used to construct a case in your favour. The best thing to do is to contact one of the organizations that specialize in helping immigrants. These are the Joint Council for the Welfare of Immigrants, the UK Immigrants Advisory Service, and the National Council for Civil Liberties (addresses on p. 283).
2. If you think you may have difficulty getting into the country, always try to arrange for friends to meet you at the port or airport.
3. If you are entering as a student, the immigration authorities will not automatically let you in because you have been accepted for a full-time course of study (despite what the rules say). They may also want proof of your ability to study the course. So be prepared for that and bring with you whatever documentary evidence you have.
4. If you get a work permit to do one sort of job, it is very difficult to change to another. It is also difficult to bargain for more pay, as you may lose your job, and if you lose your job you will probably have to leave the country. That is why immigrant labour is so often exploited.

5. If you do not have a right to stay here permanently, don't leave the country without first checking that you will be able to come back. It is best to take with you all the documents you had when you came in before: for instance, if you came in as a 'dependent wife', you might need to show copies of your marriage certificate and your husband's work permit. If your permission to stay is about to expire, apply for an extension before you leave the country and ask for a short extension while the Home Office considers your application.

6. Employers don't normally check whether their employees have work permits. Problems arise only when the employees tell them that they don't have permits and they then feel obliged to abide by the rules (that is, by refusing work or by notifying the Home Office).

Rules which affect women who are subject to immigration control

ENTERING BRITAIN WITH YOUR HUSBAND

If your husband gets permission to enter Britain (to work, study or settle here) you can enter with him as his dependant – although he may first have to prove that he is able to support you. You will be allowed to work under the same conditions as he is. If his work permit runs out, you will have to stop working. Your children under 18 can enter as well.

If you have been living with a man 'in permanent association', but are not married to him, you can come to Britain with him if the immigration authorities decide that your 'permanent association' with him is accepted as the equivalent of marriage in the country you come from. They will certainly not let you in on this basis if you come from the 'white Commonwealth' or from any country, such as India, where marriage is the norm.

IF YOUR HUSBAND COMES TO BRITAIN FIRST AND YOU PLAN TO JOIN HIM

There may be a very long delay before you are given an entry certificate or visa – up to nine months or a year. Early in 1973, Asian women wanting to join their husbands in Britain were being told they would have to wait until January 1974 before their applications could be 'processed'. So try to enter with him if possible.

CAN A WOMAN IMMIGRANT BRING HER HUSBAND WITH HER?

The Immigration Rules make no mention of the possibility. It is highly unlikely that your husband would be allowed to come to Britain with you unless he had obtained permission to enter in his own right. According to the Home Office, a husband would not be allowed in as his wife's dependant except in 'exceptional circumstances' and it is very unusual for permission to be given.

CAN A WOMAN IMMIGRANT BRING HER CHILDREN WITH HER?

You can bring your children with you, or send for them to join you, under the following circumstances:

1. You and the father of the child *both* have permission to settle in Britain. (This condition applies even if the child is illegitimate, despite the fact that in all other aspects of British law, a mother has sole rights over her illegitimate child.)
   or

2. You can prove to the immigration authorities that you have had *sole responsibility* for the child. If your child has been living with a grandparent, or has maintained some contact with the father, you will find it extremely difficult to prove that you have had sole responsibility, even if you have been supporting the child financially. The authorities are not prepared to waive the rule unless a child is 'desperately unhappy and

finds life intolerable in his own country'. Ironically, the result is that a child who is actually disturbed stands a better chance of being admitted than a child who is well-adjusted.

If you are not allowed to bring your child into the country because the immigration authorities do not accept that you have sole responsibility for the child, you may be able to overcome this problem by getting a court in your country of origin to award you custody of the child. If you want to do this you will need a solicitor in your country of origin, and the legal proceedings may take as long as a year, but it may be the only way of solving the problem. If you are awarded custody, this should be proof for the immigration authorities that you have 'sole responsibility' for the child.

These regulations apply to children under 18. Generally, children over 18 must qualify for admission in their own right. However, an unmarried and fully dependent son under 21, or an unmarried daughter under 21 who formed part of the family unit overseas, may be admitted if the whole family are admitted for settlement.

GETTING MARRIED

A woman who marries a British citizen has a right to settle in Britain. This is one of the easiest ways for a woman to get permission to stay here permanently, and a number of 'marriages of convenience' take place for that purpose. Once you get married you can apply for registration or naturalization as a UK citizen. If you get divorced later you still have a right to stay.

If a woman who is a British citizen marries a non-British citizen, she cannot extend her right to stay in Britain to her husband. If he does not have permission to stay in his own right (for instance by getting a work permit or an entry voucher) she will either have to stay in Britain without him or leave the country in order to remain with him.

In these circumstances you can only claim an exemption if you can prove to the immigration authorities that you and your husband would suffer great hardship if forced to leave. The hardship must be very great indeed, as illustrated by two cases reported in the *Guardian* (21 March 1973):

Take the case of a couple called Dumont – an English woman married to a Canadian. When they first applied for permission to stay, the adjudicator stated: 'The evidence, presented with great honesty, paints a picture of a serious, introverted family grouping, self-contained and devoted, unadaptable, far more likely to wilt than to respond vigorously to the challenge presented by family separation and life in a strange country. In my opinion, serious hardship and harm would be likely to result to the family.' But the case went to the Immigration Appeals Tribunal, where it was ruled that this did *not* amount to sufficient hardship to prevent their being expelled from the UK.

In another case, an adjudicator ruled that there was no hardship involved in sending a British woman to Cyprus to live with her Turkish husband, even though it meant returning to her mother-in-law who refused to acknowledge her because she was not a Moslem; living in the Turkish enclave surrounded by UN troops; and risking her husband's arrest by the Greek and Turkish authorities, because he had been a guerilla fighter who deserted from the Turkish forces.

IF YOU ARE ENGAGED TO BE MARRIED

As a woman, you will be allowed to enter Britain to marry your fiancé, if you can satisfy the immigration authorities that you will get married within a reasonable time. You will normally be admitted for up to three months. Once you get married you can apply to the Home Office for a right to permanent residence (or, if your husband only has a temporary right to stay, for permission to stay as long as he does). If you don't get married within three months, you can apply for permission to stay longer, but you will have to give a good reason why the marriage has been delayed and provide evidence that it will take place at an early date.

If a man comes to Britain to marry a woman he is engaged to, he will normally be allowed to stay for up to three months, on the condition that he doesn't work. He will have to show the immigration authorities proof that his marriage will take place within a reasonable time and that he will leave with his wife shortly afterwards.

DEPORTATION

If you are married and your husband is deported, you are likely to be deported with him, unless you have permission to stay in your own right (for instance, as the holder of a work permit); or unless you can prove that you have been living apart from your husband and you are not dependent on him.

If you are deported, your husband will probably be allowed to stay.

'AU PAIR' GIRLS

The Home Office makes special provision for 'au pair' girls to enter Britain – doubtless to keep middle-class households comfortably equipped with cheap domestic labour. According to the Immigration Rules, '"Au pair" is an arrangement under which a girl of 17 or over may come to the United Kingdom to learn the English language and to live for a time as a member of a resident English-speaking family.' No mention of 'au pair' boys. The arrangement can include part-time domestic work (although in practice it often amounts to full-time drudgery). A full-time domestic job officially requires a work permit. You can stay twelve months as an 'au pair' girl, and this can be extended for one more year, but no longer. If you come to Britain as an 'au pair', you cannot change to any other form of employment.

How to appeal

If you do not agree with any decision taken by the immigration authorities, you may be able to appeal – first to an adjudicator and, in certain cases, to the Immigration Appeals Tribunal. You will need help with your appeal, but legal aid is not available and few solicitors know much about immigration law. It would be best to contact one of the following organizations, which specialize in helping people with immigration appeals.

Further information

Joint Council for the Welfare of Immigrants (JCWI), 233 Pentonville Road, London N1 (01 278 6727): an independent organization, giving advice and legal help to immigrants.

UK Immigrants Advisory Service (UKIAS), St George's Churchyard, Bloomsbury Way, London WC1 (01 405 3225): for advice and help with immigration problems and appeals. Set up and grant-aided by the Government, but claims to be independent.

The National Council for Civil Liberties (NCCL), 186 Kings Cross Road, London WC1 (01 278 4575), may also be able to help in limited circumstances.

Copies of the 1973 Immigration Rules are available from HMSO bookshops, price 13½p each:
No. 79: *Commonwealth Citizens, Control on Entry*
No. 80: *Commonwealth Citizens, Control after Entry*

No. 81: *EEC and other Non-Commonwealth Nationals, Control on Entry*

No. 82: *EEC and other Non-Commonwealth Nationals, Control after Entry*

10. Women and Prison

In 1971 there were, on average, 1,035 women in prison and 38,673 men. That is, one woman for every thirty-seven men. So we have assumed that there are a lot more women with husbands and other male relatives in prison than there are women prisoners, and have dealt with the subjects in that order.

Prisoners' wives

(This section also applies if you are the 'common-law' wife of a prisoner: you are normally regarded as a 'common-law' wife if you have been living with a man for more than two years as though you were married, without actually going through the ceremony. Much of the information should be useful to anyone who has a close friend or relative in prison.)

Perhaps the most useful thing to know in the first place is where you can get information, help and advice

1. *Your local probation service* should be able to help you make sense of all the official rules and regulations that surround prisons, such as how to arrange visits. It may be a useful source of advice if you run into financial difficulties and other practical problems. Most probation services are now expanding the work they do with prisoners' families and run a variety of schemes, such as co-operative buying of basic groceries, coffee-mornings and other meetings for unsupported wives (not just prisoners' wives), and transport for taking families to out-of-the-way prisons. You will find the address and phone

number of the probation service in the telephone directory.

2. *The welfare officers at the prison* will be able to tell you how the Prison Rules are put into practice in that particular prison (this varies very much from one prison to another); to help you with your visits; and to deal with any problems or queries you may have in connection with the prison. They can also be a source of more general help and information. You can write to a welfare officer at the prison address, or arrange for a meeting when you come to visit your husband.

3. *The social services department* of your local authority may be a useful source of help if you have difficulties connected with your home or your family and other social problems. Its address and phone number are in the telephone directory in the heading of your local authority.

4. *Your local Social Security office* is the place to go if you need money. You won't get much, but it may keep you just above the breadline. If you ask at your local Post Office, they will give you the address. More is said about Social Security on pp. 113–21.

5. *Citizens' Advice Bureaux* are a good source of information and advice on most practical problems. If you have to go to court (for instance if you have trouble with your landlord, or if you want to start divorce proceedings), your Citizens' Advice Bureau will help you get in touch with a solicitor and apply for legal aid. You will find the address of your nearest CAB in the telephone directory.

6. *NACRO* (*National Association for the Care and Resettlement of Offenders*) is a registered charity which gives help to prisoners and their families both before and after release from prison. It may sometimes be able to help where government departments cannot, although it often refers people to probation officers.

Is your husband on remand or has he been given a prison sentence?

If your husband has not yet been given a prison sentence by the court, then he is in prison 'on remand'. This means that he has certain privileges. You can write to him and visit him more often. The rules applying to prisoners on remand are described on p. 297.

The rest of this section applies mainly to wives of men who are serving prison sentences.

Visits

HOW OFTEN ARE VISITS ALLOWED?

In theory, a prisoner is allowed one visit every four weeks. Before you can make a visit you must get a Visiting Order from the prison governor. If you don't know how to get one, your husband should know how to arrange it; otherwise ask your local probation officer or write or phone to the governor at the prison.

Three individuals can be named on each Visiting Order. If a prisoner's wife or common-law wife is named, the order covers any children of the marriage.

In practice, some prisons allow visits every two or three weeks. On rare occasions, prison welfare officers can arrange special visits, but this depends very much on the whim of the prison governor.

Until recently, prisoners' wives were allowed to make extra visits if they were helping their husbands with appeals. But in December 1972 the Home Office introduced new rules which put an end to this, by giving unlimited access to legal advisers helping prisoners with appeals to any court, but excluding anyone who is not a qualified legal adviser.

Mrs Margaret Tuttle, of Muswell Hill, London, is a typical case.

Her husband is in Gartree, near Leicester, serving an 18-year sentence for armed robbery, malicious wounding and carrying an offensive weapon. He is appealing against his sentence and Mrs Tuttle is also trying to get together new evidence which would allow him a new trial . . . Until the new Home Office rules were introduced last month, Mrs Tuttle used to visit her husband twice a month. 'One visit we reserved for seeing each other, for talking about my problems with the house and social security, for example, and for Jimmy, my husband, to see our 22-month-old son . . . The second we used to talk about his appeal. It is 100 miles from London to his prison. No lawyer has the time to make that trip many times. I used to see the lawyer and act as a go-between. Prisoners do not like writing to their solicitors because all their letters are read. What people do not seem to realise is that they don't just lock prisoners away – they "lock away" prisoners' families as well.' [From the *Guardian*, 23 January 1973]

WHAT ARE THE CONDITIONS?

A visit is supposed to last for twenty minutes and to take place in 'closed conditions' – which is rather like sitting on opposite sides of a Post Office counter with a glass window between you and your husband and inadequate partitions to separate you from a long row of other visitors.

In practice, conditions vary enormously. In open prisons, visits may take place in cafeteria-like rooms and last up to two and a half hours. In some other prisons, visits last for thirty minutes in cramped conditions with no privacy. In long-stay prisons, governors tend to be fairly liberal about the way visits are conducted.

Most prisons allow you to hold hands, but nothing more. Some do not even allow that. Nothing is supposed to change hands between you and your husband, although some prisons let visitors give inmates cigarettes and sweets. It is worth finding out about this from the prison welfare officer before you make your first visit. Prisoners are searched before and after visits to make sure that they have not been given anything they should not have.

Visits are rarely in private and the Prison Rules say that they must take place within the sight, but not necessarily in the hearing, of a prison officer. In practice, there are always officers on duty but they tend to be too busy to pay attention to any particular visit. Nevertheless, wives tend to feel that they are very exposed during their visits. It is worth asking the welfare officer which visiting days are likely to be the quietest, as this can make an enormous difference.

WHAT ARE THE FACILITIES FOR WIVES AND CHILDREN?

Again, this varies a great deal from one prison to another. Some prisons provide toys and voluntary helpers to run play groups for children on visits; and some have special facilities for mothers with babies. Others have very poor facilities. One of the biggest problems is that families often have to wait a long time before they can go in to see the prisoner: this can be a bit harrowing, so take plenty of toys if you have children with you. Many prisons are a long way from public transport routes, but welfare officers can often help with local transport.

IF YOU CAN'T AFFORD TO MAKE THE VISIT

If you are already receiving supplementary benefit and you are the wife or common-law wife of a prisoner, or the closest relative of a prisoner who is not married, you can get fares for monthly visits paid by the Social Security office. If you have any children by the prisoner their fares will be paid too. Unfortunately the Social Security will not pay visiting fares for you or your children if you are the fiancée or close friend of a prisoner and you have been living with him for less than two years. If the prison allows fortnightly or three-weekly visits, Social Security will only pay your fares once a month.

The Prisoners' Wives Service, which operates in the London area, is campaigning for each visiting order to be covered by a travel warrant ... 'We visit over 350 new families each year and of these about 100 are receiving invitations for extra visits. Our families are lucky as there are charities in the London area that will help with the extra fare money. This can be quite substantial. A return ticket to Hull, for example, can cost about £8. But we are really concerned about all the other wives throughout the country who are not getting help. We feel that to issue a visiting order without the funds to use it is a form of cruelty and means that the rich are in a privileged position and the poor suffer ... We have approached the Home Office, but they have said that the money is not available to cover these extra visits.' [From *Social Services*, 3 March 1973]

Fares are usually paid in the form of a railway warrant and you will not be given any other money unless the prison is too far for you to get there and back within one day. It is up to the Social Security officials to decide what is a day's journey: it could mean setting off at 7.00 a.m. and returning at 11.00 p.m. It might be worth insisting on making your visit on a Sunday, as there are fewer trains and you may not be able to get there and back on the same day.

If you have to stay overnight, the Social Security will pay for bed and breakfast but not for anything else. Arrangements have to be made well in advance, and if you write to the prison welfare department, it will usually help you find a hotel or boarding house.

Letters

IN THEORY, A PRISONER MAY WRITE ONE LETTER
A WEEK

to anyone he chooses, and it is posted by second-class mail at public expense. In practice, most prisons allow inmates who are serving sentences of more than a couple of months to pay for two extra letters a week from their earnings. Letters to official sources, such as probation officers and solicitors, are supposed to be issued free in addition to the prisoner's quota of letters to his friends and family. But this rule is not always observed, and some prisons are more lenient about it than others.

Letters written by prisoners have to be a regulation size and written on prison paper. They are posted in plain envelopes which do not give any indication of where they come from. Strictly speaking, air-mail letters should not be identifiable as letters from prison but in fact they sometimes are. In exceptional circumstances, the prison authorities can allow the prisoner to write on plain paper, for instance, if the letter is going to a child under 16.

IN THEORY, PRISONERS ARE ALLOWED TO RECEIVE ONE LETTER A WEEK,

which is restricted in length. Again, in practice they may be allowed to receive more, and restrictions on length are not as rigid as with outgoing letters. Prison officers can be quite co-operative if wives write very long letters at times of family crisis and for other special reasons. All prisons have a private postal address which you can use if you don't want your letters to be identified as going to a prison – you can get this from your local probation officer or from the prison welfare department.

ALL LETTERS TO AND FROM PRISONERS ARE CENSORED

Prisoners are not allowed to include in their letters information about prison conditions or comments about prison staff, nor to mention other prisoners by name. Like the semi-public visits, the censoring of letters is sometimes a source of great anxiety for wives. In fact, prison officers have to read so many letters that they are trained to look for specific details and usually fail to take anything else in.

THERE ARE OFTEN SERIOUS POSTAL DELAYS

If letters aren't getting through in either direction, contact your local probation officer or the welfare officer at the prison: they should be able to tell you whether the delay has simply been caused by the postal service, or by something more serious.

the prison should allow you to write and receive letters in your own language. There is sometimes a bit of a hold-up about this at first, until the prison authorities get used to the idea: after that, things should run smoothly.

Money

Unless you have a reasonable income of your own, you are entitled to supplementary benefit in the same way as any single woman. If you have children you will get additional allowances for them. We explain about supplementary benefit on pp. 113–21. If you have children and you are working you may be entitled to the Family Income Supplement, which is described on pp. 110–13. If – as is likely – you find that supplementary benefit isn't enough to live on, contact your local probation officer or NACRO: they may be able to put you in touch with organizations that can give you additional support. The WRVS (Women's Royal Voluntary Service) can be very helpful.

Housing

If you are entitled to supplementary benefit (and you can find out whether you are on pp. 114–15) the Social Security should pay your rent and rates. The local authority may give you a rent rebate: inquire about this at your local housing department (address in the telephone directory under the heading of the local authority).

If you have any trouble with threats of eviction or rent arrears, try to get help immediately. Your local probation officer should be able to advise you what to do; otherwise go to your Citizens' Advice Bureau and ask to be put in touch with a solicitor. The Social Security may pay rent arrears, especially if the alternative is to split up the family and place the children in care. In some circumstances, the social services department of the local council will pay rent arrears.

If you have a mortgage, the Social Security will not meet the full payments, but it may arrange to pay a certain amount towards the interest. Either you or your husband should write to the building society as soon as possible to see what can be arranged.

In many ways you are in the same position as a separated wife, so you may find it useful to read the section entitled 'Married Women: Your Right to the Family Home' on pp. 240–50. For general information on your rights as a tenant, read the section entitled 'Quick Guide for Tenants' on pp. 255–60.

Hire purchase and other debts and fines

You are not responsible for your husband's debts. He should write to the company or court to whom he owes money explaining that he is in prison and that he will pay a nominal amount out of his wages. This has the effect of leaving everything in suspended animation until he is released. In the meantime you are freed from the anxiety of having to keep up payments. The same is true of gas and electricity bill and local authority rent arrears: if your husband writes saying that he is responsible and that all he can do is offer a nominal amount – say 10p a month – out of his prison earnings, this is usually accepted. You will only be responsible for bills incurred after his imprisonment and for debts that are in your name.

Divorce and separation

If you want to start legal proceedings to divorce or separate from your husband, the fact that he is in prison makes no difference – if anything, it makes it easier (although while your husband is in prison he cannot be said to be deserting you, as he has no choice). You will probably be able to get legal aid. We explain how to find a solicitor and apply for legal aid on pp. 298–305; and how to get a divorce or separation on pp. 169–202.

Women in prison

I wish to be judged by my peers

What do women go to prison for?

Over half the women who go to prison each year are *on remand*. That means that they have not actually been sentenced to prison but they are either awaiting trial or have been convicted and are waiting to be sentenced. In 1970, 4,902 women went to prison. Of those, 2,703 (56 per cent) were in prison on remand but did not in the end receive prison sentences. The average period of remand was three weeks.

In 1970, 1,200 women were actually sentenced to prison. Sixty per cent of them were sentenced for various forms of stealing; 12 per cent for charges connected with prostitution; 11 per cent for drink or drugs; 9 per cent for other, mainly minor offences; and 8 per cent for some sort of violence against other people.

Shoplifting sent more women to jail than any other offence: 35 per cent, to be exact. Most shoplifting offences are very small. Home Office research carried out in 1967 showed that 'A quarter of the offences involved goods valued at less than five shillings, over half less than £1. A fifth involved sums of £5 or more. A half involved thefts from self-service stores, of which two-thirds were entirely of food.'

So women prisoners are hardly a bunch of dangerous criminals. less than a handful might need to be locked up for public safety.

The vast majority are in on very short sentences. Between 500 and 559 women serve prison sentences in Holloway each year. Allowing for remission (reduction of sentence, which usually amounts to one third) only *10 per cent* of them (between fifty and sixty) actually spend more than a year inside. That is a tiny proportion, 2 per cent, of the total number (including those on remand) who spend time in Holloway each year.

There are two closed women's prisons, Holloway, in North London, and Styal, near Manchester; and two open prisons, Askham Grange, near York, and Moor Court, near Stoke on Trent. Moor Court is soon to be closed. Holloway is being rebuilt under an ambitious multi-million-pound plan which is due for completion in 1978/9. One result of there being so few women's prisons is that many of the inmates are a long way from home.

Rules for women prisoners

Almost all prison rules are the same for women as they are for men, including the rules about visits and letters which are described in the section on Prisoners' Wives (pp. 285–94). There are two exceptions.

1. *Women are allowed to wear their own clothes* and they do not have to have their hair cut. Personal appearance is a matter left to the individual prisoner.
2. *If a woman has a baby* (either before or after she is sent to prison) she is allowed to keep it with her until it is about 9 months old. This is supposed to be the rule, but prison governors can

refuse to let mothers have their babies with them if there isn't enough room. At Askham Grange there is a mother-and-baby unit where mothers can (if there is room) keep their children up to the age of 2 years. But children older than the age limit set by the prison must be taken into the care of the local council if they cannot be looked after by relatives. The official reasoning on this issue is rather strange: that a child should not be allowed to stay in prison beyond an age where it is aware of its environment. Yet the alternative is to send it away from the mother, probably to another institution.

Research (1967) by Carole Gibb on women with children received in a year into Holloway alone showed that 35 per cent had dependent children (many in Holloway, especially on remand, are young) and that only half of the children normally lived with their mother. This still meant that over 1,000 were separated by their mother going into prison. Over a quarter had to be taken into care, almost another quarter had to move to friends or relatives and nearly half stayed in the same family situation, usually with fathers, grandparents or siblings. A considerable number of these separations proved unnecessary, as the mother was remanded and then not sentenced to prison. The distress, both to mother and children, over such separation is apparent even to the Home Office:

'It is well-known that this sort of dispersal has a traumatic effect on the children and may be a cause of their future delinquency or other forms of instability . . . To send a woman to prison is to take her away from her family; the children in particular suffer from this deprivation which can lead to the break up of the home, even where there is a stable marriage' (*Treatment of Women and Girls in Custody*, HMSO 1970). [From a report by RAP (Radical Alternatives to Prison), *Alternatives to Holloway*]

The new Holloway will have a special unit where children can stay with their mothers up to the age of 5, but that in itself will give rise to other problems. How many children can each mother bring? Will they be free to come and go if their mothers are not? How will they be affected by their time in prison? What will happen to them when they reach 5 years?

Prisoners on remand

(This applies to men as well as women, but we thought it worth mentioning since so many women prisoners are on remand.)

If you are on remand you have certain 'privileges', including:

1. You don't have to do prison work if you don't want to (although it may be better than doing nothing).
2. You can send and receive as many letters as you like.
3. You can have as many visits as you like, although you will probably be restricted to one a day.
4. You are allowed to receive some sorts of food from outside the prison.
5. You can buy writing materials, newspapers and books, unless they are considered 'objectionable' by the prison authorities.
6. You can ask for a visit from a doctor or dentist who is not attached to the prison.
7. You can see your legal adviser within normal working hours as often as you need to, in the sight but not in the hearing of a prison officer.

Read also 'Getting legal aid' (pp. 301–8).

Further information

Radical Alternatives to Prison (RAP), 104 Newgate Street, London EC1 (01 600 4793): campaigning organization to change conventional thinking and government policy towards prisons. Publishes *Alternatives to Holloway*, a very informative booklet, price 30p.

Preservation of the Rights of Prisoners (PROP), 339a Finchley Road, London NW3 (01 435 1215): prisoners' union, campaigning for prisoners' rights.

National Association for the Care and Resettlement of Offenders (NACRO), 125 Kennington Park Road, London SE11 (01 735 1151): information and help for prisoners, ex-prisoners and prisoners' wives and families.

National Council for Civil Liberties (NCCL), 186 Kings Cross Road, London WC1 (01 278 4575).

11. Approaching the Law

Going to a solicitor

Throughout this book we have often suggested that you go to a solicitor for help. Most people have never met a solicitor and wouldn't know where to start looking for one. The thought may be a little alarming. But once you know what to do, it really isn't all that difficult.

What sort of people are they?

The vast majority are men. All practising solicitors are enrolled with the Law Society, and at the last count it had 25,366 men and 803 women members. All solicitors are middle-class: most of them were born that way and the rest were educated into it. This is positively encouraged by the legal education system, which is extremely conservative.

Solicitors tend to wear suits and have their offices in the smarter parts of town. They are not allowed to advertise their services, so it is very hard to find out about them. They expect you to phone or write to make an appointment before you go to see them.

If all this sounds offputting, don't worry. It doesn't mean that they won't be helpful to you. Most of them have a reasonable knowledge of the law and some are very sympathetic and obliging.

Two warnings: almost any legal proceedings take a long time; and solicitors are *very* expensive, so you should apply for legal aid to pay your costs (see pp. 301–8).

How to contact a solicitor

Go to your nearest Citizens' Advice Bureau and ask for the names of local solicitors who would be prepared to act for you under the legal aid scheme. Not all of them will do this: they only get 90 per cent of the normal fee. If your CAB is a good one, they should be able to tell you which solicitors are best suited to help with your particular case and make an appointment for you. Otherwise you will just have to try pot luck.

You can also go to a magistrates' court or a county court and ask someone in the court office to give you the names and addresses of solicitors who work nearby.

If the case is urgent and you can't contact a solicitor, fill in the appropriate legal aid form (available from the court or from your Citizens' Advice Bureau) and leave a blank space where it asks for the name of your solicitor. Then you will be provided with one.

If you find yourself in court without a solicitor (for instance, if you are arrested and taken to court before you have time to contact one) ask to have the case adjourned: your request will almost certainly be granted. You will then have time to contact a solicitor and apply for legal aid.

How to change your solicitor

If you don't like the solicitor you've got and you want to get another one to act for you, you are perfectly entitled to do so. Don't be frightened of taking the step – it's quite common. On the other hand, don't be too optimistic: you may find that the second solicitor is no better than the first, because the law itself is a slow, expensive and unsatisfactory business.

If you're on legal aid, tell the Clerk of the Court (if you're involved in a criminal case) or the Law Society (if you're involved in a civil case), and ask them to transfer your legal aid to the solicitor of your choice. Once that is done, the first solicitor will transfer all your papers to the second one. It would be courteous to tell the first solicitor what you intend to do and ask him to transfer the papers, but he will do so even if you don't tell him.

If you're not on legal aid you will have to tell the first solicitor to transfer your papers to the second solicitor. He probably won't do this until you pay his bill, and he is entitled to keep all the papers until he gets his money.

The second solicitor will not start acting for you until your case has been handed over to him by the first solicitor.

What to do if you think your solicitor has charged you too much

If you're on legal aid, you probably won't come up against this problem. But if you're not and you think your solicitor's bill is too high, take action right away. If you don't challenge the bill within a month you will have to pay it in full. The first thing to do is tell the solicitor that you think it's too high. If he doesn't convince you that he has charged the right amount, or agree to reduce the bill, you can ask him to get a certificate from the Law Society stating that in their opinion the sum charged is 'fair and reasonable'. If the Law Society says that a lower sum would be 'fair and reasonable', you will only have to pay that.

Your solicitor cannot take you to court for not paying his bill until he has written to you telling you of the right to ask the Law Society for a certificate and a month has passed since you received this letter. He also has to tell you that you can ask for his bill to be 'taxed'. This means having it checked by the county court or high court. It may be decided that the bill should be reduced. You must ask for the bill to be taxed within a month of receiving it. The snag is that unless it is decided that you should pay less than five sixths (or in some cases four fifths) of the bill, you will have to pay the costs of having it taxed, which may mean that you have to pay more than the original sum.

You cannot ask for a certificate from the Law Society after a month from the time your solicitor told you of your right to do this; nor can you do so after you have paid the bill, or if the court has said the bill should be taxed.

Neighbourhood law centres

There is a growing number of these centres. At the time of writing there were eight in London and one in Cardiff. They are places where lawyers make a positive effort to be accessible to the community and offer free legal advice and aid in most cases. If there is one in your area, it would be well worth approaching them to see if they can help you. (For addresses, see p. 319.)

Getting legal aid

A person to see you about Legal Aid, sir

Legal aid is money paid by the state to cover the cost of having a solicitor to help you with a legal matter. If you want to get help from a solicitor and you are not so rich that you don't have to worry about the bill, you should apply for it. The amount of legal aid you get depends on what your income is.

Married women: If you are married, your husband's income is counted as part of yours when you are assessed for legal aid, *unless* you are involved in legal action against him. This can be unfair. For instance, a married woman might be injured at work and want to claim compensation from her employer; her husband may think she shouldn't bother; with his income added to hers she is not eligible for legal aid; without his financial support she cannot pursue her claim.

There are four different legal aid schemes.

1. Legal advice and assistance

This is a new scheme known as the 'green form procedure'. You can get advice and other help (such as writing letters or drawing up documents) from a solicitor, on any legal problem. It is either free or partly free depending on your financial resources. You can use it for preparing your case for a tribunal hearing, and even for getting a solicitor to accompany you to the tribunal and advise you on how to put forward your case. But it doesn't cover the cost of a solicitor actually representing you at the tribunal, as there is no legal aid for that. There is no limit to the amount of advice and assistance you can get under this scheme, but if it amounts to more than £25 worth, the solicitor must get authorization from the Law Society and satisfy himself that your case is not a trivial one.

EXAMPLES OF WHEN IT IS USEFUL

Your landlord threatens you with eviction or puts up the rent, and you want to find out what to do about it.

Your husband has walked out on you and left you without any money. You are uncertain whether to start divorce proceedings or to sue him for maintenance.

You have had your supplementary benefit book taken away because you are suspected of living with a man: you want help to prepare an appeal to the supplementary benefits appeals tribunal.

HOW DO YOU GET IT?

Ask your solicitor or the Citizens' Advice Bureau for an application form, and for help with filling it in. You will qualify if your 'disposable' income is less than £20 a week and your 'disposable' capital is less than £250 (or £375 if you have one child or £455 if you have two). However, you may still have to pay a contribution. For instance, if your disposable income is £16 a week, you may have to contribute up to £10; but if your weekly disposable income is £12, the most you will have to contribute is £1.

WHAT DOES 'DISPOSABLE' INCOME AND CAPITAL MEAN?

Your disposable income is your total weekly income, *not counting* tax, National Insurance contributions, allowances for dependants and certain other expenses.

Your disposable capital is the money you have saved or invested, *not counting* the value of your furniture, part or all of the value of your house, debts and certain other sums.

It is very complicated to work all this out and you should try to get help with it, from your solicitor or the Citizens' Advice Bureau.

2. Civil legal aid

Civil legal aid is money to cover all or part of the cost of having a solicitor act for you if you are involved in a civil case. It is administered by the Law Society.

What is a civil case? A civil case is a non-criminal case where one private individual or group of individuals sues another. Most of the areas of law dealt with in this book would involve civil cases, for instance divorce, separation, affiliation proceedings, adoption and consumer disputes.

You will get legal aid if you can convince the Law Society's Legal Aid Committee that you have good reason for proceeding with your case; and you satisfy the financial conditions. Legal aid will be totally free if:

(a) you are receiving supplementary benefit;
   or
(b) your annual disposable income is £300 or less and you have no more than £325 disposable capital.

You will get legal aid to cover *part* of your costs if:

(a) your annual disposable income is between £300 and £950;
   and
(b) your disposable capital is between £325 and £1500.

You will certainly not get legal aid if your disposable income is over £950 and you will probably not get it if your disposable capital is over £1500.

HOW TO APPLY

(a) It is advisable to get legal advice first, to find out whether you have a strong enough case to make it worth going ahead. You can get this under the 'legal advice and assistance scheme' described on pp. 302–3.
(b) You can get an application form from your solicitor, Citizens' Advice Bureau or the nearest Law Society's Legal Aid area office (addresses are in the telephone directory).
(c) The form is long and complicated to fill in. If you already have a solicitor he will probably help you, otherwise you can get help from your Citizens' Advice Bureau. Send the form off as soon as possible to the Secretary at the Law Society's Legal Aid area office.
(d) The financial section of the form is sent on to the Supplementary Benefits Commission: they assess your financial situation and tell the Law Society what is the maximum amount you can afford to pay. They will probably want to interview you.
(e) The Legal Aid Committee will then decide whether or not to grant you legal aid.

If you are granted legal aid, you will be told how much the case is likely to cost and what your contribution is likely to be. You will also be told what is the maximum you will be expected to pay if the case turns out to be more expensive. If you accept this decision you must tell the Law Society within twenty-eight days, and you will then be given a legal aid certificate. It usually takes two or three months from the time you apply to the time you are granted the certificate. Your solicitor can then go ahead with your case. You will be expected to pay your contributions (if any) in monthly instalments.

You can apply for an emergency certificate if your case is urgent, by filling in a special form (available from your solicitor, Citizens' Advice Bureau or the Law Society's Legal Aid area office). It is best to find a solicitor to act for you before you apply: you can organize this through the 'legal advice and assistance scheme' described on pp. 302–3.

You can appeal to the Law Society's Legal Aid area committee if you are refused legal aid. You should do this within four days of hearing the decision. You cannot appeal against the financial arrangements, only against the decision that your case is not strong enough to merit legal aid. Tell them about any new evidence or information that you think might be relevant. If your financial circumstances change, it is worth making a fresh application for legal aid.

Is it worth going ahead if you can't get legal aid? If you win your case, your legal costs will normally be paid by your opponent. So if you have a strong case it may be worth going ahead and borrowing the money if necessary. Your solicitor will advise you on this.

3. Criminal legal aid

Criminal legal aid is money to cover the cost of having a solicitor represent you if you are involved in a criminal case.

What is a criminal case? A criminal case is one where a person is prosecuted by the police for breaking the law, for instance for dangerous driving, shoplifting or soliciting.

If you are prosecuted by the police, be sure to get a solicitor, unless the case is very trivial indeed. If you intend to plead 'not guilty', don't assume that your innocence will protect you. It is quite possible that false evidence may be given against you – deliberately or accidentally. Never plead 'guilty' until you have spoken to a solicitor. He may advise you against it, or present 'mitigating' factors to the court so that you have a chance of getting a reduced sentence. So if you are taken to court and you don't have a solicitor, tell the magistrate that you want a solicitor and legal aid, and ask for the case to be adjourned. If you don't know of a solicitor, you will be provided with one.

If you end up being tried without a solicitor, and the magistrate is considering sending you to prison, he *must* ask you if you want legal aid. It's rather absurd that he is not obliged to offer you this until you have been convicted, but, whatever happens, don't refuse his offer.

IF YOU ARE NOT LEGALLY REPRESENTED IN COURT, YOU ARE MORE LIKELY TO GO TO PRISON

This fact was clearly shown in a book called *Silent in Court* by Susan Dell – a study of women prisoners in Holloway and how they had been represented in court before they were sentenced. Only 17 per cent of women who were sent to Holloway from magistrates' courts had been legally represented. (Eighty per cent of Holloway's inmates come from magistrates' courts.) The book was written before the new ruling which obliges magistrates to offer legal aid before sending anyone to prison, but it shows the importance of being properly represented in court. Susan Dell says:

An inexperienced defendant is at a disadvantage in court even if well-educated and articulate, but for those who have little education, who are scared, nervous and unable to express themselves in the kind of language they believe is expected in courts, the handicap can be crippling, particularly if they wish to deny the offence or plead mitigating circumstances.

The mere presence of someone to speak on behalf of the person in court, even if it is just to state the basic facts of the case and ask for bail, can have a significant effect on the number sent to prison on remand or under sentence. The study shows that an alarming number of women who were convicted but not represented in court later claimed that they were not guilty. Most of them had pleaded guilty in court, either on the advice of the police or because they didn't see any point in putting up a fight ('it's their word against mine') and wanted to 'get it over', or simply because they didn't understand what was going on.

YOU WILL BE GRANTED LEGAL AID IF THE COURT
DECIDES:

(a) that it is in the interests of justice that you should have it;
    and
(b) that you cannot afford to pay the cost of your defence yourself.

You will get legal aid entirely free if:

(a) you are receiving supplementary benefit;
    or
(b) your net income over the last year was not more than £250 after deducting tax, National Insurance, rent, rates and allowances for dependants; and your savings and investments are not more than £25.

But people who have more money than that often get legal aid free. Practice varies from one court to another: for instance, it is more difficult to get legal aid for shoplifting cases in the Marlborough Street magistrates' court than in Camberwell. Generally speaking, free legal aid is a lot easier to get than it would seem from the official requirements listed above. Free legal aid is granted almost automatically for trials in the higher courts (the Crown Courts or Central Criminal Court).

If you are not granted legal aid entirely free, you will have to pay a contribution towards your legal costs.

HOW TO APPLY

Apply as soon as possible. The application form is more straightforward than the one for civil legal aid. It is available from court offices and Citizens' Advice Bureaux. It is best to fill it in on the spot, so that you can get help if you need it. If you are in prison, you are supposed to be given the form automatically, but you'll probably have to ask for it.

If you don't have time to apply for legal aid before you are taken to court, tell the magistrate as soon as possible. He will either consider your application immediately, or adjourn the case.

The clerk of the court will probably consider your application first. If he is against granting you legal aid, he must refer it to the magistrate. If the magistrate refuses legal aid, you cannot appeal against his decision, but you may be able to make a fresh application later.

If you are granted legal aid, but you have to pay part of the costs, you may be asked to make a down-payment before the case is heard. But this doesn't often happen and the down-payment is unlikely to be more than £10 for a case heard by a magistrate, or £25 for a case heard in a higher court. When the case has been concluded, the magistrate or judge may order you to pay a contribution towards the costs, but if you are acquitted your costs should be paid for you.

In the higher courts, a legal aid order will cover the cost of a solicitor and barrister, but in the lower courts it will usually only cover a solicitor. But if it is a complex case, your solicitor can apply for the legal aid order to cover the barrister as well.

Further information

Civil Liberty: The NCCL Guide includes chapters on arrest, bail and questioning; court procedure; and legal aid. A Penguin Special, price 50p, from bookshops or from the National Council for Civil Liberties, 186 Kings Cross Road, London WC1 (01 278 4575).

Guide to New Legal Aid, free from your local Citizens' Advice Bureau or from the Law Society, Chancery Lane, London WC2.

The different kinds of civil courts

At many points in this book we have mentioned the civil courts. The diagram on p. 310 summarizes the different kinds of cases dealt with in different civil courts, and the way in which an individual case may move from one court to another if the parties concerned are not satisfied with the first verdict. If a case is 'defended' it means that the case you are bringing against somebody is challenged by them.

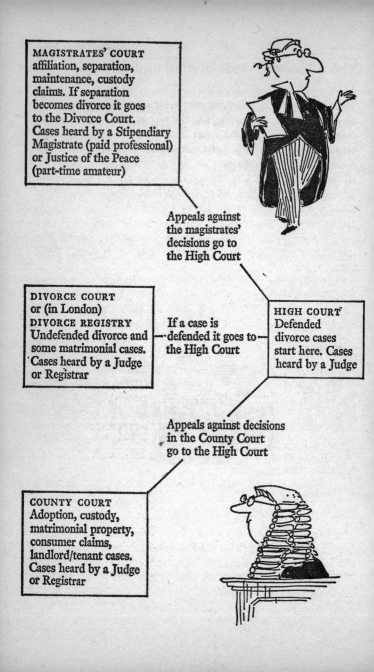

MAGISTRATES' COURT
affiliation, separation, maintenance, custody claims. If separation becomes divorce it goes to the Divorce Court. Cases heard by a Stipendiary Magistrate (paid professional) or Justice of the Peace (part-time amateur)

Appeals against the magistrates' decisions go to the High Court

DIVORCE COURT
or (in London)
DIVORCE REGISTRY
Undefended divorce and some matrimonial cases. Cases heard by a Judge or Registrar

If a case is defended it goes to the High Court

HIGH COURT
Defended divorce cases start here. Cases heard by a Judge

Appeals against decisions in the County Court go to the High Court

COUNTY COURT
Adoption, custody, matrimonial property, consumer claims, landlord/tenant cases. Cases heard by a Judge or Registrar

Tribunals

You might have to appeal to a tribunal if you have a dispute with your landlord, or if you disagree with a decision that has been made about your right to National Insurance or supplementary benefits. Here are some notes to give you an idea of what to expect.

Tribunals are not like law courts. They are supposed to be informal. They are designed so that ordinary people can appeal to them without having to get advice from a lawyer, and without having to spend any money. They can settle cases a lot more quickly than law courts – a complex case might take as much as three hours, but most cases are settled much more quickly than that.

It all sounds great. But the truth is that in almost any tribunal hearing, you, the person who is appealing, will have to argue your case against people who are experts in the field. You will have to understand a lot of complicated rules and regulations if you are going to get the better of them. So you may be at a considerable disadvantage if you just turn up on your own and rely on their good will and understanding. Legal aid is not available for tribunal hearings (although it should be) but under the new 'green form procedure', described on pp. 302–3, you can get considerable help from a solicitor without actually having legal representation at the hearing. Otherwise, take a friend or a representative from your trade union, claimants' union or the Child Poverty Action Group, or anyone you can find who has experience of the way tribunals work.

National Insurance Tribunals

You can appeal to this tribunal if you are claiming a National Insurance benefit (such as unemployment benefit or maternity allowance) and you disagree with the decision made by the National Insurance officer – because he is not giving you enough, or giving you nothing at all.

Get an application form from your local National Insurance office. That is normally in the same place as the Social Security office. You return the completed form, and will then be told the date of the hearing.

The tribunal consists of three members: a chairman, who is usually a lawyer, and two others, drawn from two panels representing employers and workers, and appointed by the Department of Health and Social Security. None of the members of the tribunal is employed by the DHSS. You will sit at the same table as the tribunal members and you will not have to take an oath or stand up when you are giving evidence.

The tribunal knows the basic facts of the case before the hearing starts. You are allowed to call witnesses and produce documentary evidence such as letters, doctor's certificates, pay-slips, time sheets, etc. The tribunal will ask you questions and the National Insurance officer will probably do so as well. You may question witnesses and study documents produced by the Insurance officer.

The tribunal will tell you its decision at the hearing, or afterwards by post. It is not obliged to give its reasons for the decision unless you ask, so make sure that you ask to be given them in writing – in case you want to appeal.

You can appeal against the tribunal's decision to the National Insurance Commissioner, but appealing is a complicated business, so you should first get expert advice from a solicitor or your trade union. You must appeal within twenty-one days of the tribunal's decision.

You can claim travelling expenses and compensation for loss of earnings. See the Clerk of the tribunal about this.

Supplementary Benefit Appeal Tribunals

If you think you are not getting enough supplementary benefit and you are entitled to more, make an appeal to this tribunal. You should appeal within twenty-one days of the decision you disagreed with. Get an application form from your local Social Security office or simply write a letter to them saying 'I wish to appeal against the decision made on [date], as my benefit is not enough.' You will be told the date of the hearing.

The tribunal consists of a chairman and two other members from panels representing workers and employers. The chairman is often a lawyer. The hearing will be in private unless you give permission for research workers to attend. It is just as informal as the National Insurance tribunal.

You are allowed to produce documents and witnesses to back up your case, and to question the officials from the Supplementary Benefits Commission and any witnesses they produce. You may be asked questions by the members of the tribunal and by the Supplementary Benefits officials.

You will hear the tribunal's decision at the end of the hearing, or later by post. They are obliged to give their reasons for the decision, in writing. You may be able to appeal to the High Court if the tribunal has made a mistake on a point of law, but you should get expert advice on this.

You can claim travelling expenses and compensation for loss of earnings. See the Clerk of the tribunal about this.

Rent Tribunal

You can appeal to this tribunal if you are living in furnished rented accommodation and you think your rent is too high; or you are given notice to quit and you want to stay; or both.

You have to apply to have a fair rent fixed. You cannot apply just for security against eviction: it must be as part of an application for a fair rent. Application forms are available from your local Citizens' Advice Bureau or from the tribunal office. You will be told the date of the hearing.

Members of the tribunal are selected from panels appointed by the Department of the Environment. The chairman is almost always a lawyer. The hearing will be less formal than a law court, but more formal than some other tribunals. The chairman and members sit at one table and you and your landlord sit at two separate tables with your representatives. Nobody has to speak under oath.

The members of the tribunal visit your home on the morning of the hearing. Make sure you are there so you can draw their attention to relevant details that might affect the rent. At the hearing, you are allowed to call witnesses and produce documents such as letters, plans and rent books. The tribunal will question you. You or your representative may question the landlord and his witnesses; he may question you.

The tribunal gives its decision either at the end of the hearing or later, by post. You should always ask for its reasons, in case you have grounds for an appeal. You may appeal to the High Court if you think the tribunal has made a mistake on a point of law. But get expert advice first.

Rent Officer and Rent Assessment Committee

If you live in unfurnished rented accommodation, you can't appeal to the Rent Tribunal if you think your rent is too high. Instead you can apply to the Rent Officer and, if you don't agree with his decision, to the Rent Assessment Committee. (Your landlord can also appeal, if he wants to put the rent up.)

First of all, apply to the Rent Officer. Application forms are available from your Citizens' Advice Bureau or from the Rent Office (address in the telephone directory). You must say that you think the present rent is too high and suggest a new rent.

When the Rent Officer gets your application, he will notify the landlord. He will then try to get you both to agree, first by talking to each of you separately and, if that fails, by calling you to a meeting. The discussion will be fairly informal. You are each allowed to have someone to represent you, and to produce documentary evidence. After the meeting, the Rent Officer will decide on a 'fair rent', notify you and the landlord, and register the rent.

If you don't agree with the Rent Officer's decision, you must send a written objection to him within twenty-eight days. The case will then be referred to the Rent Assessment Committee. If you get to this stage you will really need expert advice from a surveyor or valuer. Ask your Citizens' Advice Bureau how to get in touch with one.

Members of the Rent Assessment Committee are chosen from panels nominated by the Minister for the Environment: the chairman is usually a lawyer. The hearing is fairly formal – comparable to a Rent Tribunal.

The committee may first ask you and your landlord for further information. It will then give you both a date before which you must submit your case in writing or ask for an oral hearing. If either of you asks for an oral hearing, there will be one. Each of you will have a chance to argue against the other's case. The committee usually inspects the premises before the hearing. You will be allowed to call expert witnesses, such as a surveyor, and if the landlord calls witnesses, you can question them.

The committee then either confirms the Rent Officer's decision or decides on a new 'fair rent' which is then registered. You should always ask the committee to give reasons for its decision, in case you have grounds for an appeal. You can appeal to the High Court, but only on a point of law, and you would need a solicitor's help for this.

Other tribunals

We don't have enough space to discuss all the tribunals here. The others are:

Immigration Appeal Tribunal – for appeals against decisions of Immigration Officers and the Home Office concerning the entry of immigrants etc.

Industrial Tribunal – deals with disputes between workers and employers over unfair dismissal, redundancy pay, etc.

Medical Appeal Tribunal – to determine compensation if you are injured at work.

Mental Health Review Tribunal – for appeals for discharge from mental institutions.

Tribunals of the National Health Service – for complaints against doctors, dentists, etc.

Local Valuation Courts – for disputes over rates.

Appendix 1

Organizations for further help and advice

Adoption Resource Exchange, 39 Brixton Road, London SW9 (01 735 8941): deals with adoption of children with special needs.

Advisory Centre for Education (ACE), 32 Trumpington Street, Cambridge CB2 1QY (Cambridge 51456): for information on most aspects of education.

Age Concern, 55 Gower Street, London WC1 (01 637 2886): information and campaigning centre for old people's welfare rights.

Association of British Adoption Agencies, 4 Southampton Row, London WC1 (01 242 8951): for general advice on adoption and a list of all adoption agencies.

Association of Local Advice Centres, c/o Joe O'Hara, 54 Lisburn Road Belfast BT9 6AF.

Belfast Housing Aid Society, 16 Howard Street, Belfast BT1 7PA.

British Pregnancy Advisory Service, Guildhall Buildings, Navigation Street, Birmingham B2 4BT (021 643 1461): charitable organization which arranges low-cost abortion.

Brook Advisory Centre, 233 Tottenham Court Road, London W1 (01 580 2991): headquarters for Brook clinics in London and six major cities, which provide advice on contraception and general sexual problems, especially helpful to younger people.

Building Societies Association, 14 Park Street, London W1 (01 629 0515): for information about mortgages.

Catholic Housing Aid Society, 189a Old Brompton Road, London SW5 (01 373 7276): helps homeless people find homes, with special department for single parents.

Catholic Marriage Advisory Service, 11 College Street, Belfast.

Child Poverty Action Group (CPAG), 1 Macklin Street, London WC2 (01 242 3225): for information on welfare benefits.

Citizens' Advice Bureaux: headquarters at National Citizens' Advice Bureaux Council, 26 Bedford Square, London WC1 (01 636 4066), with 500 bureaux throughout the country, which give advice on a wide range of subjects including legal aid, welfare benefits, landlord/tenant and other legal problems.

Citizens' Advice Bureaux (Northern Ireland headquarters): 28 Bedford Street, Belfast BT2 7FE.

Citizens' Rights Office, 1 Macklin Street, London WC2 (01 405 5942): helps poorer families with legal problems (such as appeals to tribunals) and provides practical advice on welfare rights, etc.

Claimants' unions: community-based organizations to help people claim welfare benefits. No headquarters, but one of the most long-standing ones, which may be a possible source of information, is the South-East London Claimants' Union, The Albany, Creek Road, Deptford, London SE8 (01 692 1047).

Consumers' Association, 14 Buckingham Street, London WC2 (01 839 1222): for information on consumer subjects. Publications are available to the general public, but it caters mainly for members.

Cruse Organization for Widows, 6 Lion Gate Gardens, Richmond, Surrey (01 940 2660): information and advice for widows.

Down and Connor Family Welfare Society, 43 Falls Road, Belfast 12.

Family Planning Association: headquarters at 27–35 Mortimer Street, London W1 (01 636 7866), with clinics throughout the country, for contraception.

Family Planning Association of Northern Ireland, 28 Bedford Street, Belfast.

Gingerbread, 9 Poland Street, London W1 (01 734 9014): practical help and moral support for single parents.

Independent Adoption Society, 160 Peckham Rye, London SE22 (01 693 4155): for adoption without religious specifications.

Islington Free School, 57 White Lion Street, London N1 (01 837 6379): for information on how to set up a free school.

Joint Council for the Welfare of Immigrants (JCWI), 233 Pentonville Road, London N1 (01 278 6727): advice and legal help for immigrants.

Law Society of Northern Ireland, Chichester Street, Belfast BT1 3JE.

Law Society of Scotland, 26/7 Drumsheugh Gardens, Edinburgh EH3 7YR.

London Pregnancy Advisory Service, 40 Margaret Street, London W1 (01 409 0281): a charitable organization which arranges low-cost abortion.

Marie Stopes Memorial Clinic, 108 Whitfield Street, London W1 (01 388 0662): for help and advice on contraception and abortion.

National Association for the Care and Resettlement of Offenders (NACRO), 125 Kennington Park Road, London SE11 (01 735 1151): information and help for prisoners, ex-prisoners and prisoners' wives and families.

National Council for Civil Liberties (NCCL), 186 Kings Cross Road, London WC1 (01 278 4575): campaigning organization for protection of civil rights, information and help on immigration, legal aid, etc.

National Union of Students, 3 Endsleigh Street, London WC1 (01 387 1277): for information about grants and general advice for students.

Neighbourhood Law Centres: Adamsdown Community and Advice Centre, 103–4 Clifton Street, Adamsdown, Cardiff (Cardiff 498117); Brent Community Law Centre, 161 Church Road, London NW10. (01 451 1122); Camden Community Law Centre, 146 Kentish Town Road, London NW1 (01 485 6672); Islington Community Law Centre, 161 Hornsey Road, London N7 (01 607 2461); Newham Rights Centre, Durning Hall, Earlham Grove, Forest Gate, London E7 (01 555 0142); North Kensington Neighbourhood Law Centre, 74 Golborne Road, London W10 (01 969 7473); Paddington Neighbourhood Advice Bureau and Law Centre, 465 Harrow Road, London W10 (01 969 9425); Stepney Green Neighbourhood Law Centre, Dame Colet House, Ben Jonson Road, London E1 (01 790 6721); West Stepney Neighbourhood Law Centre, 59 Watney Street, London E1 (01 790 6311).

Northern Ireland Civil Rights Association, 2 Marquis Street, Belfast.

One-Parent Families, 255 Kentish Town Road, London NW5

(01 267 1361): help for one-parent families. Formerly called the National Council for the Unmarried Mother and her Child.

Pre-School Playgroups Association, Alford House, Aveline Street, London SE11 (01 582 8871): advice on how to set up play groups.

Preservation of the Rights of Prisoners (PROP), 339a Finchley Road, London NW3 (01 435 1215): prisoners' union, campaigning for prisoners' rights.

Radical Alternatives to Prison (RAP), 104 Newgate Street, London EC1 (01 600 4793): campaigns for the abolition of prisons. Information on women's prisons.

Release, 1 Elgin Avenue, London W9 (01 289 1123): advice on abortion, landlord/tenant disputes, drugs arrests and general social and legal problems.

Scottish Association for the Care and Resettlement of Offenders (SACRO), 1 Strathmore House, East Kilbride, Glasgow G74 1LF.

Scottish Child Poverty Action Group, 11 Castle Street, Edinburgh 2.

Scottish Council for Civil Liberties, 314 Clyde Street, Glasgow, C1.

Shelter Housing Aid Centre, 189a Old Brompton Road, London SW5 (01 373 7276): helps to house homeless families.

TUC, Congress House, 23–28 Great Russell Street, London WC1. (01 636 4030): for a list of maternity leave arrangements in the public sector, plus information on trade unions.

UK Immigrants Advisory Service (UKIAS), St George's Churchyard, Bloomsbury Way, London WC1 (01 405 3225): for advice and help with immigration problems and appeals.

Ulster Pregnancy Advisory Association, 198 Stranmillis Road, Belfast BT8 5DT.

Women's Aid, 369 Chiswick High Road, London W4: for advice and assistance to women assaulted by their husbands.

Women's Group on Public Welfare, 26 Bedford Square, London WC1 (01 636 4066): publishes a duplicated sheet of over 100 women's organizations, price 20p plus 5p postage.

Women's Liberation Workshop, 38 Earlham Street, London WC2: for information on the women's liberation movement and addresses of local groups.

Appendix 2

Notes on Scotland and Northern Ireland

The laws in Scotland and Northern Ireland differ considerably from those in England and Wales. It is impossible in one chapter to cover adequately all the differences – ideally there should be a separate guide for each country. These notes are an attempt to highlight the differences where they are most marked – they cannot be regarded as comprehensive. They should be read with reference to the relevant sections of the main text.

Scotland

Money

All the subjects dealt with under this heading apply to Scotland, except as follows.

WIDOWS' INHERITANCE (p. 108)

If your husband has made a will but has left little or nothing to you, you are guaranteed one half of your husband's estate if you have no surviving children or grandchildren. If there are children or grandchildren, you are entitled to one third and they are entitled to one third, to be divided between them. If your husband dies without leaving a will, you will normally have a right to a share in the value of the family home up to £15,000; a share in the value of the 'furniture and plenishings' of the family home up to £5,000; and further financial provisions up to £5,000 if there are no surviving children, or up to £2,500 if there are. If there is anything left after that, you will not inherit any of it if your husband has left surviving parents, brothers or sisters, or any direct descendants of those relatives; if he has not, you will inherit the remainder of the estate. The procedure for claiming inheritance (p. 109) is completely different in Scotland. Get advice from a solicitor on this.

SUPPLEMENTARY BENEFIT (p. 113)

For further information contact the Scottish Child Poverty Action Group, 11 Castle Street, Edinburgh 2.

Sex

SEX UNDER 18 (p. 130)

If you are under 17 and are having sexual intercourse or 'in danger' of having it, you will not be taken to court, because the whole procedure for dealing with juvenile offenders and children in need of supervision is different in Scotland: if you are under 16 and considered to be exposed to moral danger you may be brought before a Children's Panel and put under a supervision order. The procedure is explained more fully below (pp. 324–5).

There is no assumption in Scots law that a boy under 14 is incapable of sexual intercourse.

CONTRACEPTION (p. 134)

Under Scots law, it is not illegal for a doctor to give a medical examination to a girl under 16 without her parents' consent.

RAPE (p. 150)

A boy under 14 can be found guilty of rape under Scots law. Example (b) of rape carried out under false pretences does not apply to Scotland. Penalties for indecent assault are not the same, and differ according to the court in which the prosecution is brought.

PROSTITUTION (p. 152)

The situation is the same as in England and Wales, except that the procedure for cautioning and arresting prostitutes does not apply in Scotland; and a man who solicits a woman to have intercourse with him may be guilty of an offence under the Immoral Traffic (Scotland) Act of 1902.

Marriage

GETTING MARRIED UNDER 18 (p. 159)

If you are 16 or over you can get married without your parents' consent anywhere in Scotland.

In limited circumstances, a marriage may be constituted in Scotland where a man and woman are living together with the result that they are generally believed to be husband and wife. This is known as 'cohabitation with habit and repute'.

The Married Women's Property (Scotland) Act was passed in 1920.

Divorce (p. 171)

The Divorce Reform Act, 1969, does not apply to Scotland. Grounds for divorce are similar to the grounds for getting a separation order in a magistrates' court: adultery, wilful desertion for three years, incurable insanity, cruelty, sodomy and bestiality. Divorce cases can only be tried in the Court of Session (equivalent to the English High Court). A wife is entitled to maintenance (called aliment) for herself and her children until a final settlement is made by the court.

Children

HOW YOUR CHILD COULD BE TAKEN INTO CARE (p. 211)

Procedures for taking children into the care of the local authority are governed by the Social Work (Scotland) Act, 1968. The first two ways in which your children might be taken into care, described on p. 211, are broadly similar in Scotland. The third way is entirely different, as follows.

Young people who get into trouble with the law, and whose parents are not considered to be looking after them properly, are dealt with by a system of Reporters and Children's Panels set up under the 1968 Act. The scheme was first put into practice in April 1971 and varies considerably from one area to another.

Reporters are appointed by the local authorities. Usually they are lawyers or have experience in social work or criminology. Children's Panels are appointed by Children's Panels Advisory Committees, which are made up of three representatives nominated by the Secretary of State for Scotland and two representatives nominated by the local authorities.

If a child under 16 commits an offence she or he is normally referred to the Reporter by the police or the Social Work Department. Children up to the age of 18 may also be dealt with in this way if they are already under a supervision requirement from a Children's Hearing. The Reporter considers the case and if he decides that further action should be taken he can do one of the following things: write directly to the child's parents; arrange with the police to give the child a formal warning; refer the case to the Social Work Department for further investigation; or refer the case to a Children's Hearing. In practice, most cases which come before the Reporter are not referred to Children's Hearings. If the reporter decides to refer the case to a Children's Hearing, he sets out his 'Grounds for Referral' and sends a copy to the parents, with seven days' notice of the date of the hearing. The hearing consists of a chairman and two members of the Children's Panel – one man and one woman. The child, the parents, a social worker, the Reporter and deputy Reporter attend the hearing. The Chairman reads out the Grounds for Referral, and if the parents or child dispute them the case then goes to the Sheriff Court (for which the parents may claim legal aid). If the Sheriff Court does not uphold the objection, the case is referred back to a Children's Hearing.

The hearing may decide to dismiss the case or to impose a supervision requirement: this would mean that the child undergoes compulsory supervision, either by a social worker while she or he remains at home or in a residential establishment. A supervision requirement may be imposed if the child is considered (a) to be beyond the control of her or his parents; (b) through lack of parental control, to be falling into bad associations; exposed to moral danger; suffering unnecessarily; suffering damage to health or development; (c) to be truanting; (d) to have committed an offence; or (e) to have been the victim of a sexual offence. If the parents wish to appeal against the decision, they can ask for written reasons for the decision from the Reporter and make their appeal to the Sheriff within twenty-one days of the hearing.

The supervision order must be renewed annually. It does not last for any fixed period of time, but is intended to be related to the needs of the child. However, it automatically lapses on the child's 18th birthday. The child or parent can make a request at least once every six months for the order to be reviewed.

ADOPTION (p. 227)

Adoptions are supervised by the social work department of the local authority and cases are heard by the Sheriff Court or the Court of Session. Otherwise the procedure is the same.

LEAVING HOME WHEN YOU'RE UNDER 18 (p. 236)

Cases are heard by the Children's Hearings, not by the courts. The procedure is explained above. Children's Hearings have no jurisdiction over young people aged 16 or over unless they are already under a supervision order.

Housing

MARRIED WOMEN: YOUR RIGHT TO THE FAMILY HOME (p. 240)

The law in Scotland is quite different and is too complex to explain here. Get advice from a solicitor.

WHAT ARE YOUR RIGHTS IF YOU HAVE SET UP HOME WITH A MAN WHO IS NOT YOUR HUSBAND? (p. 250)

Your relationship may be recognized as a marriage under Scots law (see above, p. 323). The Acts referred to in this section do not apply in Scotland.

Women and prison

In 1971 there were on average 157 women in prison in Scotland and 4,933 men.

PRISONERS' WIVES (p. 285)

There is no probation service in Scotland. The social work departments of local authorities are the nearest equivalent.

The Scottish equivalent of NACRO is the Scottish Association for the Care and Resettlement of Offenders (SACRO), 1 Strathmore House, East Kilbride, Glasgow G74 1LF.

Extra visits in connection with prisoners' appeals (p. 287): wives are not excluded in Scotland. Legal advisers have virtually unlimited access and there can be visits from any other people provided these are in connection with the appeal. Conditions for visits are slightly different. Visits to convicted prisoners by relatives must be in the sight and the hearing of a prison officer. They are supposed to last thirty minutes. A prisoner may be permitted to embrace his wife.

WOMEN IN PRISON (p. 294)

In 1971, 42·5 per cent of women in prison in Scotland were there on remand. The most common reason for imprisonment, other than remand, was for non-payment of fines following conviction for breach of the peace (usually drunkenness) – those amounted to 18 per cent of the total. All convicted women are at Greenock Prison.

The Scottish Council for Civil Liberties is at 214 Clyde Street, Glasgow C1.

Approaching the law

GOING TO A SOLICITOR (p. 298)

Scottish lawyers belong to the Law Society of Scotland, 26/7 Drumsheugh Gardens, Edinburgh EH3 7YR. If you're on legal aid and you want to change your solicitor, tell the Clerk of the Court or the appropriate legal aid committee. 'Taxation' of lawyers' bills in Scotland is carried out by the Auditor of the Court of Session or of the Sheriff Court.

GETTING LEGAL AID (p. 301)

Civil legal aid is administered by the Law Society of Scotland. The procedure is more complicated than in England and you will need a solicitor to help you fill in the forms. Criminal legal aid is not available for proceedings in police courts, but is available in the Sheriff Court. If you are in custody you will automatically get free legal aid for your first appearance in the Sheriff Court. If you are eligible for legal aid you will not have to pay any contribution towards the cost of your defence. The new legal advice and assistance scheme (p. 302) applies to Scotland.

TRIBUNALS (p. 311)

This section applies to Scotland except that the official bodies involved, such as the Department of the Environment and the High Court, are the Scottish equivalent of those mentioned (e.g., members of Rent Tribunals are selected from panels appointed by the Secretary of State for Scotland; there is a right of appeal from tribunals to the Court of Session, not the High Court). There is no Mental Health Review Tribunal in Scotland. The Local Valuation Court is called the Valuation Appeal Committee.

Northern Ireland

Money

All the subjects dealt with under this heading apply to Northern Ireland, except as follows.

WIDOWS' INHERITANCE (p. 108)

If your husband does not leave you enough to live on (assuming that the value of his estate should enable him to do so), the court has power under the Family Provisions (N.I.) Act, 1960, to order appropriate payments to be made to you from his estate. The order ceases if your dependency ceases (for example, if you remarry). If your husband dies without leaving a will, you are entitled to inherit his personal belongings and up to £7,500 before paying death duties.

SUPPLEMENTARY BENEFIT (p. 113)

The equivalent to the Social Security office is the local office of the Ministry of Health and Social Services, known as the Social Services office. The equivalent of the claimants' unions are the local advice centres. The Association of Local Advice Centres can be contacted c/o Joe O'Hara, 54 Lisburn Road, Belfast BT 6AF.

Sex

SEX UNDER 18 (p. 130)

The age of consent in Northern Ireland is 17. If a man under 24 is charged with having illegal sexual intercourse with a girl under 17, it is not a defence for him to claim that he thought she was 17 or over.

CONTRACEPTION (p. 134)

Family planning advice is available from family health centres, which are held in group practices or in local authority clinics (listed in the telephone directory under the Area Boards for Health and Social Services). Health visitors, including those attached to the School Health Service, will also give advice suitable to people of each religious denomination. The Catholic Marriage Advisory Service holds clinics in Belfast and in many regional areas, which provide family planning advice and general advice on marriage problems. Its headquarters are at 11 College Street, Belfast. The Family Planning Association of Northern Ireland is at 28 Bedford Square, Belfast.

IF YOU ARE PREGNANT AND YOU WANT TO HAVE THE BABY (p. 145)

Your local Social Services office will be able to help you, although they have no obligation to provide any particular type of help. In some areas, help will be in the form of referring you, with your consent, to a voluntary society which will provide a hostel or flatlet, or counselling to help you decide about your baby's future. Two Social Services departments have their own hostels for mothers and babies, and others may keep a list of sympathetic landladies. If you want to go to a Catholic agency, the appropriate one is the Down and Connor Family Welfare Society, 43 Falls Road, Belfast 12.

ABORTION (p. 142)

The 1967 Abortion Act does not apply to Northern Ireland, so it is extremely difficult to get an abortion there. Some abortions are done on the National Health under the 1861 Offences Against the Person Act, but only in extreme cases, for what are considered really 'convincing' medical or psychiatric reasons. If you have a dozen children and varicose veins, that apparently isn't sufficient. The usual reply to women who are refused abortions is 'We'll support you through your pregnancy' (see above). Doctors may help if there is a genetic risk to your baby, or if you can convince them that you have been exposed to German measles at a time when the foetus might be damaged by it. Mental subnormality would probably qualify you for an abortion, too. If you can't get an abortion for any of these reasons, your best bet is to go to England and contact one of the pregnancy advisory services listed on pp. 148–9. Each year about 1,000 women from Northern Ireland have abortions in England. A sympathetic GP may arrange for you to have a 'voluntary' abortion under the National Health Service in England, but you will have to pay your own travelling expenses to and from the hospital. For advice in Northern Ireland, contact the Ulster Pregnancy Advisory Association, 198 Stranmillis Road, Belfast BT8 5DT. They charge £5 for counselling, but this is waived where appropriate.

Marriage

GETTING MARRIED UNDER 18 (p. 159)

The courts have no general powers to give consent to the marriage of a minor where the parents refuse to do so.

HOUSEKEEPING MONEY (p. 166)

The English legislation of 1964 does not apply to Northern Ireland, so a wife does not have any legal right to keep what money she saves from an allowance that her husband gives her.

Divorce and Separation (p. 169)

The Divorce Reform Act, 1969, does not apply to Northern Ireland. Grounds for divorce are similar to the grounds for getting a separation order in a magistrates' court: adultery, wilful desertion for three years, incurable insanity, cruelty, sodomy and bestiality. A decree absolute is normally granted six months after the decree nisi.

Children

CLAIMING MAINTENANCE FROM THE FATHER (p. 204)

Under the Maintenance and Affiliation Orders (N.I.) Act, 1966, a woman can apply to the magistrate for an affiliation order at any time during her pregnancy, or within twelve months of the birth, or within twelve months of the putative father's return to Northern Ireland if there is proof that he has been away. She must swear in writing that he is the child's father. Otherwise the procedure is similar to that in England and Wales.

HOW YOUR CHILD COULD BE TAKEN INTO CARE (p. 211)

The situation in Northern Ireland is somewhat different, since the Children and Young Persons Act, 1969, does not apply. The ways that your child could be taken into care are set out in the Children and Young Persons Act (N.I.), 1968.

ADOPTION (p. 227)

The procedure is similar, except that the courts in Northern Ireland have wider discretion to dispense with the consent of the natural parents. For instance, if the natural mother withdraws her consent when she discovers the identity of the adoptive parents, this may be deemed unreasonable and disregarded.

NURSERIES AND OTHER CHILD-CARE FACILITIES (p. 212)

There are no day nurseries run by the state, and in general there are very few child-care facilities available. Some foster mothers registered with the Social Services departments take children daily. In cases of hardship, it is sometimes possible for a child to be cared for on a daily basis in a residential nursery run by a voluntary society. Your local Social Services office will tell you what is available.

Housing

MARRIED WOMEN: YOUR RIGHT TO THE FAMILY HOME (p. 240)

The laws in Northern Ireland are substantially different. For instance, there is no system whereby a married woman who has no legal interest in the family home can register her right of occupation. If you suspect that your husband might sell the home against your will, the best you can do is to take proceedings under Section 17 of the Married Women's Property Act of 1882. You will need a solicitor's help for this.

FINDING A PLACE TO LIVE – RENTED ACCOMMODATION (p. 253)

All public housing is controlled by the Northern Ireland Housing Executive, which has district offices, listed in the telephone directory.

QUICK GUIDE FOR TENANTS (p. 255)

The Rent Act of 1964 does not apply to Northern Ireland. There are no Rent Tribunals, Rent Officers or Local Valuation Courts. However, limited provisions do exist to protect tenants of furnished and unfurnished accommodation. Get advice on this from your local Citizens' Advice Bureau, or from a solicitor.

MORTGAGES (p. 260)

The Northern Ireland Housing Executive makes loans to people who would not normally be considered by a building society. They claim in their publicity to give equal consideration to male and female applicants. The Belfast Housing Aid Society is at 16 Howard Street, Belfast BT1 6PA.

Women and immigration (p. 276)

The immigration laws apply to Northern Ireland. The only immigrants who can work in Northern Ireland without permits are those with professional qualifications.

Women and prison (p. 294)

Where political prisoners, known as 'Special Category' prisoners, are concerned, the prison system in Northern Ireland is quite different from that in England and Wales. Women and men can be detained and interned without trial, and visits are limited. In theory, 'Special Category' prisoners are supposed to be treated as prisoners on remand but there are some important differences. For example, they are not allowed to receive anything which may conceal any object 'injurious to public safety' and that would include cooked meals.

Prisons are administered by the Ministry for Home Affairs.

Approaching the law

GOING TO A SOLICITOR (p. 298)

Solicitors in Northern Ireland belong to the Law Society of Northern Ireland, Chichester Street, Belfast BT1 3JE.

GETTING LEGAL AID (p. 301)

The 'green form procedure' does not yet apply to Northern

Ireland. Thirty minutes of oral advice is available, free or partly free according to means, from solicitors who participate in a scheme run by the Law Society. For further information about legal aid and advice, contact your Citizens' Advice Bureau, or the Law Society of Northern Ireland Legal Aid Department, Chichester Street, Belfast BT1 3JE.

Appendix 3

A draft contract for marriage or living together

If you live with a man, whether you are married or not, you may find that there are many ways in which your rights are not protected. One way of tackling this problem is to come to a clear agreement about the terms of your relationship at the outset, preferably before you move in together or marry, and draw up a legal contract setting out in black and white exactly what your rights and responsibilities will be. Love and understanding may not solve all your problems and you may find it very useful to devote some hard, clear thinking to the subject and to commit your understanding to paper.

Below, we give an example of a contract drawn up by one (imaginary) couple. Gloria and Sam are getting married but you could make a similar contract if you just wanted to live together. However, there is a danger that the courts would not enforce a 'cohabitation contract' because they might consider it immoral in threatening the institution of marriage!

It's up to you to decide which terms to include. For instance, you might want to have a joint family name instead of keeping separate names. You might want to include an agreement that you will devote a certain amount of time to discussing your relationship, so that channels of communication are kept open. You might want to include a clause providing that you should review the agreement from time to time to see if you wish to amend it. There will probably be areas of your relationship that you do not want to deal with in a legal contract – such as religion and sexual fidelity.

A contract of this kind has not yet been tested in the courts of Britain, so it is impossible to know exactly how far it would be legally enforceable. Some of the terms would be more acceptable in a court of law than others. For example, the law cannot and will not enforce an agreement to share housework, to look after children, or to oblige one partner to encourage the other in the pursuit of training or a career. However, if you are married and your husband has consistently flouted these terms of the agreement you might (if things got that bad) be able to use this as part of the evidence of his unreasonable behaviour in divorce proceedings.

Terms dealing with property rights would have more legal force. As a clear expression of the intent of both parties to set out specific property rights, they would normally be enforceable in a court of law. Courts dealing with divorce and separation would have to overrule the agreement if they considered the terms were not fair and equitable, but the terms stated in the sample contract would probably be upheld by the courts.

In any event, a contract is a useful way of reminding you both of the agreement you made at the start of your relationship. In the event of a disagreement, it could have considerable force in helping you and the man to work out your own solutions without having to go to court. And, if the relationship does break down, it could make it easier to sort out money matters and other practical arrangements, which can otherwise cause great difficulty.

In order for the contract to have as much legal force as possible, it's best to have it drawn up by a solicitor. Some solicitors may be surprised at your request, or may even refuse to deal with it – so you may have to look for one who is sympathetic. If you show the solicitor the sample contract given here it will help to explain the sort of thing you want.

THIS AGREEMENT IS made on the 1st day of January BETWEEN GLORIA SMITH of Manchester, England (hereinafter called 'the Woman') and SAM BLOGGS of London, England (hereinafter called 'the Man').
WHEREAS:—
1. The Woman and Man intend to marry.
2. The Woman and Man wish to enter into an Agreement which they intend to be legally binding upon them, as to their own respective rights within marriage, obligations towards each other, obligations

towards any children of the marriage and interest in any property owned jointly and separately by them.

3. The Woman and Man wish to establish the principle that they both have equal rights in all matters concerning their life together and their respective development as individuals and that all such matters should be settled between them in mutual agreement.

4. The said principle shall be the guiding principle even when it conflicts with financial considerations.

NOW in consideration of the above agreement and of the intended marriage IT IS HEREBY AGREED:—

1. The Woman and Man agree that each shall be entitled to retain for all purposes after the marriage their own respective names before the marriage. They agree that when they have children they will adopt a joint family name, there being no prior assumption that this should be the name of the Man.

2. The Woman and Man shall each be entitled to work and to engage in vocational and social activities as each chooses. Should either of them who has not previously been working outside the home decide to take up an occupation, or should either of them decide to continue her or his education, they agree to support each other in attaining their objectives.

3. The Woman and Man agree to plan their lives in such a way that the Woman may combine her work and any vocational and social activities with motherhood and that the upbringing of any children of the marriage shall not disrupt or restrict the work and vocational and social activities of one party more than of the other.

4. The Woman and Man agree that the responsibility for the upbringing of any children of the marriage and for the domestic work of the home shall be shared equally between them.

5. The Woman and Man agree that they shall decide jointly where the family home shall be with equal consideration as to the needs of each. The fact that one of them may earn more than the other as a result of employment in a certain place shall not allow that one to decide where they shall live.

6. The Woman and Man agree that they shall have equal interests in any premises occupied by them as the family home so that if the legal title to such premises is vested in one party such title shall be held in trust for both parties in equal shares.

7. The Woman and Man agree that all property owned separately by them before the marriage shall remain their separate property unless such property shall be occupied as the family home, in

which case the above clause applies. Any property owned jointly by them before the marriage shall remain their joint property and on sale the proceeds shall belong to them in equal shares.

8. The Woman and Man agree that all property acquired after the marriage for their joint use shall be jointly owned. All property acquired after the marriage for the sole use of either party shall remain separate property of that party.

9. (a) The Woman and Man agree that while they both maintain separate bank accounts the monies in each bank account shall belong to the party whose name it is in.

(b) Should they decide at any time to open a joint bank account the monies in that account shall belong to both in equal shares.

(c) If at any time one of them is not in full-time paid employment because of childbirth or responsibilities of caring for the children of the marriage, they both shall transfer all monies into a joint bank account but failing this half the monies earned during such a period by the one who is employed shall belong to the other.

10. The Woman and Man shall, as far as it is reasonable to do so, share equally in the management and control of any jointly held income and property.

11. The Woman and Man agree that they shall be equally liable to meet the common expenses of the family home including all necessary outgoings such as rent and mortgage payments, rates, electricity and the expenses of maintaining the children, in proportion to their respective incomes.

IN WITNESS whereof the parties have hereunto set their hands and seals the day and year first above written.

SIGNED SEALED AND DELIVERED
by the said GLORIA SMITH in the presence of

                         Witness ....

                         Address ....

                         Occupation............

SIGNED SEALED AND DELIVERED
by the said SAM BLOGGS in the presence of

                         Witness ....

                         Address ....

                         Occupation............

Index

For more general guidance, see the special contents table on pp. 8–10.

Bold figures are used for the more important entries.

More about Penguins and Pelicans

Penguinews, which appears every month, contains details of all the new books issued by Penguins as they are published. From time to time it is supplemented by *Penguins in Print*, which is a complete list of all titles available. (There are some five thousand of these.)

A specimen copy of *Penguinews* will be sent to you free on request. For a year's issues (including the complete lists) please send 50p if you live in the British Isles, or 75p if you live elsewhere. Just write to Dept EP, Penguin Books Ltd, Harmondsworth, Middlesex, enclosing a cheque or postal order, and your name will be added to the mailing list.

In the U.S.A.: For a complete list of books available from Penguin in the United States write to Dept CS, Penguin Books Inc., 7110 Ambassador Road, Baltimore, Maryland 21207.

In Canada: For a complete list of books available from Penguin in Canada write to Penguin Books Canada Ltd, 41 Steelcase Road West, Markham, Ontario.

A Penguin Special

Civil Liberty: The NCCL Guide

Anna Coote and Lawrence Grant

Second Edition

No constitution or charter protects British rights. At the mercy of any piece of hasty or prejudiced legislation, they must be upheld in every generation.

Do you possess the 'eternal vigilance' required to safeguard liberty? Do you know, for instance, what your rights are if you are arrested or need legal aid; if you are discriminated against or evicted; if you want ...ncel a hire purchase agreement or make a ...r doctor; if you are getting a ...a baby; if you hold a public meeting or go on s...

If you are unsure, this Penguin Special will supply the answers. You will find detailed here all those questions of liberty, justice and human rights about which most men in the street are ignorant or, at best, doubtful. In effect this well ordered and useful guide distils the long experience of the National Council for Civil Liberties in standing up (both politically and through case-work) for 'us' against 'them'.